The Complete
Root Cellar
Book

The Complete
Root Cellar
Book

Building Plans, Uses and 100 Recipes

Steve Maxwell and Jennifer MacKenzie

Robert
ROSE

For complete cataloguing information, see page 256.

Disclaimer
Neither the publisher nor the author can be held responsible for errors, omissions or negligence in construction and/or operation of the root cellar.

The recipes in this book have been carefully tested by our kitchen and our tasters. To the best of our knowledge, they are safe and nutritious for ordinary use and users. For those people with food or other allergies, or who have special food requirements or health issues, please read the suggested contents of each recipe carefully and determine whether or not they may create a problem for you. All recipes are used at the risk of the consumer.

We cannot be responsible for any hazards, loss or damage that may occur as a result of any recipe use.

For those with special needs, allergies, requirements or health problems, in the event of any doubt, please contact your medical adviser prior to the use of any recipe.

Design and Production: Kevin Cockburn/PageWave Graphics Inc.
Editor: Sue Sumeraj
Proofreader: Sheila Wawanash
Indexer: Gillian Watts
Illustrator: Len Churchill
Photography: Colin Erricson
Food Styling: Kathryn Robertson
Prop Styling: Charlene Erricson

On the cover: Preserved Lemons (page 238), Preserved Oranges (page 240), Preserved Limes (page 242) and Rumtopf (page 253)

We acknowledge the financial support of the Government of Canada through the Book Publishing Industry Development Program (BPIDP) for our publishing activities.

Published by Robert Rose Inc.
120 Eglinton Avenue East, Suite 800, Toronto, Ontario, Canada M4P 1E2
Tel: (416) 322-6552 Fax: (416) 322-6936

Printed and bound in Canada

1 2 3 4 5 6 7 8 9 TCP 18 17 16 15 14 13 12 11 10

Mixed Sources
Product group from well-managed forests and other controlled sources
www.fsc.org   Cert no. SW-COC-000952
©1996 Forest Stewardship Council

Contents

Introduction
Why a Root Cellar?

The true test of an idea is how durable it is, and root cellars have proven to be a surprisingly resilient concept. Despite the proliferation of convenience foods, the steady decline of domestic skills and our habit of eating out more often than in, root cellars are somehow still here. Still here and coming on strong again. Why? For all the traditional reasons of economy and food security, plus a few new ones.

Root cellars are cool, usually humid places ideally suited to storing vegetables, fruits, nuts and other foods, preserving them for weeks, or even months, without the use of additives or outside energy inputs. It's an ecologically sound, age-old technology that's simple, reliable and practical. But root cellars are more than the food storage equivalent of a sensible pair of orthopedic shoes. They are also romantic. Yes, romantic, especially for those of us who live with an otherwise rather clinical and modern food system.

Instant access to food on store shelves is an astonishing development. Yet like so many of our conveniences, we take it for granted. If people from ages past could stand in front of even an ordinary grocery store shelf, the variety and abundance would floor them. We have a range of food choices from every corner of the globe, ready to eat regardless of the season, sitting in coolers, freezers and attractive aisle displays. But as remarkable as this blessing is, our current approach to food leaves some people hungry for another way. It's not just a return to old food values, though that's certainly part of the attraction. And it's not just about saving money on food, as much as using a root cellar will do that for you. Underneath these obviously practical motivations, there are two other reasons some of us want more: an opportunity for the deepest kind of food craftsmanship and a way to contribute to effective environmental stewardship. These are motivations both personal and global, and they're rewards that our modern, convenience-focused food system struggles to provide.

While root cellars aren't convenient in the typical, microwavable sense, they do allow us to connect personally with food in ways nothing else can match. Modern food purveyors are starting to recognize our longing for deeper food experiences, enticing us with new apple varieties, vegetables from Asia and fascinating organic foods with a story behind

European colonists arriving in New England and Chesapeake Bay in the early 1600s quickly adopted the Native American practice of storing foods in underground pits.

The earliest written record of beets dates back 2,800 years ago, to Mesopotamia.

them. But the system's only able to go so far, and many of us are left wanting more. Does this strike a chord with you? Do you have an interest in seeking out food from new sources? How would you like to tap into seasonal abundance to save money and take greater environmental responsibility for the food you eat? If these ideas make you smile and nod your head, you probably need a root cellar.

A good cellar is the gateway to experiences and a food philosophy that's more important to some of us than 24/7 wall-to-wall convenience. A root cellar is to carrots, beets and salsify what a wine cellar is to Chardonnay, Merlot and Cabernet Sauvignon. It provides a necessary storage space for both wholesome food staples and culinary treasures.

Imagine you've just spotted a bushel of crisp Maiden's Blush apples at the Saturday farmers' market. Originating in New Jersey and dating back to the early 1800s, this variety does it all: it's good for fresh eating, it's a champion drying apple, and it's the featured ingredient in spectacular pies. But you can't do justice to such a find without a cellar to keep it in. You can't just stick a treasure like this in the corner of your kitchen.

Or maybe you've discovered a local heritage grower who offers Italian Bassano beets or that most ancient and famous beet of all, the French Crapaudine — a variety dating back to the days of Charlemagne. Can you possibly put gems like these in the crisper of your fridge, reducing them to wrinkly softness in less than a week? No. Absolutely not. You've got to have some sort of a cellar — a cool, humid, dark storage space. The advantages of such a place go beyond just storage, too. Root cellars help make the most of your food dollar by allowing you to stock up big-time at low prices during seasonal harvests.

Root cellars offer a lifestyle, and the bigger the cellar, the more encompassing the experience. Even the seemingly simple act of visiting your cellar regularly to examine your stores, remove droopy specimens and carry something delicious up to the kitchen affords simple satisfactions that can't be sealed in cellophane. Successful root cellaring delivers an opportunity to cultivate skills and hone gourmet insights in a way that is both fulfilling and globally responsible.

It's easy to miss the fact that most of us survive, in large measure, on crude oil. Our food may not look, smell or taste like black gold, but your next supermarket meal probably wouldn't exist without a lot of diesel fuel and gasoline burned in the background to produce, process and deliver it. In fact, global food production and delivery systems involve hidden energy inputs so huge that they usually far exceed the energy contained in the food itself. For every calorie of food in your next imported

The carrot is believed to have originated in Afghanistan before 900 AD.

Researchers at the University of Alberta concluded that the environmental impact of transporting food over long distances outweighs the benefits of organic production.

According to a study at the Leopold Center for Sustainable Agriculture at Iowa State University, American food travels an average of 1,500 miles (2,400 km) between farm and consumer.

The average grocery store shopping trip of 5 miles (7.8 km) uses more energy per pound (500 g) of food delivered than does the 620 mile (1000 km) average trip food takes from farms to cities by truck.

It takes 6000% more energy to transport food by air than it does by barge.

mouthful, approximately 10 calories were used to make it. And of this, a great portion was expended in transportation.

Once you understand that it takes about one calorie of diesel fuel to move two pounds of food a mile, a few simple calculations show that food can't travel far before it "runs out of gas." Go farther than several hundred miles from the source of production, and you become absolutely dependent on a steady supply of finite fossil fuels just to stay fed. Do you really want to remain this vulnerable?

Root cellars won't solve the problem, but they certainly do help, perhaps more than any other single course of action. Because a root cellar offers an option for long-term storage, you can grow your own foods and/or purchase locally produced foods in large quantities when they're in season, thereby both supporting the local economy and doing your part to reduce energy used to haul, process and refrigerate food in the usual way.

Root cellars are also versatile and, in a holistic sense, convenient. No matter where you live, they're appropriate. In cold climates, cellars protect food against frost. In hot climates, they protect against heat. In rural agricultural areas, they enable food storage within a few dozen yards of the soil where the food was produced. In urban areas, they offer a year-round home for local produce from garden plots and nearby farms. Even if you do nothing other than take advantage of supermarket specials on bushels of fruit and imported vegetables, some kind of cellar space makes sense. In this regard, a root cellar is a home improvement feature that boosts convenience. Instead of running out to the store every time you run short of something, you just go down (or out) to the cellar. It saves time, gas and parking hassles, and cuts down on traffic.

Food Cellarbration

Even though the original raison d'être for root cellars has evolved, many people still don't consider a home quite complete without some kind of underground realm that includes a food storage component. Perhaps it's a cultural throwback, or the practical realization that it just makes sense. Maybe it's something more primordial.

Regardless of your motivation, root cellaring, even on a small scale, can enhance the opportunities for culinary adventures, because a root cellar offers you the storage space to gather foods beyond the usual supermarket fare, and time beyond the immediate in which to keep those foods before consuming them.

This book delivers both the vision and the know-how to empower you to make some kind of root cellar a part of your life, and to enjoy richer food experiences because of it. How much a part depends on you, but be warned: the more you bring food adventures into your home, the more important really good food becomes. There's something hard-wired into the human heart that loves to lavish care and attention on food, and in turn to love food that has had care and attention lavished upon it. If this resonates with you, you're part of a growing fraternity. *The Complete Root Cellar Book* will show you how to construct a root cellar that will work for you, how to keep the food stored in your cellar wholesome and how to prepare that food in fabulous ways.

> Remember to check local building codes and regulations before you start construction. Always seek professional assistance where appropriate.

About the Metric Conversions in This Book

While it's easy to use formulas to figure out strict conversions from imperial units to metric, you won't necessarily end up with measurements that make sense in the real world. For example, different countries use different conventions to express lumber size. Then there's the challenge of converting general guidelines for length and width in one system into the nice round numbers you'd use to eyeball something in the other. And cookbooks have their own conventions for metric equivalents in recipes.

Since the aim of conversions is always to be as practically useful as possible for the greatest number of people, metric and imperial equivalents must go beyond what the calculator says. Mathematics alone can never deal with the complex and varied conventions of measurement that have developed in different industries and in various parts of the world, so an explanation is needed for the decisions we made in this book.

For imperial lumber sizes, we follow the North American standard of nominal thickness by nominal width, even though the actual dimensions of the wood are always smaller (e.g., a 2x6 actually measures $1\frac{1}{2}$ by $5\frac{1}{2}$ inches). For metric lumber sizes, we follow the British convention of nominal width by nominal thickness (e.g., a 150x50 actually measures 140 by 38 millimeters).

For other building materials, the measurements we use in both systems reflect how these items are sold. For example, a screw sold as #10 by 3-inch in North America is sold as 75 by 5 mm in Europe. Lengths of building materials and structural dimensions are direct conversions, with metric equivalents rounded to the nearest whole number and expressed in either millimeters or meters as per the European convention.

For temperature conversions, the Celsius equivalents in the construction and storage sections of this book are rounded off to the nearest whole number for ease of reading when precision is unnecessary. In the recipes, oven temperatures are based on actual oven settings, while meat doneness temperatures are strict conversions rounded to the nearest whole number.

Part 1

Root Cellaring in the 21st Century

Does your house sit on top of a basement? If you live in a temperate climate, chances are good that you have not only a basement, but also some kind of small, separate room that's sectioned off for food storage. This is a cold room, though you probably don't like it much.

Designs vary, but most cold rooms are small spaces that extend out one side of the basement, typically capped by a set of precast concrete front steps outside the entrance door. It's an admirable attempt at providing a basic root cellaring zone, but there's usually a problem. Several problems, in fact.

If your home is like thousands of others, that little cold room probably doesn't work like it should for proper food storage. Too cold in winter (perhaps even frigid enough to freeze vegetables and form frost on walls and the ceiling) and too warm in summer, a standard-issue cold room is more often than not just a tantalizing glimpse of what a true domestic food storage facility should be. But it doesn't have to stay that way. Upgrading a dysfunctional, under-the-steps cold room is not only possible, it's also relatively simple. Start with a brief history lesson, continue with an understanding of basic physics and put a few hands-on renovation techniques into practice, and you'll have your cold room working like it should.

> Between 1630 and 1660, 50% of houses in the Massachusetts Bay area featured root cellar storage.

A Short History of Basements

Basements evolved from the days when frost-proof, underground food storage (especially of root crops) was a matter of basic survival for most folks living in places that get cold winters. Every house worthy of the name traditionally included a place to safely store the potatoes, carrots, beets, cabbage and other frost-sensitive foods that the family's life depended upon until the next growing season rolled around. Why so much fuss about avoiding frost? After all, isn't freezing a great way to preserve food?

Freeze most kinds of vegetables, let them thaw and sit around for a while, and you have an ugly, putrid mess. That's why frost is the enemy of all things root-cellared. Since homes in cold climates typically require footings that extend down below the point of frost penetration into the soil, our forebears began excavating some of the soil bounded by these foundation walls so they could use the subterranean space to keep food out of Jack Frost's reach.

This is the age-old thinking behind traditional basements and the cellars that were often part of them, and the underground approach serves a useful purpose at the warm end of the seasonal spectrum, too. Underground spaces keep foods cool enough and moist enough during hot weather to preserve them for months after harvest, without any energy inputs.

As useful as an old-time cellar is (or was), building technologies and evolving lifestyles combined to make working cellars an endangered species. Homebuilding materials changed, allowing basement spaces to be finished as warm, dry living zones instead of the cool, moist areas suitable for preserving foods long-term. Modern basements are good news for couch potatoes, but not so great for a supply of Yukon golds.

As our lifestyles trended away from the domestic food arts and toward convenience, eating out and buy-as-you-eat grocery shopping, the root-cellaring tradition seemed doomed. And perhaps root cellars would have become extinct, but for one fundamental human impulse: somewhere, deep down inside, a good many of us still love to stock up. It feels prudent and wholesome and right. And though root cellaring is now often as much about the pleasure and culinary variety it brings as it is about survival, the practice endures. In fact, it's on the upswing, as more and more people become aware of the advantages offered by a working root cellar. It's one of those things that make you sit up and think that maybe those old-timers were smarter than we thought.

> Standard cold rooms are usually too cold in winter and too warm in summer. Simple do-it-yourself renovations can even out seasonal temperatures to make the cold room usable for food storage.

Stocking for an Emergency

It's easy to take our steady supply of grocery store food for granted, but you might not want to bet your next meal entirely on it. As significant weather events become more common, isn't it prudent to keep at least a little food in storage, just in case? Typical basement cold rooms might not be large, but they can certainly make a vital difference to your household if steady supplies of food for sale ever become disrupted. So what foods make the most sense as an emergency supply?

Root crops such as potatoes, carrots, turnips, beets and squash are certainly good keepers and pack lots of nutrition into a small space. Dried fruit, nuts and a 5-gallon (20 L) jug of water also make good sense. For more information on emergency preparedness, see page 110.

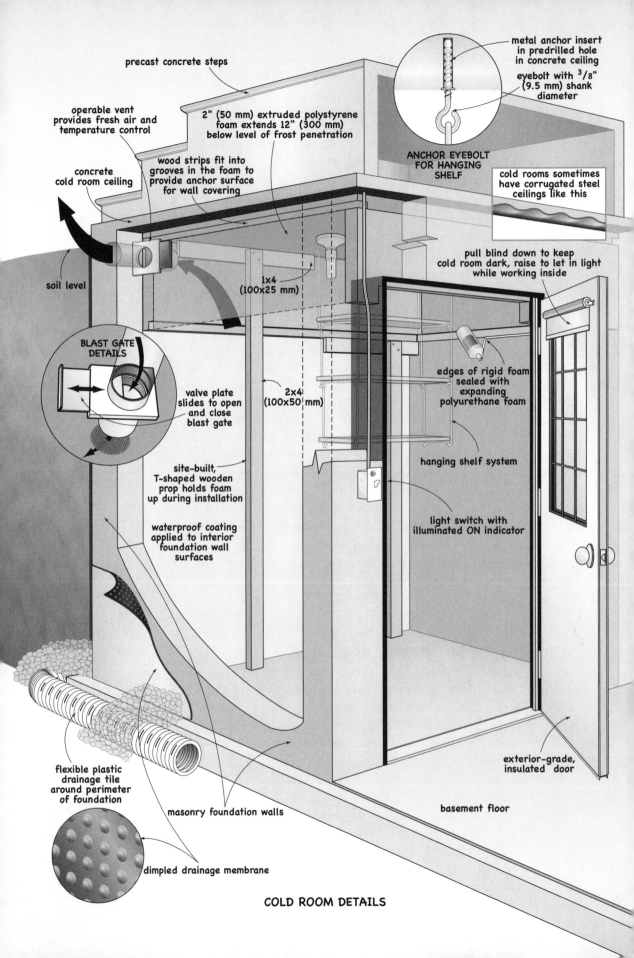

precast concrete steps

metal anchor insert in predrilled hole in concrete ceiling

eyebolt with ³/₈" (9.5 mm) shank diameter

ANCHOR EYEBOLT FOR HANGING SHELF

operable vent provides fresh air and temperature control

2" (50 mm) extruded polystyrene foam extends 12" (300 mm) below level of frost penetration

wood strips fit into grooves in the foam to provide anchor surface for wall covering

concrete cold room ceiling

cold rooms sometimes have corrugated steel ceilings like this

soil level

1x4 (100x25 mm)

pull blind down to keep cold room dark, raise to let in light while working inside

BLAST GATE DETAILS

2x4 (100x50 mm)

valve plate slides to open and close blast gate

edges of rigid foam sealed with expanding polyurethane foam

site-built, T-shaped wooden prop holds foam up during installation

hanging shelf system

waterproof coating applied to interior foundation wall surfaces

light switch with illuminated ON indicator

flexible plastic drainage tile around perimeter of foundation

masonry foundation walls

exterior-grade, insulated door

basement floor

dimpled drainage membrane

COLD ROOM DETAILS

Tuning Up Your Cold Room

Our growing desire to have a basic basement food storage zone, even if we live near a grocery store, hasn't gone unnoticed. Homebuilders realize that the call for space to keep at least a few bags of potatoes isn't going to disappear, and that's why they usually include a cold room in new home designs. Or at least, they try to. Few of these modern cold rooms, typically located underneath a set of concrete stairs at the front of the house, actually work the way they're supposed to — at least, not without some serious souping up. While even a fully functioning cold room won't be able to maintain the 32°F to 40°F (0°C to 5°C) temperatures and 80% to 90% relative humidity levels that are the ideal conditions for certain vegetables, renovating a cold room so that it functions as a cold room is still worth the effort. This is especially true if you don't have a lot of food storage space in other parts of your house.

If you have an under-the-front-porch cold room, you probably know all too well that it has some limitations. Poor cold-weather performance tops the list of troubles in many standard-issue cold rooms, especially in regions where wintertime temperatures drop below 15°F (–10°C). Cold rooms are typically way too cold in winter. Most designs sit high enough out of the soil that frost penetrates at least the top 25% and sometimes even 50% of the structure. Besides making the cold room too cold, inadequate soil buffering also leads to the formation of frost on the interior walls and ceiling as internal masonry surfaces drop below freezing. On its own, frost on walls might not seem like a disaster, but when it melts and runs onto the floor, it comes close. Besides soaking the floor, the added moisture can boost airborne humidity high enough to promote mold and mildew. Not good.

Poor warm-weather performance usually goes hand in hand with a cold room that's ineffective in winter. This is problem number two. Without the moderating effects of enough soil around the structure, cold room temperatures are likely to get much too high in the summer for effective root cellaring of any kind.

Water leakage into under-the-steps cold rooms is the third most common cold room headache. It has two sources. Water can seep in through the walls of the structure or down from the top, through or around the precast steps. Despite their solid appearance, ordinary concrete blocks and poured concrete aren't fully waterproof. Often they're not even close.

While wide swings in cold room temperatures are a more common problem than water leaks, and temperature problems are easier to fix, water leakage is a more serious problem because a wet space can never function as a cold room. Water

It takes less than two days' work for an average homeowner to modify a typical cold room so that it functions as intended.

Most basement water leaks are caused by water pooling against the building.

causes mold and rot, so making things reliably dry is job number one.

Stopping Water Leaks

If water is leaking into your cold room, there are several things you can do to upgrade it. First, make sure all surface water drains away from the area around your cold room (and your whole house, for that matter). Eavestroughs offer a good start, but they're effective only if the soil is sloped so that water runs away from the foundation after it hits the ground.

Even with proper grading on your side, water can still leak into your cold room. If it does, there's a quick fix that's worth trying before you get involved in a more troublesome, excavation-focused repair scenario. If the inside surfaces of your cold room walls and ceiling are bare, unpainted masonry, there are effective waterproofing products you can paint on them to stop minor water leaks. What's minor? That's not easy to say, but a fix this simple is almost always worth a try. The best products work by sealing the masonry surface pores from the inside, so they're super-easy to apply. Ordinary paint offers virtually no benefit as far as waterproofing goes, so don't bother putting any on. In fact, paint will prevent you from getting good results with dedicated masonry waterproof coatings.

Leaks can sometimes be localized, coming from cracks or individual holes in the foundation wall rather than oozing in through the entire surface. Watch your leaks for a while and learn all you can about where the water is coming from. Polyurethane caulking often seals small holes perfectly. Longer cracks can be repaired with an epoxy injection process, done either professionally or as a DIY project.

Let's say you have appropriate grading, you've sloshed something waterproof on your cold room walls, you've repaired cracks and holes, and water still gets in during wet weather. What next? Well, it's time to get out the big guns and consider something called vertical drainage membrane as part of a larger basement waterproofing strategy.

Invented by Cosella-Dörken Products Inc. and now offered by a handful of manufacturers, this dimpled, plastic sheet material goes against the outside face of foundation walls, creating thin, vertical drainage pathways for water to trickle down without interference from soil. Without pressure from the soil, water isn't driven through the masonry with the same vigor, so it's much more likely to move downward into the drainage tile system around the bottom of the wall, rather than sideways into your cold room or basement. That's the good news. The bad news is that you'll need to excavate the soil away from the foundation wall to install drainage membrane, then

If you see white, fluffy growths on your cold room walls, it's probably a mineral buildup called efflorescence. Caused by the slow movement of water through the masonry, it's a sign that you need to apply a waterproof coating before you do anything else. Scrub the area with a brush and water to remove the fuzz and let the surface dry. Apply the coating only when active water leaks have stopped.

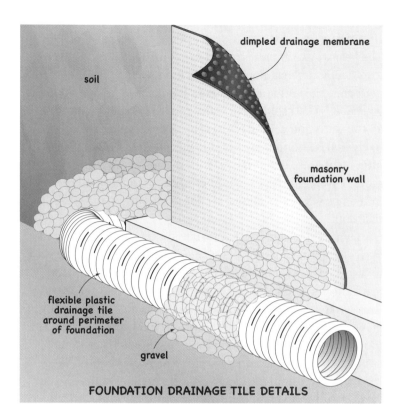

dimpled drainage membrane

soil

masonry
foundation wall

flexible plastic
drainage tile
around perimeter
of foundation

gravel

FOUNDATION DRAINAGE TILE DETAILS

backfill with sandy soil that has good drainage properties. In order to work, the drainage membrane also needs to connect to perforated horizontal pipes (that's the drainage tile) around the perimeter of the footing. After all, the water needs someplace to go after it drains downward. Excavation and basement waterproofing of this sort is not do-it-yourself work for most people, so you'll need to find an experienced contractor.

Despite the installation hassles, drainage membrane does perform admirably. Chances are, if your cold room leaks, other parts of your basement leak too, so you'll want to make a big job of it and do the whole thing. All of the techniques that turn a wet space into an effective root cellar also work to prepare a wet basement for finishing as living space. One way or the other, a leaky cold room won't ever make a very good root cellar. If you can't dry things out, don't outfit the space for food storage (or a finished basement, for that matter).

Recent innovations in building materials make it much easier to keep water out of basement cold rooms and root cellars.

Reducing Seasonal Temperature Fluctuations

Temperature fluctuations occur because too little of the cold room surface area is moderated by soil and because most cold room access doors aren't up to the task of keeping warm, heated basement air out. Each of these issues requires a different strategy. The first task is to install insulation on the ceiling and the upper part of the walls. When that's done, you can look at improving your cold room door.

Installing Insulation

The best way to approach the issue of inadequate soil cover is to add a moderate amount of insulation, watch how the cellar performs, then add more insulation if needed. You could make your overly cold cold room warmer in the winter by covering all the walls and ceiling with insulation, though that would likely make it too warm, in both summer and winter. But a little insulation of the right kind, especially over frost-prone areas of the cold room walls and ceiling, can make all the difference while still allowing cool soil temperatures to chill the room.

So what's the right kind of insulation, and how much is the correct amount? First of all, whatever you use must be non-toxic, impervious to water (in case of an unexpected water leak) and impermeable to warm, moist indoor air percolating through to the cold wall surface underneath. This last point is an easily overlooked detail, but it's absolutely crucial. If warm, moist air is allowed to seep into the insulating layer, it may cool down enough to condense, forming water behind the insulation. Without an effectively air-sealed insulation layer, this air infiltration and condensation process will continue long-term, forming a wet, nasty, moldy mess behind the foam. It can even lead to water pooling on the floor.

Rigid extruded polystyrene foam is the best insulation for correcting temperature problems in a cold room. It's available at every building supply outlet, comes in rigid sheets (typically 24 by 96 inches, or 600 mm by 2450 mm in metric countries) and is reasonably priced. It's easy to work with and is perfect for regulating the temperature swings that plague typical residential cold rooms. The material's cell structure is closed, which means it's impervious enough to water vapor that it won't lead to condensation, as long as the seams around the sheets are sealed. Extruded polystyrene is also surprisingly strong.

Whatever you do, don't use the white, beady, expanded polystyrene insulation for your cold room upgrade campaign. It's cheaper, but it does not provide enough protection against the passage of water vapor, which can lead to large, troublesome internal condensation problems behind the foam. You should also stay away from any kind of fiber-based batt insulation for cold rooms. Some people use it, but the risk is high. Batt insulation may be fine above ground, but it's too vulnerable to moisture and prone to mold growth for prudent use in any kind of root cellar application.

Even with the right kind of foam on your side, there still are dangers to avoid. The key to success is in the installation details. There are three points in particular that really matter: the proportion of the cold room surface that's covered in

For information on the metric conversions used in this book, see page 9.

Rigid foam is such a good insulator that simply putting your hand against it makes your skin feel warm.

foam; the way the foam is fastened to walls and ceilings; and the method used to seal the foam to prevent cold-weather condensation behind it.

If you live in a cold climate, wintertime frost is one of the best indications of where to put foam on the interior surfaces of your cold room: simply apply foam wherever you see white patches of frost during the coldest winter weather. If your region doesn't get cold enough to frost up the inside of your cold room, plan to insulate the ceiling (especially if that ceiling has a masonry or corrugated metal surface), as well as the exterior walls down to about 12 inches (300 mm) below the level of the soil outside. You may have to expand the area covered by foam later, but you won't know for sure until you see how the temperature of your new and improved root cellar ranges over the course of a year.

For most root cellar applications, you'll find that 2-inch (50 mm) thick extruded polystyrene delivering an insulation value of R10 (1.76 RSI) works well (see Insulation Education, page 40, for information on insulation values). Versions that include grooves along adjoining edges to allow space for wooden anchor strips are great. Start by cutting the pieces of foam required to cover the ceiling. A full-size handsaw of the sort used to cut wood is ideal for this job. You could use a power saw, but that's unnecessarily noisy and messy. Foam also has a tendency to grab spinning circular saw blades and kick them back.

Since extruded polystyrene foam typically comes in sheets of 24 by 96 inches (600 by 2450 mm), it takes three or four sheets to cover the ceiling of an average cold room. As you cut each one to size, be sure to leave $1/2$- to $3/4$-inch (13 to 19 mm) gaps at each end (but not between pieces of foam). This is crucial for the all-important step of air-sealing the installation (more on this on page 22).

Polyurethane construction adhesive is the best product for securing pieces of foam insulation to the walls and ceiling, at least initially. Start by applying a continuous bead $1/2$ inch (13 mm) away from the edges of each piece, then in a zigzag pattern across the surface of the foam that touches the masonry. The perimeter bead acts as an initial sealing barrier, to keep warm air from sneaking in behind the foam. Be sure the construction adhesive forms a continuous line, without breaks. For tips on making it easier to dispense construction adhesive, see Cordless Caulking on page 20.

Construction adhesive is viscous enough, and foam insulation lightweight enough, that you might not have to do anything other than press the pieces of foam into place against the ceiling, especially if it's a smooth concrete surface.

Handsaws with a Japanese tooth pattern cut much better than anything else. You can tell them apart from other handsaws by their exceptionally sharp tooth tips and the fact that they're designed to cut on the pull stroke.

Cordless Caulking

Construction adhesive offers a lot of advantages when it comes to building any kind of root cellar. Trouble is, it can also be very hard on your hand to squeeze out three or four tubes of this thick, sticky stuff using a manual caulking gun. Luckily, power tool companies have created battery-operated, cordless caulking guns, and several models in particular are priced to make the most sense for casual home improvement work. Look for models that use the same rechargeable battery packs as other cordless tools, such as drills and circular saws, and also offer variable speeds for controlling the rate that the caulking gets squeezed out of the gun.

To use a battery-operated caulking gun, just slice open the plastic tip of the caulking tube, use a 4-inch (100 mm) long deck screw to poke a hole through the inner sealing membrane, then pull the trigger and watch the caulking or adhesive ooze out.

If you don't have a power caulking gun, you can heat the caulking to a manageable viscosity. Just don't heat it too much.

If the wooden subfloor above your cold room has nails sticking through from the floor above, use a multi-tool with a hacksaw blade to trim the metal flush before applying rigid foam sheets. You can also try pounding the nails flush with the wood using a hammer or trim them using a pair of wire nippers.

However, some cold room ceilings are made of corrugated metal, and since these offer much less contact area, you will definitely need to hold the foam up while the glue dries. In any case, regardless of whether your ceiling is smooth or wavy, it's prudent to prepare some T-shaped wooden props ahead of time (see the illustration on page 14). These will rest on the floor and extend up, holding the foam tight to the ceiling while the adhesive hardens. They don't need to be fancy, just a crossbar screwed to an upright piece, with the upright piece long enough to extend from the floor to the foam as it sits tight against the ceiling. Use 2x4s (100x50s) for the upright pieces, and make them about $\frac{1}{4}$ inch (6 mm) longer than necessary, so they'll jam tightly between the foam and floor when installed vertically. Use two deck screws to secure a crosspiece to the top of each upright, forming a big T that spreads pressure over a wide area — 18-inch (450 mm) pieces of 1x4 (100x25) lumber are ideal for the crosspieces. Make as many of these props as you need to hold the ceiling foam securely. One placed every 24 to 36 inches (600 to 900 mm) usually works well.

If you're using the kind of rigid foam that has grooves along the edges for wooden anchoring strips, install these after the adhesive begins to harden. Besides holding the foam very securely, these strips also provide a convenient surface onto which you can easily fasten drywall or cement board later, using conventional drywall screws. To install the wooden strips, squirt a bead of expanding polyurethane foam (see Spray Foam in a Can, page 21) into the middle of the gap on the joint line, filling the space, before setting the strips in place and fastening them with Tapcon screws (to learn more about these great screws, see The Amazing Tapcon Screw on page 23). Drill through the wood and foam and into the masonry all at once, using a hammer drill and carbide bit, then drive the screws tight using an impact driver.

If your foam doesn't have grooves for wood, the screws that secure the wallboard (see page 23) will do double duty, anchoring the foam, too. While this approach seems simpler than using wooden strips, on balance it's more troublesome, because you will need to go through the rather slow process of predrilling holes through the wallboard and into the masonry while holding the wallboard in position the entire time. Anchoring into wood, on the other hand, requires no predrilling, and the first few screws hold each sheet up.

A hammer drill bores holes in masonry many times faster than a regular drill. You can recognize a hammer drill by a control ring or lever with a hammer symbol next to it. Hammer drills make vibrating sounds as they operate, so wear hearing protection as well as safety glasses.

Spray Foam in a Can

A can of polyurethane spray foam is one of the best products for sealing your home, and it offers particular benefits for root cellar construction and cold room renovations. Available at home improvement stores, polyurethane spray foam is safe and comes in two types: regular and low-expansion (Steve's personal favorite). As the name suggests, low-expansion foam swells up less as it cures, creating a more firm final product that's also less likely to distort surrounding surfaces.

If you have just a few gaps to fill, ready-to-use cans of polyurethane foam make good sense. Just stick the application wand into the can valve and press the trigger. If, however, your root cellar project involves more sealing than two or three cans can accomplish, it makes sense to use a more economical system of foam delivery: a large canister of spray foam with a removable and reusable application gun. This approach costs less per unit of foam delivered, and the results are much neater. The gun has a valve right at the application tip that stops the flow of foam the moment you release your finger from the trigger. Ready-to-use spray foam cans, on the other hand, have a valve at the top of the can, so foam continues to expand and dribble out of the long nozzle for a while after you have released the trigger.

Regardless of the application system you choose, there are precautions you need to take when using spray foam. First, and most important, always wear safety goggles. Even the smallest stray drop in your eye will cause big problems. In addition, you'll want to don a pair of disposable rubber gloves before you begin the application. Polyurethane spray foam is very sticky, and you don't want to get it on your skin.

In the fairly likely event that some foam does go where it's not supposed to, you'll be glad to have a can of polyurethane foam solvent on hand. You'll also need it to clean the application gun, if you're using one. Solvent comes in a pressure can with the same kind of threaded top as the foam. To clean the applicator, screw it onto the gun in place of the foam canister and trigger a few shots of solvent through the gun after removing a spent can of foam and before installing a new one. The solvent only works until the foam is cured, so use it quickly.

With your pieces of rigid ceiling foam in place, you're almost ready to apply wall foam. But first you'll need to use spray foam to fill the gaps you left around the perimeter of the ceiling sheets, thereby air-sealing the installation. Don safety glasses and disposable gloves, put the extended tip of the nozzle into the gap between the perimeter of the ceiling foam and the wall, then gently squeeze the trigger. Move the nozzle tip along fast enough to fill about half the depth of the gap with fresh foam as it comes out. It will expand as it hardens, and if you've applied the correct amount, the foam will grow to fill the gap entirely, bulging outward as it does. In a couple of hours, this foam will be fully hardened, ready for excess to be removed. A hacksaw blade taken out of its frame is the perfect tool for this job. It's flexible enough to saw through the excess foam, flush to the surrounding foam sheets. Simply saw back and forth, then sweep up the strips of hardened foam that fall to the ground.

Now is the time to insulate the upper portion of your walls with rigid foam. If the walls are too rough or uneven for construction adhesive to form a complete perimeter seal, use expanding polyurethane foam behind each sheet to fill the gaps and seal against air infiltration. This foam sticks well enough to act as its own adhesive. Cut pieces of rigid foam for the walls slightly smaller than required to cover the space, leaving a $1/2$- to $3/4$-inch (13 to 19 mm) wide gap between neighboring pieces of foam in the corners and between the wall foam and the ceiling foam above. You will also need to cut an opening for the vent, if you have an existing one (see page 24). Cut a piece of foam to fit in the space surrounding the vent, then press it in place firmly over the vent to mark where the foam needs to be cut. Next, shorten the T-shaped props you used earlier for the ceiling so that they'll hold up the wall foam from the bottom edge while you're cutting and installing wooden anchoring battens (if you're using them).

Dealing with a Wood Frame on the Ceiling

If the ceiling of your cold room has an exposed framework of wood, you can still use rigid pieces of foam to insulate it, but you'll need to cut the foam into pieces that fit between the joists. As you cut each piece, leave a gap around the perimeter to accept beads of air-sealing spray foam.

A faster, though more expensive option is to spray the entire surface of the ceiling between the joists with a two-part spray foam kit designed to cover larger areas. This replaces the need to cut and seal pieces of foam individually, and it seals out drafts perfectly.

The Amazing Tapcon Screw

Originally patented in 1976, and since copied by various manufacturers, the Tapcon screw grips directly into predrilled holes in most kinds of masonry, without the need for plastic or metal anchors. All brands are used in the same way: predrill a hole that matches the diameter of the screw at the bottom of the threads, then tighten the screw into the hole. That's it. Tapcon screws can be used to secure all light and medium-weight items, such as pipe anchors, electrical conduits and small shelves, to masonry surfaces in your cellar. Choose a screw length that puts between 1 and 1¾ inches (250 and 450 mm) of threads into the masonry, and drill the hole slightly deeper than required for the screw. Without sufficient hole depth, Tapcon screws bottom out before tightening down on the object they're anchoring.

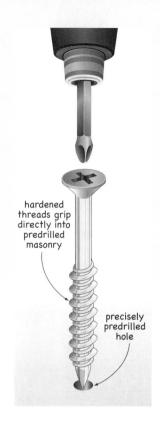

hardened threads grip directly into predrilled masonry

precisely predrilled hole

With the foam up, you have two things left to do. First, use expanding polyurethane foam from a hand-held spray can to fill all of the remaining gaps you left between pieces of foam. Let it harden, then cut off the excess flush with the surrounding foam sheets, as you did for the ceiling, using a hacksaw blade taken out of the saw frame.

Next, you must cover the entire foamed area with wallboard. Since there's a small chance that extruded polyurethane foam sheets could ignite, building codes require that foam be covered to reduce the risk of fire. In addition, the wallboard will protect the foam from getting crushed and torn over time.

An excellent material for covering foam in a cellar is cement board, a masonry sheet material that's typically ½ inch (13 mm) thick. Secure it with drywall screws driven into the underlying wooden anchor strips or, if you opted to use foam alone (without the wooden strips), with Tapcon screws driven through the foam into predrilled holes in the underlying masonry.

Cement board is very tough, though heavy. It also makes your cold room look like something from a Soviet army barracks. You can paint it, but the rough surface will remain visible. If you want a more refined look, cover the foam with water-resistant, mold-resistant drywall instead. Often used in bathrooms, traditional water-resistant drywall is usually green, but you can paint it any color you want. An even better option is fiberglass drywall, which uses a thin layer of fiberglass over a gypsum base, eliminating all organic material that mold might grow on. Whatever you do, don't use conventional paper-faced drywall in a cold room — it's too vulnerable to moisture and mold growth.

Although not yet mainstream, fiberglass drywall is highly mold-resistant and is excellent for root cellar applications.

Getting More Door

The door to a standard cold room is typically just an ordinary, interior passage door, which is completely inadequate for a working cold room. This type of door doesn't seal well enough (not at all, in fact) and doesn't have a high enough insulation value (see Insulation Education, page 40).

The most effective solution is to install an insulated exterior door. These are typically made with a steel skin inside and out, with foam insulation factory-injected in between. These "prehung" doors come in various sizes, with the door already hinged on a wooden frame that gets set into the rough door opening, then anchored to your walls. Highly effective weatherstripping and a door sweep are included. Installing a prehung door of this kind involves removing the existing door and frame, setting the new unit in place in the opening, straightening and plumbing up the sides of the door frame with wedges, then securing the new frame into the surrounding door opening. More detailed installation instructions appear on page 43.

If all this seems beyond your DIY skills, don't feel bad. Changing doors is one of the more advanced home improvement skills. Don't be afraid to bring in a pro, though even that's not always a guarantee of success. Whether you do it yourself or hire a contractor, be sure that low-expansion foam is injected into the gap between the new frame and the surrounding rough opening (with the door shut and wedges temporarily placed in the gap immediately around the door to brace the frame against bowing inward from the expansion of the foam) before the trim goes on. You want this installation to be as airtight as possible.

If you'd rather not change the door of your cold room, you can improve its performance by adding rigid foam to the inside surface. Use the same kind of extruded polystyrene foam that you applied to the ceiling and walls of your cold room. You'll also need to apply weatherstripping around the sides and top of the door. A heavy door sweep works best along the bottom.

Will your new door need a new handle? If it does, choose a lever-style handle. When your hands are full of stuff, it's much easier to grab and open a lever than a round knob.

Venting Your Cold Room

Standard cold rooms usually have a wall vent somewhere up near the ceiling, opening out above ground level. Although this kind of vent isn't adequate for a full-sized root cellar, it's often enough for a small, under-the-steps cold room. The only prerequisite is that the set-up offers a way to open and close the

Remove the threshold from a prehung exterior door before installation to make it easier to sweep your cold room floor.

Install an automatic closer to ensure that the door of your cold room is never left open accidentally.

Condensation Elimination

Most of the time, ventilation is a good thing in the root cellar business, but not always. When it's hot and humid outside, allowing this type of air to enter your cold room or root cellar can cause the relative humidity to skyrocket way beyond what's ideal. The reason has to do with how the moisture-holding capacity of air changes with temperature.

Let's say it's 85°F (30°C) outside and 80% relative humidity. If this outdoor air is allowed to enter your cold room or root cellar with an ambient temperature of 50°F (10°C), the outdoor air will cool as it enters. Cooler air has a reduced ability to hold water. Even though the cooler air is not taking up any additional evaporated water from the surroundings, its relative humidity will rise as its temperature declines. When its relative humidity reaches 100% and the outdoor air continues to cool off (as it certainly can do), water will appear on surrounding surfaces. This is condensation, and it's not what you want.

This dynamic happens in a lot of basements during the summer. As it turns out, the solution is the same for basements, cold rooms and root cellars: prevent warm, moist air from entering. This typically means closing outdoor vents (either partially or fully) during times of hot, humid weather, then opening them again as needed when the air gets fresher and less muggy. Whatever you do, don't make the mistake of thinking that the solution for a too-humid root cellar involves admitting more warm summertime air. This air is almost certainly the source of the excess moisture that's causing your grief. The less you let in, the better.

vent. That's key. You'll want to admit fresh air during certain seasons, but not others. The amount and extent that the vent is left open depends on outdoor temperatures and humidity levels. See Condensation Elimination, above, and Root Cellar Vent Control on page 34 for help understanding how and when to use a manual cellar vent. Success is definitely about more than just temperature.

If your cold room doesn't have an operable vent, you'll need to add one, which, as you've probably realized, involves knocking a precise hole through your masonry foundation. Before you do that, find an operable hardware louvre or vent, then mark out the space it requires, on both the interior and the exterior wall surfaces. See page 30 for important instructions on creating an accurate vent hole.

A rotary hammer of the sort used to bore holes for large masonry anchors is the tool of choice for punching vent holes through the relatively weak structure of a concrete block foundation. Bore a series of holes around the perimeter of the opening you want to create, working through the insulation inside the cold room and from the outside of the foundation wall, then replace the drill bit in the rotary hammer with a straight chisel or point to break out the waste.

Be sure to have your new vent on hand before drilling, and use it to mark the size of hole you need to create. It's difficult to enlarge a hole that has been drilled too small.

Stellar Cellar

Your cold room is now ready to stock, though it's not going to win any decor contests. At least not yet. Want a cold room that looks great inside, kind of like a fancy wine cellar, but filled with food? Take a look at Finishing Touches for Your Root Cellar, page 74, for hands-on electricity, plumbing, flooring, wall treatment, work table and shelving ideas that make for a stunning space.

If your foundation is poured concrete, stone, brick or any other solid masonry construction, a coring drill makes more sense. This tool removes a cylindrical plug of masonry, usually using a water-cooled carbide bit. Rental outlets everywhere offer coring drills, though you may want to hire a professional to do the work if you're not used to wrestling large, spirited power tools.

Option 2
Building a Walk-In Basement Root Cellar

If you have a basement — any kind of dry, subterranean basement — you can have a great root cellar that's much more useful than even a properly functioning cold room. Although modern basements are often too warm for storing roots and fruits, by walling off a section of your basement and adding ventilation, you can create the cool, humid conditions that are the hallmark of an excellent root cellar.

Location, Location, Location

Although every basement is different, there are universals when it comes to choosing a good location for your root cellar. The first of these has to do with ventilation. Since you'll need access to the outdoors for fresh air, it's essential to choose a spot that includes either a window or an exterior wall you can put a vent through (see Boring Through a Foundation Wall on page 30 for help determining what kind of wall you have and the process and tools required to get through it).

When it comes to any kind of basement root cellar, the soil-covered portion of the exterior walls is what delivers the all-important cooling action. The more soil covering you have, the better. That's why, if you can, you'll want to choose a corner location for your root cellar. Corners offer maximum exposure to exterior walls while minimizing the number of interior walls you'll need to build and insulate to separate the cellar from

The earliest recorded use of the term "root cellar" is found in a 1767 advertisement for a farmhouse near New York City.

In 1943, the U.S. Department of Agriculture published detailed plans for walling off a section of basement for use as a root cellar.

Optimal Root Cellar Conditions

Cold and humid: these are the best conditions for storing most root crops and many other vegetables. More specifically, the key is to create a space that offers three vital features: a year-round temperature range between 32°F and 40°F (0°C and 5°C); positive and controllable ventilation; and a relative humidity that hovers between 70% and 90%, depending on what you plan to store. Just understand that these are ideal conditions. If your root cellar is a bit warmer or dryer, all is not lost. You can still enjoy very good storage capabilities, especially if you use crop-specific storage systems that create microclimates directly around the foods being stored (see page 93). Invest in a good thermometer/hygrometer combination to monitor root cellar temperature and humidity.

the rest of the basement. If you have a choice, select a spot with the highest possible soil height outside the foundation. If more than 18 inches (450 mm) of foundation wall is exposed above the surrounding earth, consider adding more light, well-drained topsoil around the outside of the building, to a maximum height of 8 inches (200 mm) below the top of the basement wall. Slope this new soil gradually away from the foundation walls, and it'll encourage better drainage, too.

As a final location consideration, if one of your options includes northern exposure, go for it. The less sunlight warming the area, the better. (In the southern hemisphere, southern exposure is best.)

Designing Your Cellar

After you've selected your cellar location, it's time to start thinking about design. Grab a sheet or two of plywood or waferboard and a helper, then get ready to use your imagination. It's amazing how temporarily propping up a few pieces of plywood can help you get a sense of the floor plan of a new room, leading you to a better design. How long should your cellar be? How deep? Is a 3-foot (0.9 m) wide door big enough? These kinds of questions become much easier to answer when you have something to hold up, look at, move around and tweak.

Generally speaking, a floor plan of 12 by 16 feet (3.6 by 4.8 m) makes an ample basement root cellar space. You can certainly go smaller if necessary, but don't underestimate the amount of room you'll need, especially if you plan to include a sink and a prep table in your cellar. Whatever you do, regard these numbers as starting points only. And remember that the inside dimensions of your cellar will be smaller than the outside because of the thickness of the walls. Use your plywood, your helper and your imagination to fine-tune overall dimensions to suit your location. As you make decisions, try to settle on length and width figures that are multiples of the size of standard sheet goods (for example, the width of plywood and drywall is always 48 inches, or 1220 mm). Once you've finalized the footprint and door location, draw relevant outlines on the basement floor with a big felt-tipped marker or masking tape.

Installing Vents

With wall locations decided, it's time to create vent holes to the outdoors for fresh air, humidity control and temperature management. Depending on your situation, creating these holes may be relatively easy or challenging.

If you're having soil trucked in for use around your basement walls, buy topsoil for the job and take the time to examine it before the trucks are loaded for delivery. Look for smooth, lump-free dirt, with no stones or roots. Good topsoil costs more than ordinary fill, but it's easy to handle, rakes out smoothly and grows new grass quickly.

If you're not quite sure how big to make your cellar, stick strips of masking tape onto the floor to mark out what you think is a good size, then live with the space for a while. It even makes sense to install a few shelves and park a few crates and bins in the area, so you can get an accurate sense of the size and shape your cellar will be. Be sure to mark the inside wall dimensions, because these are the ones you'll be living with.

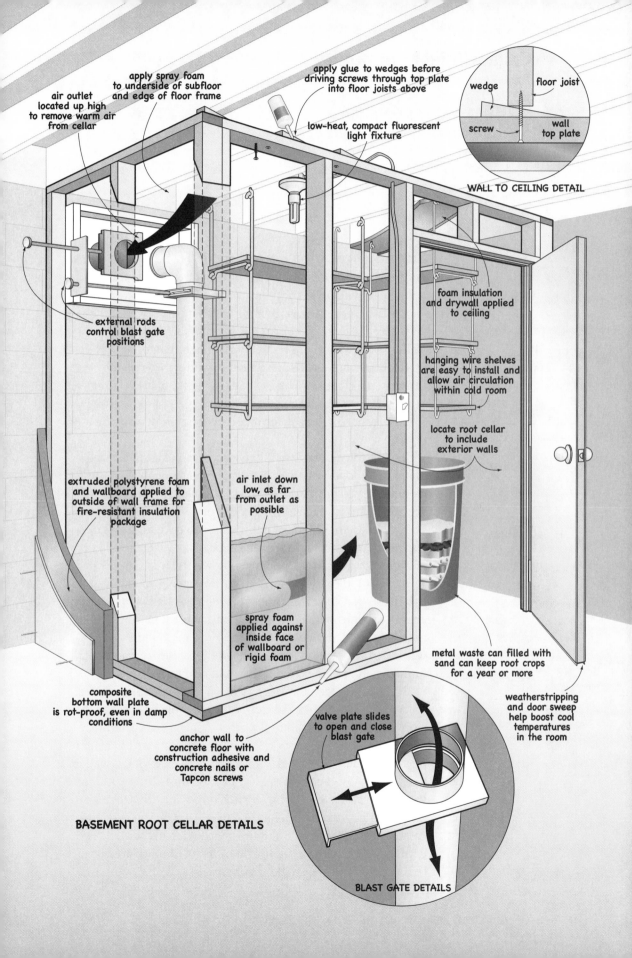

apply glue to wedges before
driving screws through top plate
into floor joists above

apply spray foam
to underside of subfloor
and edge of floor frame

air outlet
located up high
to remove warm air
from cellar

low-heat, compact fluorescent
light fixture

wedge | floor joist

screw | wall
top plate

WALL TO CEILING DETAIL

external rods
control blast gate
positions

foam insulation
and drywall applied
to ceiling

hanging wire shelves
are easy to install and
allow air circulation
within cold room

locate root cellar
to include
exterior walls

extruded polystyrene foam
and wallboard applied to
outside of wall frame for
fire-resistant insulation
package

air inlet down
low, as far
from outlet as
possible

spray foam
applied against
inside face
of wallboard or
rigid foam

metal waste can filled with
sand can keep root crops
for a year or more

composite
bottom wall plate
is rot-proof, even in damp
conditions

weatherstripping
and door sweep
help boost cool
temperatures
in the room

anchor wall to
concrete floor with
construction adhesive and
concrete nails or
Tapcon screws

valve plate slides
to open and close
blast gate

BASEMENT ROOT CELLAR DETAILS

BLAST GATE DETAILS

Cellars Build Community

There are many people who'd like a root cellar who don't have the resources or living space to create one for themselves. That's where you can help, if you have the room to do so. Whatever cellar design you're pursuing, make it bigger than seems necessary. You'll probably appreciate having more space than you thought you needed, but you'll also have enough room to invite a friend or neighbor to store food in your cellar. The pursuit of food has brought people together since the dawn of time, and it's still a powerful way to build connections.

A high-performance root cellar vent must be more than just a hole in the wall. For the best results, you need *two* holes: one to let fresh air in and another to let stale air out. This detail is crucial for creating a reliable flow of fresh air.

Ask about a support stand when you rent a tool for boring through a concrete or stone basement wall. The process takes several hours, and a stand makes the work easier.

Boring Through a Foundation Wall

Regardless of the design of your basement walls, it's always possible to bore holes through an exterior foundation wall for the two 3- or 4-inch (75 or 100 mm) diameter vent pipes you'll need. Always possible, yes, but not always easy. Some walls are definitely simpler to bust through than others. Your exterior basement walls are almost certainly made of one of five materials: concrete block, poured concrete, brick, stone or preserved wood. The process of boring vent holes through to the outdoors will be determined by the type of wall you are dealing with.

Concrete block is one of the most common basement wall materials, and it's relatively easy to punch through, because blocks are typically hollow (though occasionally these cavities are filled with concrete during construction to boost strength). You know you have blocks if the wall surface has a series of staggered, recessed mortar joints about 7 or 8 inches (180 or 200 mm) apart as you look up and down the wall, and 15 or 16 inches (380 or 410 mm) apart as you scan horizontally. You'll find that the easiest route through the wall is in the zone about one-third of the way over from a vertical mortar joint. Avoid the solid areas of block at the ends and middle of the wall. (Pick up a concrete block at your local lumberyard; you'll immediately see where drilling would be easiest.)

The best approach for getting through a block wall involves boring a single $\frac{1}{2}$-inch (13 mm) diameter hole right through from one side of the wall to the other, using a rotary hammer (available at any rental outlet). This first hole marks the center of a larger hole you'll need to make on both sides of the wall for your vent. Most block walls are 8 to 12 inches (200 to 300 mm) thick, so plan on using a bit slightly longer than this. Use a large felt-tipped marker to outline the vent hole you're going to create on both the inside and the outside face of the wall. The diameter of the outline should be $\frac{1}{2}$ inch (13 mm) larger than that of the vent pipe you'll be using.

Bore a series of holes around the perimeter of these circular outlines, but don't go right through. Stop each hole just past halfway through the wall, drilling first from one side of the wall and then the other. This two-stage approach makes for a more accurate drilling job, since it eliminates problems caused by the bit wandering up, down or sideways, as it would if you were drilling all those holes through the entire thickness of wall from one side. Don't try to overlap the holes as you work; just leave $1/4$ to $1/2$ inch (6 to 13 mm) of undrilled block between each hole. When you're done, use a sledge hammer to bust out the perforated disks of concrete block, then clean up the edges of the hole with a masonry chisel and a 2-pound (1 kg) mason's hammer. Don't forget to wear safety glasses.

Another common basement wall material, poured concrete, requires more time and effort to get through because it's solid, not hollow. Your basement wall is poured if it's a more

Rotary hammers work fastest when you use lots of pressure to push them into masonry. For best results, position yourself safely and comfortably so you can lean into the tool. Rotary hammers are loud enough that you'll need hearing protection in addition to safety glasses.

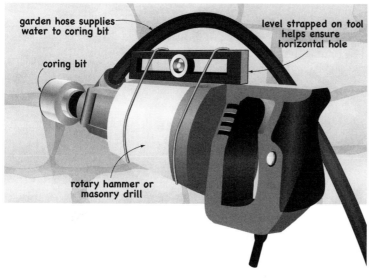

garden hose supplies water to coring bit

level strapped on tool helps ensure horizontal hole

coring bit

rotary hammer or masonry drill

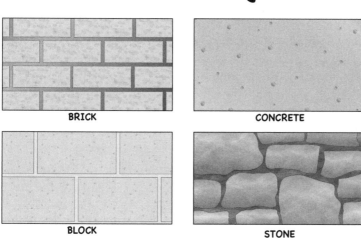

BRICK

CONCRETE

BLOCK

STONE

TYPICAL BASEMENT WALL TYPES

or less smooth gray surface, sometimes with small circular depressions here and there left behind by the forms that held the concrete while it cured. There are no mortar joints in a poured wall, though wood grain textures from the forms sometimes show up on the finished surface.

A coring bit is the best option for boring large holes through a poured wall or a structural brick foundation wall. Both types are non-hollow, so you can deal with them in the same way. A coring bit removes a cylindrical plug of concrete and is made to cut through any metal reinforcing rod that may be embedded in the wall. Coring bits are designed to work with rotary hammers or similar large masonry drills. They can be rented, along with an adjustable floor stand that will hold the tool while you're using it.

The same approach might work with a stone foundation, depending on the stone and the thickness of the wall. If your blocks are roughly rectangular, they are probably a sedimentary rock such as limestone or sandstone; these are relatively easy to bore through. Round fieldstone is much harder and requires more drilling time. However, all traditional stone foundations are beefy enough to pose challenges because of their thickness, which often ranges from 18 to 24 inches (460 to 600 mm). You can rent boring equipment for this work, though it might take some searching around. Look for drilling rigs that have a support stand to hold them up. It can take an hour or more of continuous drilling to get through a thick stone wall. If you can't find a coring bit long enough to go through your stone foundation in one pass, bore as deeply as you can, remove the bit, break the cylindrical plug out with a hammer, then continue boring deeper with an extension on the coring bit.

In some cases, you may be able to make vent holes just above a tough foundation wall, through the edge of the wooden floor frame and any siding that may be on the outside of the building. This might be an easier approach, but it all depends on how accessible the outside face of the floor frame is from your cellar location. If there's a floor joist near the edge of the frame, it may obscure access to the area you plan to put the hole through. The sides of the basement where the ends of floor joists rest offer the greatest possibility for vent hole installation without going through the foundation wall.

Occasionally, a house has a wooden foundation made of preserved studs and plywood. In this case, cutting a vent hole is easy. Select a location that's away from any studs, then mark the size of hole required. Bore a 1-inch (25 mm) hole through the plywood as a starting point for a reciprocating saw blade, then cut along the layout lines.

Root cellars aren't just for keeping bins of food fresh; they're also perfect for foods preserved by lactic fermentation, with salt and by corning.

Tape a 6-inch (150 mm) bubble level to a flat part of your rotary hammer or masonry drill to help you keep it horizontal as you bore holes through your wall.

Running Vents Through a Window

If you have a basement window you don't mind giving up for your root cellar, it's a whole lot easier to simply remove the glass, replace it with an insulated plywood panel, then run your vent pipes through holes in the wood before sealing around the surface.

To make a terrific insulated panel for vent pipe access, first laminate two pieces of $\frac{1}{2}$-inch (13 mm) thick exterior-grade plywood on each side of a 4-inch (100 mm) thick piece of extruded polystyrene foam. Polyurethane construction adhesive is perfect for holding this foam and wood sandwich together. Be sure to use a continuous bead of adhesive all around the perimeter of the foam to create an airtight, condensation-proof seal between the plywood and foam.

To achieve proper temperature and humidity levels, keep out insects and rodents, and prevent condensation problems in cold climates, it is crucial to seal all gaps to the outdoors.

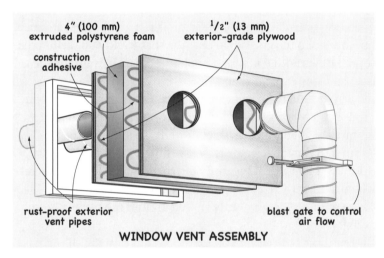

4" (100 mm) extruded polystyrene foam

$\frac{1}{2}$" (13 mm) exterior-grade plywood

construction adhesive

rust-proof exterior vent pipes

blast gate to control air flow

WINDOW VENT ASSEMBLY

Ventilation Pipes

The ideal root cellar ventilation system puts fresh air into the entire cellar space, not just part of it. To function well and promote air circulation, the interior ends of the pipes should be as far apart as possible inside your cellar. Install one short pipe that opens into the cellar near the ceiling, and make the other one long enough to end some distance away at the floor (see illustration, page 29). Separating the ends of the pipes forces air to circulate throughout the entire cellar, not just in one corner. And by arranging the outdoor ends of the pipes so they angle in different directions, you can take advantage of prevailing winds to promote air movement into and out of the cellar.

Galvanized metal pipes are the best choice for a root cellar ventilation system. They're strong, easy to work with and pose no risk of leaching chemicals into your food. There are two types of metal vent pipes to choose from: conventional metal ducting with a snap-together seam running along the middle of each length (available at building supply stores) or, for the

Root cellar ventilation is essential because stored vegetables are alive and give off gases. These gases can promote premature ripening and decay unless you vent them off, and some don't smell great. In most cases, the tiniest bit of ventilation is all that's required.

hyper-diligent root cellar builder, a stronger, spiral-joined pipe (available at commercial heating and ventilation equipment suppliers). Typically used for dust collection systems in woodworking shops, spiral-bound pipe is much more damage-resistant and looks cooler, in an industrial kind of way. Use tin snips to cut straight pieces of straight-seamed pipe to length before snapping the seam together. A power hacksaw is the best tool for cutting spiral-seamed pipe. You can rent one if your supplier won't cut pipe to length for you.

In addition to straight lengths of pipe, you'll need to work some elbows into the network, and this means joints. For straight-seamed pipes, use three $1/8$-inch (3 mm) diameter pop rivets to secure each joint. A pop rivet looks something like a small nail, except that its end expands when activated with a special pop rivet gun. Assemble the pipe joints, drill one hole in an overlapped section of the joint, insert a pop rivet into the hole, then slip the gun down over the shank and pull the handle several times until you hear a popping sound. This means the rivet has fully expanded and you're ready to move one-third of the way around the perimeter of the pipe to drill and rivet again. Three equally spaced rivets are sufficient to secure each joint.

Spiral-seamed pipe has thicker walls, so joints are best secured in this material with self-drilling screws. These have a tip shaped like a drill bit, and bore their own hole in the metal when spun with an electric drill and an appropriate driver bit. Three of these screws evenly spaced around the perimeter of each joint does the trick.

Regardless of whether you use pop rivets or self-drilling metal screws, seal each joint with aluminum tape. This self-sticking, heavy-gauge foil works better than duct tape for sealing joints because it never shifts or creeps after installation. Foil tape works best applied to the joint after pop rivets are applied but before screws go in.

A magnetic driver bit works best for installing self-drilling screws. It holds the screw head engaged and ready to drive so you don't have to hold the screw with your fingers. Magnetic driver bits fit all hand-held drills and impact drivers.

Root Cellar Vent Control

Root cellars require several kinds of hands-on management, including seasonal adjustment of the vents, which must be opened and closed depending on relative outdoor temperature and humidity. For this purpose, you can't beat metal blast gates. Designed as shut-off valves for dust collection systems in woodworking shops, blast gates are strong, effective and last many lifetimes of constant use. Blast gates include a metal framework that gets spliced into the vent pipe in a convenient location, with a metal slide that moves back and forth within the frame. Close the slide completely during very cold or humid weather, or open it up varying amounts depending on how much outdoor air you want to move into your cellar.

Vent Screens

Be sure to incorporate some kind of screen to prevent unwanted critters from getting into your cellar through the vents. Galvanized hardware cloth with $\frac{1}{4}$-inch (6 mm) mesh is perfect for keeping out rodents. Galvanized metal lath of the sort used as a ceramic tile underlay or base for plaster also works well. Cut out a circular piece with anchoring tabs, set it into the pipe just before the angled end pieces, then secure the screen with pop rivets and washers. To deny entry to flies and crawling bugs, supplement the hardware cloth with a layer of aluminum window screen installed inside the pipe behind the hardware cloth. Also make sure to use expanding polyurethane foam or caulking to seal around pipes where they go through holes in the walls to the outside.

Building the Interior Walls

Before you get busy with tools, you have more decisions to make. Will you build a stud frame wall insulated with spray foam? Or will you use structural insulated panels? Will your partition walls include wiring for lights? What about running water and a utility sink in your cellar for washing produce before bringing it upstairs? Once you have all these details sorted out in your mind, it's time to build your walls and doorway!

Stud Frame Walls

Stud frame walls are commonly used for residential house construction in temperate regions. If houses in your area are built this way, modified stud framing is an option for the interior walls of your root cellar, too.

Start by taking a look at the illustration on page 36 to become familiar with the parts of a stud frame wall. Vertical pieces of wood or steel — called studs and spaced 16 inches (410 mm) or 24 inches (600 mm) apart, measured from the edge of one stud to the corresponding edge of the next — are connected at the top and bottom to horizontal pieces called plates, which attach to your floor and ceiling. Once the frame is up, insulation and wallboard are added to complete the wall. Stud frame walls are a familiar construction option and work pretty well in root cellar applications, as long as you incorporate specific design modifications.

First of all, although you could use wood 2x4s (100x50s), or the equivalent steel stud components, to divide your basement and root cellar, 2x6s (150x50s) are better because they allow more room for insulation — almost 60% more, in fact. Also, unlike with regular, above-ground stud wall designs, in a basement it makes sense to use two bottom plates instead of

Electricity and plumbing must be added to your cellar during the earliest stages of construction. Although this work requires additional planning, time and money, lights and running water will make your cellar much more pleasant to live with. See Finishing Touches for Your Root Cellar on page 74 for details on planning electrical and plumbing features.

Although most people are more comfortable working with wood, steel-framed walls are also an option. Steel studs are made of thin metal that's easily cut with hand-held snips. You can also cut them with a chopsaw or a hand-held circular saw fitted with a specific carbide bit. Joints are held together with screws.

one, so you can fasten the lower plate to the (likely concrete) floor before securing the assembled wall on top.

For information on the metric conversions used in this book, see page 9.

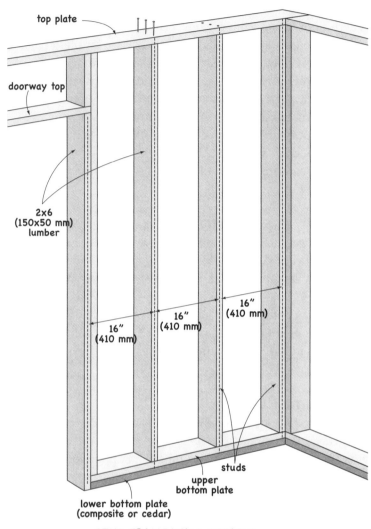

top plate

doorway top

**2x6
(150x50 mm)
lumber**

**16"
(410 mm)**

**16"
(410 mm)**

**16"
(410 mm)**

studs

**upper
bottom plate**

**lower bottom plate
(composite or cedar)**

STUD FRAME WALL DETAILS

In some jurisdictions, a strip of 6-mil vapor barrier plastic must be installed between the floor and the bottom plate to protect against moisture. Your local building inspector can tell you whether you need to do this. However, a composite bottom plate glued and pinned to the floor without a layer of plastic will be more secure and better sealed, and will be at least as moisture-resistant as a wooden bottom plate with a vapor barrier.

Because basement floors are often damp, consider using composite deck material or cedar lumber instead of ordinary wood for the lower bottom wall plate. If you're using a composite, choose a brand that's solid all the way through (as opposed to hollow), then cut and pin it down to the basement floor just as you would regular lumber (see below). Composites are rot-proof and won't contribute musty smells to your cellar even if they get damp.

To determine the proper stud length for partition walls, cut and stack three plates (two bottom plates and one top plate) on the floor in the wall's ultimate location. Measure the distance between the top of this stack and the bottom edge of the lowest part of the ceiling in the area where your wall will go. Yes, theoretically the distance between joists and floor should be the same no matter where you measure, but in practice the level of the floor and/or the joists may vary, typically by $\frac{1}{4}$ to $\frac{1}{2}$ inch (6 to 13 mm), though sometimes more. You need your wall to fit comfortably underneath the shortest part of the ceiling, so measure along the entire wall length to find where that is. As you cut wall studs to length, make them short enough to leave a $\frac{1}{4}$- to $\frac{1}{2}$-inch (6 to 13 mm) gap between the top of the wall and the shortest ceiling height when the studs are combined with the top and bottom plates. That way, you'll have no trouble tilting the wall up into position later.

One of your walls will unavoidably run parallel to the joists, so you probably won't be able anchor the wall to the joist at the top. Solve this problem by installing pieces of lumber blocking every 18 to 24 inches (460 to 600 mm) between pairs of joists flanking the wall (see illustration, at right).

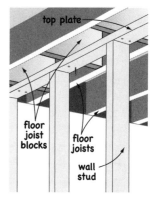

FLOOR JOIST BLOCKING

Explosive Results

Most basement renovations require wall frames to be fastened to a concrete floor. This fundamental work is best handled with a powder-actuated tool — PAT for short — also generically called a Ramset after the company that made the technology popular. All brands work in the same way. A small charge of gun powder is used to propel a nail-like pin directly into concrete without any predrilled holes. In addition to fast installation, powder-actuated tools provide strong results at a low cost. They are also a whole lot of fun to use, in a Clint Eastwood kind of way. Simple PATs cost less than $50 to buy, or you can rent one.

The most practical, lowest-cost way to fasten root cellar walls to a concrete floor is with a single-shot, hammer-activated PAT. Loading the tool involves inserting a pin into the muzzle, opening the chamber, inserting an explosive cartridge, then closing the chamber before placing the muzzle of the tool against the wood you're anchoring. You're now ready to fire the tool with a sharp hammer blow to the firing pin on the top of the handle. Firing the tool again involves manually unloading the spent cartridge case, inserting another pin into the tool, loading a new cartridge, then striking with the hammer once more. Even with this multi-step process, simple single-shot tools like these are still much faster than screws or nails for hard-surface anchoring, and they're safe. Just remember to wear safety glasses and hearing protection. Keep bystanders completely out of the area.

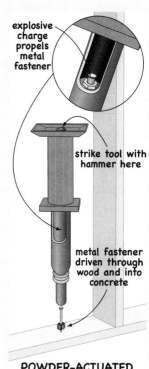

POWDER-ACTUATED TOOL

Continue by attaching the first bottom plate to the floor with construction adhesive and powder-driven fasteners. These are used all the time to secure building materials to concrete floors. See Explosive Results on page 37 for a closer look.

Next, lay the frame parts flat on the floor and assemble them as in the illustration on page 36. Tilt the frame up into place on top of the secured bottom plate, then anchor the frame with screws driven down through the upper bottom plate into the secured lower bottom plate. Use a level to make sure the wall frame is plumb (straight up and down), then secure it at the top with #10 by 3-inch (75 by 5 mm) screws driven up through the top plate and into the bottom edge of the overhead joists. Drive a softwood wedge into the gap left between the frame and the joists and secure it with a little glue before driving the screws home.

Once the stud frames are up, insulation is your next challenge. Fiberglass or mineral wool batts installed within the wall frame are simple and cheap, and builders everywhere are familiar with the stuff. But fiber-based insulation is also susceptible to moisture infiltration and damage, especially in the high-humidity environment of a root cellar. This can lead to mold growth inside wall cavities and reduced root cellar performance.

To insulate a framed root cellar partition wall in the best possible way, you'll want to use spray foam. Although it's more expensive than batts and rigid foam sheets, it's more effective, too. Much more effective. Superior air sealing is one reason why. Spray foam seals every nook and cranny as it expands and hardens, completely preventing any air transfer between basement and root cellar, boosting energy performance and making your root cellar as cool as it can possibly be.

Spray foam is applied when the stud frames are up and one side (it makes no difference which one) is covered by finished wallboard (see page 42). Contractors in more and more areas are offering spray foam application services. Products are also available for spraying your own foam in wall cavities. Although spray foam kits aren't cheap, they're typically less costly than hiring a contractor to do the work. Liquid foam comes in pressurized tanks connected to a spray gun with a hose. Put on safety glasses and a mask, then build layers of foam inside the stud frame cavities. Make your first passes around the perimeter of the cavity, then sweep back and forth inside the outline. To avoid building up too much foam at the end of each sweep, take your finger off the trigger every time you reverse direction.

You can boost the performance of your insulated stud frame partition even more by adding a 2-inch (50 mm) layer of rigid foam sheets to the wall (see sidebar, page 39). Secure the rigid foam to the frame using 3½-inch (89 mm) framing

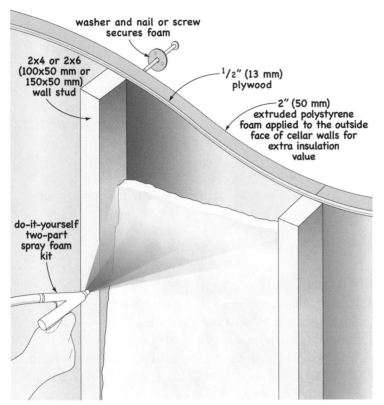

washer and nail or screw secures foam

2x4 or 2x6 (100x50 mm or 150x50 mm) wall stud

1/2" (13 mm) plywood

2" (50 mm) extruded polystyrene foam applied to the outside face of cellar walls for extra insulation value

do-it-yourself two-part spray foam kit

STUD WALL CAVITY SPRAY FOAM INSULATION

When applying spray foam, cover the perimeter of the space first, then fill in the center.

nails and washers. The foam not only adds insulation, but adds it in a continuous way, uninterrupted by the thermal bridging that would otherwise occur wherever studs span the gap between cellar space and basement space. Extruded polystyrene foam is especially good for this purpose because it's highly impervious to the migration of moisture vapor. It's also a highly effective thermal insulator. Just remember that most jurisdictions require that rigid foam be covered with some kind of sheet material to meet building code specs. A 2x6 (150x50) frame wall with 2 inches (50 mm) of rigid foam over spray foam yields an insulation value of R37.5 (6.6 RSI), compared with R27.5 (4.8 RSI) for a wall insulated with spray foam alone (see Insulation Education on page 40). When it comes to building a high-performance root cellar, the more insulation the better.

As you plan your insulation strategy, be sure to include the ceiling of your cellar. Warmth coming down from the floor above will raise cellar temperatures too high unless you have some insulation up there. You'll need to work vapor barrier plastic across the underside of the subfloor and joists if you're using batts — a nasty job that probably won't turn out very well no matter how careful you are. Spray foam is a much better choice for basement cellar ceilings. It acts as its own vapor barrier, simplifying the ceiling insulation job enormously.

It's best to install rigid foam on the outside face of the wall, because you'll want to have studs available immediately behind the wallboard on the inside face so you can anchor shelves to the wall. Therefore, if you plan to use rigid foam, you'll want to put up plywood and rigid foam on the outside face (see illustration, above), then fill the cavities with spray foam and finally add wallboard to both the inside and outside faces.

Insulation Education

The effectiveness of thermal insulation — that is, how well a material prevents heat from moving through it — is measured differently in different countries. In the United States, it is expressed as a resistance value, or "R value," based on imperial units. Countries that use the metric system use a similar scale, called RSI. (In Canada, insulation products might be labeled with either an R value or an RSI value, or both.) In both cases, the numbers refer to the amount of energy transferred over a given area at a given temperature over a specific period of time. High-density extruded polystyrene foam has a value of R5 per inch, or 0.88 RSI per 25 mm. Brick, by contrast, offers just R0.2 per inch (0.03 RSI per 25 mm). Vacuum-insulated panels, an up-and-coming building material, deliver a whopping R50 per inch (8.8 RSI per 25 mm). At the moment, vacuum-insulated panels are too expensive for use in root cellars, but that likely won't be true forever.

Structural Insulated Panels

Structural insulated panels (SIPs) offer a completely different way to build root cellar partition walls — different and superior in a number of ways. SIPs are factory-made sandwiches of foam in the middle with oriented strand board (OSB) or plywood glued on both faces. Since the rigid foam is permanently bonded to the sheet material, the combination resists flexing and is strong enough that it needs no studs. SIPs are meant for use as load-bearing features in homes — both above and below ground — so they're certainly strong enough for root cellar partition walls.

The foam in SIPs is factory-recessed along panel edges, so they straddle standard widths of construction lumber such as 2x6s (150x50s) and 2x8s (200x50s). Panels of these thicknesses yield R27.5 (4.8 RSI) and R36.25 (6.4 RSI) insulation values, respectively.

One reason SIPs work so well is that all joints are sealed with expanding polyurethane spray foam that's applied immediately before the panels get set in place. A generous bead down each side of all joints creates a connection that resists all air leakage. For highest accuracy and lowest cost, use a professional foam gun. See Spray Foam in a Can, page 21, for more information.

Although SIPs are self-supporting and require no framework for strength, they do need solid wood top and bottom plates to anchor them to the floor and ceiling. You'll also need to install wood in the recessed edges around door openings. To determine the proper length for the SIPs, measure the distance between floor and ceiling in various places along the wall location before cutting the panels to size. The best way to cut SIPs is with a circular saw equipped with a chainsaw-type bar and chain (the Prazi Beam Cutter is the best-known tool of

Structural insulated panels aren't usually found in building supply outlets. You'll need to seek out specialty dealers or go directly to the manufacturer.

In July 2000, Elliston, Newfoundland, declared itself root cellar capital of the world. The town of 591 people boasts 135 verified root cellars, some dating back 200 years.

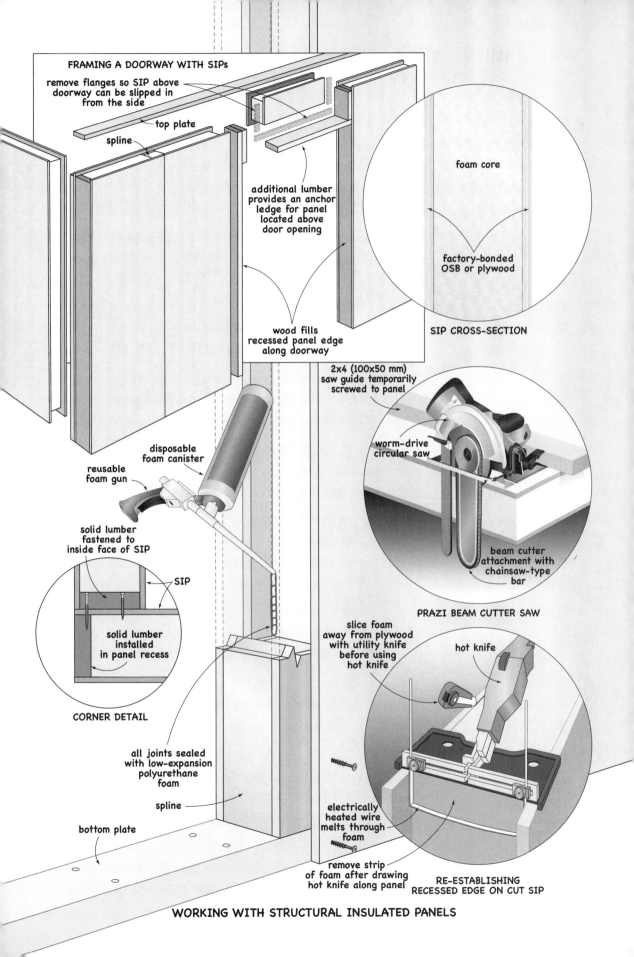

FRAMING A DOORWAY WITH SIPs

remove flanges so SIP above doorway can be slipped in from the side

top plate

spline

additional lumber provides an anchor ledge for panel located above door opening

foam core

factory-bonded OSB or plywood

SIP CROSS-SECTION

wood fills recessed panel edge along doorway

2x4 (100x50 mm) saw guide temporarily screwed to panel

worm-drive circular saw

beam cutter attachment with chainsaw-type bar

disposable foam canister

reusable foam gun

PRAZI BEAM CUTTER SAW

solid lumber fastened to inside face of SIP

SIP

solid lumber installed in panel recess

slice foam away from plywood with utility knife before using hot knife

hot knife

CORNER DETAIL

all joints sealed with low-expansion polyurethane foam

spline

electrically heated wire melts through foam

bottom plate

remove strip of foam after drawing hot knife along panel

RE-ESTABLISHING RECESSED EDGE ON CUT SIP

WORKING WITH STRUCTURAL INSULATED PANELS

this kind), though you can also cut them with a regular circular saw in two passes, one from each side. SIPs are too thick to cut in one go using a conventional saw. Once the SIPs are the right length, use a circular saw to cut out the wood on one side of the top of each panel so that the panel will slide into place under the top plate when you tip it up into position. When the panel is in place, replace the wood strip with spray foam and nails.

It's not uncommon to have to re-establish the recessed edges on SIPs you've cut in the field. A tool called a hot knife uses an electrically heated wire to slice a section of foam from panel edges, recreating the recess. You'll get the best results if your panels are perfectly dry and if you use a utility blade to slice the foam where it meets the OSB before turning on the hot knife.

When the SIPs are ready to go, fasten the bottom plates to the concrete floor of your basement (see Explosive Results on page 37 for instructions), applying expanding polyurethane foam to the underside of each plate before it goes down, to seal any gaps along the floor. Attach the top plates to the ceiling joists with #10 by 3-inch (75 by 5 mm) screws. Then tilt each SIP into position, apply expanding polyurethane foam on all joints and drive nails or screws through the side of the OSB or plywood and into the edge of the bottom plate to anchor the panel. Install joint connectors (called splines) in the recessed edges between neighboring panels as they go up. Finally, anchor the top end of each panel to the top plate with more screws driven in through the side of the SIP.

Once the SIP installation is complete, the foam is hidden and all you see is OSB on the inside and outside faces of the partition walls. Drywall fastens to SIPs with screws (drive them anywhere you like).

Wallboard

If you're using spray foam insulation inside a stud frame, you'll need to cover one side of the frame with wallboard first, then apply the spray foam, then cover the other side. With SIPs, both sides can be covered at the same time, once the SIP installation is complete.

For the outer side of the walls (the side facing the rest of your basement), you can use either drywall or solid wood or plywood paneling. Water-resistant drywall (usually green in color) or fiberglass drywall is best for the internal side of the walls and the ceiling because of the ongoing high humidity levels in a root cellar. Use hot-dipped galvanized or stainless steel nails or screws to secure the interior drywall, then tape the seams and apply a vapor barrier paint as extra insurance against humid air infiltrating the structure and causing unseen problems.

Cutting SIPs makes a mess, and the cut line will be obscured by bits of foam and wood within seconds of beginning a cut. You'll get the best accuracy if you temporarily screw a straight piece of lumber to the SIP, then use it as a guide for sliding the saw.

To make your cellar as versatile as possible, consider dividing the interior space into two or three sections. For more information, see Cellar Division on page 92.

Installing a Root Cellar Door

The access door you choose for a basement root cellar must be well insulated, and it must seal tightly. A window in the door is a nice option, as it allows you to admit ambient light into the cellar when you're working in there, though you will need to cover the window with a blind between visits (produce keeps better in the dark).

Install an illuminated light switch outside the cellar so you know at a glance if you have accidentally left the light on.

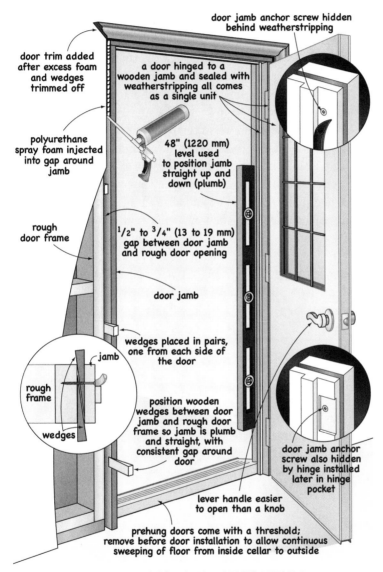

door jamb anchor screw hidden behind weatherstripping

door trim added after excess foam and wedges trimmed off

a door hinged to a wooden jamb and sealed with weatherstripping all comes as a single unit

polyurethane spray foam injected into gap around jamb

48" (1220 mm) level used to position jamb straight up and down (plumb)

rough door frame

$1/2$" to $3/4$" (13 to 19 mm) gap between door jamb and rough door opening

door jamb

jamb

rough frame

wedges

wedges placed in pairs, one from each side of the door

position wooden wedges between door jamb and rough door frame so jamb is plumb and straight, with consistent gap around door

door jamb anchor screw also hidden by hinge installed later in hinge pocket

lever handle easier to open than a knob

prehung doors come with a threshold; remove before door installation to allow continuous sweeping of floor from inside cellar to outside

INSULATED DOOR INSTALLATION DETAILS

For the best root cellar performance, you'll need a high-quality insulated exterior door. These come prehinged on a frame, with weatherstripping built right in. Installing this kind of door is more than a basic job, but it's nothing you can't handle if you're building the rest of the cellar. Buy an insulated, prehung exterior door and get it down to your basement.

That's the first step, and it should happen even before you've framed the opening for the door, because the job of installing the door is much easier if the amount of gap around the frame is just right. Aim for an opening that's $1\frac{1}{2}$ inch (38 mm) wider ($\frac{3}{4}$ inch/19 mm on either side) and $\frac{3}{4}$ inch (19 mm) taller than the outside dimensions of the frame.

When it's time to install the door, get some wooden wedges. Hardware stores and building centers sell them in bundles. These wedges fill the space between the door frame and the wall, and they provide a way to anchor the door and frame assembly. Slip the door into the opening, then grab a 24-inch (600 mm) carpenter's level to make sure it is plumb. Install wedges in pairs to fill the gap between the door frame and the wall — one wedge from each side, so they overlap. Place wedge pairs at the bottom and top of both sides of the frame, directly behind the hinges, and at the same level as the latch connected to the handle. Slide the wedges to create more or less overlap, moving the finished door frame as necessary to create an equal amount of gap all around the door (see the illustration on page 43). Anchor the door frame by driving screws or nails through the frame and wedges and into the rough wall frame, placing the screws underneath the weatherstripping so they don't show. Finish up by injecting low-expansion polyurethane foam into the gap. After the foam has hardened fully, which will take several hours, use a hacksaw blade to cut off the excess.

Wedges used in pairs provide continuous support across the width of the door frame; a single wedge would provide support at only one point.

Stellar Cellar

Your cellar is now ready to stock, though it's not going to win any decor contests. At least not yet. Want a root cellar that looks great inside, kind of like a fancy wine cellar, but filled with food? Take a look at Finishing Touches for Your Root Cellar, page 74, for hands-on electricity, plumbing, flooring, wall treatment, work table and shelving ideas that make for a stunning space.

Option 3
The Walk-In, Stand-Alone, Underground Root Cellar

Let's say you want a heavy-duty root cellar in your life, but you don't have a basement. Or maybe your basement is already completely finished. Perhaps your basement doesn't get cold enough for food storage because it's covered inside and out with foam insulation. Many basements sit too high above grade to receive enough cooling action from the earth. Any one of these situations should get you thinking about a stand-alone root cellar — one of the oldest and best options for keeping foods cool and preserved without additional energy inputs. They make especially good sense if you grow lots of food. A cellar right next to your garden saves a lot of labor moving produce around.

Imagine a small basement with no house above it, just a roof. That's a stand-alone root cellar. Typically accessed through a door in the side, this design is highly effective, though you will need to incorporate building techniques with a different emphasis from those used for above-ground structures. You'll also need to commit considerable time and resources to building an outdoor cellar. It's a serious amount of work.

Besides offering economical, convenient and ecologically sound food storage, a walk-in, underground root cellar also provides emergency shelter during a storm or natural disaster.

Location, Location, Location

A spot with good drainage is the most essential prerequisite for a stand-alone cellar, even more important than a hillside location, as helpful as that is for surrounding the structure with soil. Even though most fruits and vegetables require high humidity for long storage life, water is never good on the floor of a cellar. It's messy and dangerous, and leads to excess humidity. The area you choose must be reliably free of standing water or waterlogged soil year-round. No compromises. Although you can and should incorporate design details to keep water out (more on this later), nothing can protect you from waterlogged soil, because the floor of any good cellar sits at least somewhat below grade. Look for a slightly elevated locale, ideally with sandy, well-drained soil. Clay soils are much more difficult to dig than sand, and they hold water longer, making for a messier construction process and a less stable completed cellar installation. Avoid them if you can.

If a steel stake is easy to pound into the ground, the soil is probably light, easy to dig and good for a root cellar.

If you live in the country, and your property has been home to people for many generations, hunt around and ask area old-timers if they know of any cellars on your property. Chances are pretty good that you'll find an old cellar that will make a perfect location for cellaring now.

You'll also need to think about the seasonal dynamics of your yard. Where do people walk? What's the handiest place for a cellar you'll be visiting over and over in all weather conditions every time you carry produce back to the house? Is the location usually free of drifting or cleared snow? If you haven't paid close enough attention to your yard to answer these questions, take extra time to observe. It's worth it. There's no rush. Your cellar should last at least a century, so it's worth starting well.

Mark out your choice of a good location with something tangible — such as four 2x4s (100x50s) laid on the ground. An outdoor root cellar with an external dimension of 8 by 12 feet (2.4 by 3.7 m) yields a usable inside space of about 6 by 10 feet (1.8 by 3 m). That's plenty. You can certainly go bigger, but this size is large enough to store serious quantities of food. With care, you can stash about 60 bushels inside.

Live with your tentative location for a few months, watching the spot, walking back and forth to it, doing your usual yard chores and imagining life around it before committing to anything.

If you can find a hillside spot that has good drainage, is accessible and isn't in the way of any other activities, that's ideal. The only thing better would be a north-facing hill (south-facing if you live in the southern hemisphere). The less sunshine, the lower the cellar temperature, all else being equal.

Design Decisions

Four subterranean walls with a small door, earth banked up around the sides and a temperature-moderating roof on top — this is the age-old root cellar recipe in a nutshell. Though building it well takes more effort than meets the eye, a good stand-alone root cellar is a home improvement feature of great value. Whether you're constructing the cellar yourself or hiring the work out, your project needs to incorporate specific details if it's to succeed. Since the essential design features aren't typical of those found in regular house construction, you must be your own watchdog to make sure the project gets done right.

There are many ways to make your root cellar a reality — some very simple and rough, others more refined. Permanence, quality and performance are behind the recommendations you'll find here. The most durable designs use masonry walls of one kind or another. Stone was used traditionally for root cellar walls, and though this is still an excellent and beautiful choice, there are faster masonry alternatives. Concrete block is the most practical. It goes up quickly, requires no forms (as a cellar made of poured concrete would) and can be made very strong if you fill the hollow spaces within blocks with reinforced concrete. Getting rid of these internal air spaces

You'll probably need a building permit to construct a root cellar, but that's nothing to worry about. In fact, it's a good thing. Part of the price you'll pay for the permit will be allocated to inspections by an experienced professional at various stages of construction. And though these pros are probably not used to assessing the quality of root cellar projects, you can still expect them to provide sound advice as technical issues arise.

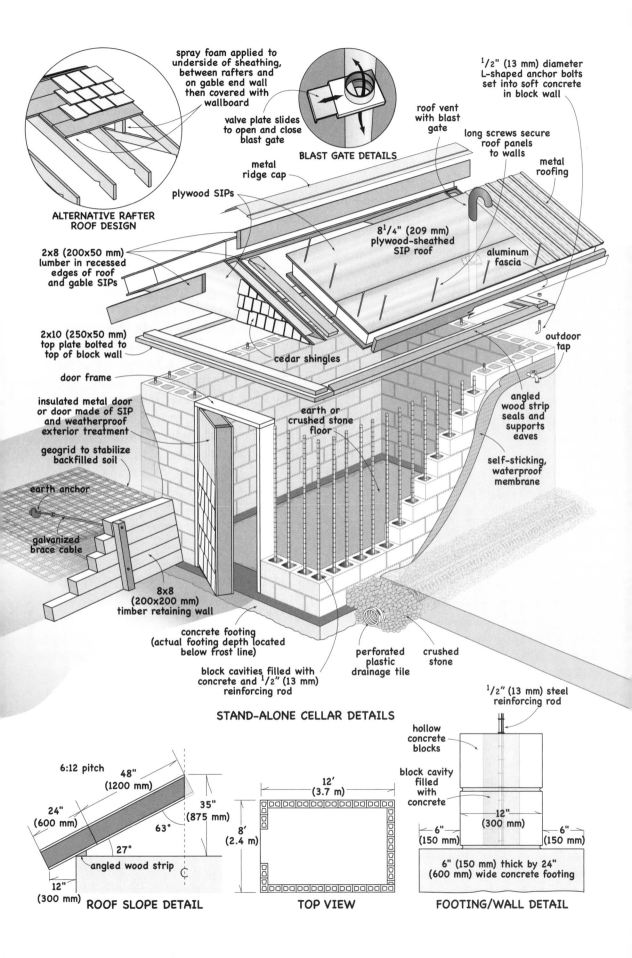

spray foam applied to underside of sheathing, between rafters and on gable end wall then covered with wallboard

valve plate slides to open and close blast gate

BLAST GATE DETAILS

ALTERNATIVE RAFTER ROOF DESIGN

1/2" (13 mm) diameter L-shaped anchor bolts set into soft concrete in block wall

roof vent with blast gate

long screws secure roof panels to walls

metal roofing

metal ridge cap

plywood SIPs

8 1/4" (209 mm) plywood-sheathed SIP roof

aluminum fascia

2x8 (200x50 mm) lumber in recessed edges of roof and gable SIPs

2x10 (250x50 mm) top plate bolted to top of block wall

cedar shingles

door frame

outdoor tap

insulated metal door or door made of SIP and weatherproof exterior treatment

earth or crushed stone floor

angled wood strip seals and supports eaves

geogrid to stabilize backfilled soil

self-sticking, waterproof membrane

earth anchor

galvanized brace cable

8x8 (200x200 mm) timber retaining wall

concrete footing (actual footing depth located below frost line)

block cavities filled with concrete and 1/2" (13 mm) reinforcing rod

perforated plastic drainage tile

crushed stone

STAND-ALONE CELLAR DETAILS

1/2" (13 mm) steel reinforcing rod

hollow concrete blocks

block cavity filled with concrete

6:12 pitch

48" (1200 mm)

24" (600 mm)

35" (875 mm)

63°

27°

angled wood strip

12" (300 mm)

ROOF SLOPE DETAIL

12' (3.7 m)

8' (2.4 m)

TOP VIEW

12" (300 mm)

6" (150 mm)

6" (150 mm)

6" (150 mm) thick by 24" (600 mm) wide concrete footing

FOOTING/WALL DETAIL

also increases the cooling action of the surrounding earth by minimizing the insulating value of the walls. Only above-ground components should have insulation.

Some people build root cellar walls with wooden timbers or logs set horizontally or vertically below the ground, but that's not the best choice. Soil in contact with wood always fosters rot and mold. An all-wood design won't last long enough to make the construction effort worthwhile unless that wood is treated with preservatives, and who wants to eat food stored beside something like that? Besides, wood is a pretty good insulator (which is bad in this case), and your cellar temperatures will be higher in the summer and lower in the winter with wooden walls.

There are two distinctly different root cellar roof options: an exposed and insulated sloped roof or an earth-covered design. Before the advent of effective insulation products, most root cellar roofs were covered in soil. Soil moderates internal temperature swings from summer to winter, but it also requires a strong, rot-proof structure for long life. Exposed roofs, on the other hand, are easier to build. It's easier to extend a weatherproof vent through their surface, and exposed roofs are more likely to keep rainwater out of the cellar in the long term.

Plans for a stand-alone root cellar are found on page 47. The instructions you'll read below apply to that drawing. Take the time to study the plans now and the instructions will make much more sense.

Step 1: Dig In

Whether you're building into a hillside or on flat ground, construction begins by marking out and excavating your spot. Dig out an area at least 12 by 16 feet (3.7 by 4.9 m) on flat ground, and larger if you're digging into a hillside. How much larger? Depending on the height of the soil and its consistency, angle the excavation back enough to eliminate the dangers of a cave-in. An angle of 30 degrees from horizontal is safe for even the least stable soils. If your location is flat, dig down 4 to 5 feet (1.2 m to 1.5 m) to create a level recessed floor that's accessible by stairs. A hillside location works fine with a completed internal floor that's level with the bottom of the doorway, though you will initially need to dig below floor level to create footings, which must be situated below the level of anticipated frost penetration in the completed cellar.

If your cellar site has sandy soil, and you're fit and strong, it's reasonable to excavate by hand with a shovel. If you'll be renting machinery to do the work, look for a mini-excavator. They're cute little versions of the big diggers you see on large construction sites. The best models have rubber tracks, so they

Square Corners

It's amazing how far from square you can be when you're laying out the sides of a building by eye, and no carpenter's square is big enough to help you accurately locate corners. This challenge emerges when you're marking lines to excavate for an outdoor root cellar, again as you're creating forms for concrete footings, and yet again (with greater importance) when you're laying out wall locations on those footings. But a simple technique lets you easily make perfectly square corners, guaranteed.

Mark one side of the root cellar as your starting side, then use what Steve calls the "two-tape method" to determine the location of adjoining walls. In the example illustrated below, we're assuming an 8-foot by 12-foot (2.4 by 3.7 m) overall external cellar size, with the 8-foot (2.4 m) wall, extending from corner 1 to corner 2, on the left as the starting side. Anchor the hook of one tape measure (tape A) on top of a 12-inch (300 mm) spike pushed into the ground at starting corner 1 (get a helper to hold the end of the tape there), then unroll the measuring tape as you walk a little more than 12 feet (3.6 m), just past the spot where you figure the spike for corner 3 should go. Hold the tape taut so that the tension will keep it hooked to the spike at corner 1, allowing your helper to let go. Now have your helper hold the hook of your second tape measure (tape B) over the spike at starting corner 2, then extend it on a diagonal toward corner 3 until tape B overlaps tape A. To find the magic crisscross point that determines a square corner, turn to the Pythagorean theorem:

$$(\text{length of starting wall})^2 + (\text{length of adjoining wall})^2 = (\text{length of tape B})^2$$

The lengths of the starting wall and the adjoining wall are known quantities: in this case (working with imperial measures), 8 feet and 12 feet; it's the proper length of tape B you need to determine. To do so, add the squares of 8 and 12 (64 + 144) to get the square of the length of tape B: 208. Once you figure out the square root of 208 (for which you'll need a calculator unless you're a math whiz), you'll know the correct length for tape B: 14.42 feet, or 14 feet $5\frac{1}{16}$ inches.

Now you simply need to adjust the relative angles of tape A and tape B until the 14-foot $5\frac{1}{16}$-inch mark on tape B crosses the 12-foot mark on tape A, at which point you've got a perfectly square layout at corner 1. Guaranteed.

Once you've determined the placement of corner 3, walk over to where you think corner 4 should be, holding both tapes tightly so that they stay hooked over their respective spikes. As you walk, tape A will extend farther while tape B retracts. When you reach the correct location for corner 4, the 14-foot $5\frac{1}{16}$-inch mark on tape A will cross the 12-foot mark on tape B.

This technique works on everything from excavation layout to the location of cellar walls on the footing. Just plug in appropriate numbers as you go.

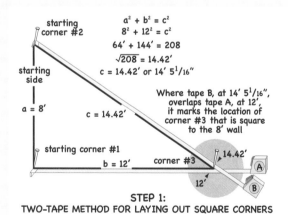

$$a^2 + b^2 = c^2$$
$$8^2 + 12^2 = c^2$$
$$64' + 144' = 208$$
$$\sqrt{208} = 14.42'$$
$$c = 14.42' \text{ or } 14' \, 5^1/16''$$

starting corner #2

starting side

a = 8'

c = 14.42'

Where tape B, at 14' 5¹/16", overlaps tape A, at 12', it marks the location of corner #3 that is square to the 8' wall

starting corner #1

b = 12'   corner #3

14.42'

12'

A

B

STEP 1:
TWO-TAPE METHOD FOR LAYING OUT SQUARE CORNERS

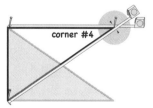

corner #4

STEP 2:
FLIP THE PROCESS TO DETERMINE CORNER #4

won't hurt your lawn. You can rent one to operate yourself, or hire a machine and operator.

Regardless of how you dig out the dirt, you must mark the excavation location. These marks needn't be exact, since the size and shape of the hole doesn't determine the precise wall location. All you need at this stage to get the job done is a handful of 12-inch (300 mm) metal spikes, a ball of string and a can of white spray paint.

Mark each of the four corners of the excavation site with a spike pushed into the ground. When opposite sides of the shape are the same length, and diagonal measurements taken corner to corner are also equal, the shape you've marked out has square corners (see page 49 for more information). Stretch strings between spikes and follow them with your can of spray paint, marking the ground. If you're digging into a bank, you may need to use more spikes to keep the strings straight as they traverse what may be uneven ground.

Step 2: Build Footings

Footings distribute the weight of a building onto a wide enough area of soil to support the structure without it moving, and creating footings is the first real building work you'll do.

The illustration at left shows how to use 2x6 (150x50) lumber and wooden stakes to create forms for the concrete that makes up the footings. Consult your building inspector about the required footing thickness for your project and substitute wider lumber for the 2x6s if thicker footings are required. Although you'll be setting this lumber onto dirt, do whatever it takes to get the top edges of the forms level and in the same plane. You'll be making two rectangles of wood, one forming the inner edge of the footing and the other forming the outer edge. Make the total width of the footing 24 inches (600 mm). That's plenty wide for a root cellar, and it allows more than the usual amount of leeway for orienting the walls square on the footing later.

It's essential that the forms be built on undisturbed soil. If you need to add small amounts of soil to get the wooden forms up to the correct level, add it only under the wood itself, leaving undisturbed soil where the bulk of the concrete will go.

Start with an outside edge of the outermost form rectangle, choose one outside corner as your starting point, then lay a 2x6 (150x150) down along what will be an outside edge of the footing. Place a 4-foot (1.2 m) carpenter's level on the top edge of this board and use a trowel as necessary to add and remove soil so that the 2x6 is more or less level. Pound a single sharpened 2- by 2- by 12-inch (38 by 38 by 300 mm) long wooden stake into the ground right next to the outside face of

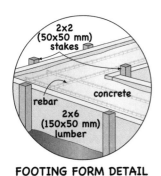

FOOTING FORM DETAIL

2x2 (50x50 mm) stakes

rebar

concrete

2x6 (150x50 mm) lumber

the 2x6, 3 to 4 inches (75 to 100 mm) back from the ends. You'll add more stakes later, to support the edge of the form every couple of feet, but for now all you need is one stake at each end.

Continue by adding another 2x6 adjoining the first one. Use the two-tape method to orient this second piece of wood square to the first (see Square Corners on page 49 for details), then pound a stake into the ground at each end. Continue the process for the other two sides of the outer form, then repeat for the inner form.

At this stage, you have your 2x6s more or less level, with corner stakes pounded into the ground, though not supporting the lumber yet. To anchor the 2x6s, drive 3-inch (75 mm) deck screws through the stakes and into the 2x6s, holding the lumber solid and in a level plane. Make this happen by driving a single screw into a predrilled hole through one corner stake, lift the 2x6 up $1/2$ to 1 inch (13 to 25 mm) higher than it sits on the soil, then lock it there by driving the screw all the way home. Raise the other end of the same 2x6 until it's level (use your carpenter's level to check), then lock it there with a second screw through the neighboring stake. Continue raising, driving screws and leveling the form lumber until all four sides of each rectangle are level and in the same plane (within $1/4$ inch/6 mm). Add more stakes every 24 inches (600 mm) along the outside face of each 2x6, driving two screws into each one. Pack loose soil around the outside faces of the forms to add support to them and keep the concrete contained, then call in a concrete truck or get your own mixer, gravel and Portland cement ready (see Mixing Your Own Concrete, page 52, for details).

When it comes time to pour concrete, enlist a helper or two and grab a couple of shovels, garden rakes and 24-inch (600 mm) long scrap pieces of 2x4 (100x50). Shovel concrete into the forms until they're about half full, then place lengths of $1/2$-inch (13 mm) diameter steel reinforcing rod on top. Use two lengths of rebar along each side of the footing, about 10 inches (250 mm) apart, crisscrossing in the corners. Shovel more concrete on top, rake it level, then pull 2x4s across the top edge of the forms to level the concrete. Let it sit for at least two days, then take out the screws, pull out the stakes, peel back the boards and get ready to make walls.

Still a little unsure about how concrete pouring works? Check out *Working with Concrete* by Rick Arnold. Although it covers much more ground than is required for making simple root cellar footings, it includes lots of confidence-building detail.

With your footings complete, consider adding drainage tile immediately around the perimeter of your cellar to give water a route *away* from the cellar rather than into it. Not all cellars

An 8-pound ($3\frac{1}{2}$ kg) sledge hammer is the perfect tool for driving wooden stakes into the ground.

For information on the metric conversions used in this book, see page 9.

Ready-mixed concrete is sold by the cubic yard or cubic meter (though these terms are typically shortened to just "yard" or "meter"). If you take careful measurements of the total width, length and thickness of your forms, a concrete supplier can usually provide a very close estimate of how much concrete you'll need.

Mixing Your Own Concrete

Depending on where you live and how accessible your outdoor cellar is, mixing your own concrete for footings might be your only option. The process is simple, and though you can mix by hand using a garden hoe and a wheelbarrow, a small power mixer will speed up the work considerably.

The best portable cement mixer for small jobs like root cellar footings uses an electric motor to spin a $3\frac{1}{2}$-cubic-foot (0.1 m³) drum. Pour sand, cement and crushed stone into the drum, let it revolve and mix, then dump the concrete out, either directly into your footing forms or into a wheelbarrow and then into the forms. Steve finds it works best to add a gallon (16 L) or so of water to the drum first, then one shovelful of Portland cement, then $2\frac{1}{4}$ shovelfuls of sand and 3 shovelfuls of crushed stone. As everything mixes, continue adding water until it's all wet, though not so wet that the mixture becomes soupy. Too much water reduces the cured strength of the concrete. Add another shovelful of Portland, $2\frac{1}{4}$ shovelfuls of sand and 3 of crushed stone, then let it all mix some more. Continue adding water and ingredients in these proportions until the mixer drum has reached capacity (about half full), then let everything mix until smooth. Concrete should be dry enough that it mounds up on a shovel, yet wet enough that it can be worked into every part of the forms. You know you have it right when the concrete looks a little too dry as you put it into the forms but develops a wet look after you rake it out and smooth the surface.

Immediately after pouring concrete out of the mixer, raise the drum back to the mixing position, then rinse the inside of the drum clean with a garden hose while it's rotating. Don't pour this dirty water out — keep it in the drum for the next batch.

Fresh cement is easier to mix into concrete and is stronger than stale cement. If the powder is soft when you pick up the bag, you know it's good.

need drainage tile to keep them free from leaks, but you won't know whether yours does until it's done, and by then it will be too late to add any conveniently. The 4-inch (100 mm) diameter, flexible perforated pipes that are at the heart of the drainage tile system should be installed so that the top of the pipe sits slightly below the top of the footing. The pipes should go all the way around the footings, sloped slightly toward one corner, where a non-perforated pipe will lead away as an outlet, ideally to a ditch or slope. To encourage continued drainage around the pipes, surround them by 6 inches (150 mm) of clean crushed stone all around. Building supply outlets offer the necessary hardware for this job, and installing it isn't difficult.

Step 3: Raise the Walls

Since most of the wall surfaces will be in contact with soil, masonry is the material of choice for an outdoor root cellar. It's strong, rot-proof and unsurpassed at transmitting cool soil temperatures to your cellar space. You could use poured concrete, brick or stone, but concrete block is the easiest, most beginner-friendly option.

Block thickness is the first decision you'll need to make as you plan your walls, and you should consult your local building authority for a recommendation. Strictly speaking, 12-inch (300 mm) thick block is typically specified for walls supporting up to a 7.2-foot (2.2 m) height of soil, though your cellar design might not involve holding back this much dirt. Then there's the big strength boost that comes from filling the block cavities with concrete and reinforcing rod. Each root cellar situation is unique, so if you're in any doubt about block thickness, get a professional opinion before you begin.

Another decision you need to make now has to do with esthetics. Standard concrete block may be relatively easy to use, but it's also pretty ugly, and unnecessarily so. For the little extra money it will cost, consider using a textured block for those small areas of your cellar that will remain exposed to view after backfilling. These would be the top course of blocks around the three buried walls (unless you're planning to build a concrete roof covered with soil) and part of the front wall, where the door is. Textured block has a factory-broken surface that looks much better than the smooth, molded surface on standard blocks.

Anyone can lay blocks, but it takes attention to detail to get the installation to look good. Each block must be level, mortar joints must be of consistent thickness, and block surfaces must remain free of mortar mess. If you've never worked with block before, you're likely to fall prey to one of two problems: either you'll think the work is beyond you (though it probably isn't), or you'll forge ahead with overconfidence and make a mess. Either way, check out the book *Building with Masonry: Brick, Block and Concrete* by Dick Kreh before you start. It'll give you the insights necessary to do a good job and the wisdom required to temper excessive confidence.

Before you get started, precisely mark the location of the outside corners of your cellar on your footings. Use the two-tape method again (see Square Corners on page 49), this time beginning with one corner marked on top of the footing. You'll find it easiest if you use a hammer drill to drill a hole in the concrete at each outside corner of your first wall, then install plastic anchors and wood screws to mark the locations. You can hook the ends of your tapes securely over the heads of the screws. Find the locations of the other two outside corners, mark them, then get ready for your root cellar to become three-dimensional.

Laying blocks successfully involves installing and following strings to guide block location, then respecting those lines as blocks go up. Three blocks go up in each corner, strings are raised to the top edge of the first course of blocks, then the

Start with the three hidden walls to gain practice before building the front and most visible wall.

Always begin by building adjacent corners partway up, then lay blocks between them by following a taut string extending from corner to corner. Build up the corners again before making the wall between them higher.

Hammer Drilling

There are two ways that boring holes in masonry is different than with wood. Besides a different drill bit, you also need a different drilling action. Drill bits for masonry always have an insert of extra-tough metal called carbide at the tip. Carbide resists wear much better than regular tool steel, offering a long working life. But a carbide masonry bit alone is not enough for efficient drilling. You also need a hammer drill. In addition to spinning, the business end of a hammer drill vibrates back and forth dozens of times a second as the chuck rotates. This vibration imparts a pounding action to the tip of the carbide bit, pulverizing concrete, brick or stone at the bottom of the hole and speeding up the drilling process many times over. Many ordinary cordless wood drills can be operated in hammer mode with the flip of a lever. Hammer drilling is three or four times faster than ordinary rotational drilling.

Blocks are usually delivered by a boom truck that sets a pile of them down in one go. Have the area in front of your cellar clear so blocks can be delivered as close as possible to where you'll use them.

Mortar hardens more quickly in warm weather and more slowly when it's cool outside. Before tooling mortar joints, let the mortar harden just enough to avoid staining neighboring blocks, however long or short a time that may be.

space in between is filled with more blocks. But even with strings and a careful mindset at the ready, you still need to have proper mortar for the job. Mortar is always mixed on-site because it's used in small quantities and must be fresh.

Standard mortar for block is a mixture of 1 part masonry cement to 3 parts sand, combined with just enough water to make a buttery, trowelable concoction. You know your mortar has the correct amount of water when it has the same consistency as cake icing. Although drum-style cement mixers aren't designed to mix mortar, they do an excellent job for a fraction of the cost of a mortar mixer, as long as you understand one trick. Since mortar contains no crushed stone, it has a tendency to stick to the sides of the mixer drum as it rotates. But if you orient the mixer drum more horizontally by putting a couple of 2x6s (150x50s) underneath one pair of legs, the rotating mortar blob flops and folds into itself perfectly.

Start by troweling about $\frac{3}{4}$ inch (19 mm) of mortar onto one corner of the footing, then nestle a block into it until it's level and the mortar joint is about $\frac{3}{8}$ inch (10 mm) thick. The block must be level in both a side-to-side and front-to-back orientation. Keep a 6-inch (150 mm) level in your back pocket to check each block.

Mortar always squeezes out between blocks as they're laid, but just ignore it for now. Neatness is the name of the game, so allow the mortar enough time to harden a bit. After a few hours, scrape off the excess mortar with your trowel, then mold the joint to a smooth, concave profile using a jointer (a hand tool made especially for this job).

You'll get the best cellar performance if you fill all the block cavities with concrete reinforced with steel rods after the mortar has fully cured. This makes the wall much stronger

Cutting Blocks

You will have to cut some blocks to length as you work. The low-tech option is to use a 3-inch (75 mm) brick chisel and a 2-pound (1 kg) mason's hammer. Mark lines on all four sides of the block where you want it to break, then give the chisel crisp hammer blows with the blade held on the lines. Just keep hammering your way around the block, and eventually it will break nicely.

A gas-powered masonry saw is a bit easier to use. The best ones are fitted with a spinning diamond abrasive blade and include a fitting to connect a garden hose to the saw. Shooting water onto the blade during use keeps dust down and makes the saw much more pleasant to operate. Without water, you will always create huge billows of dust when cutting masonry.

while also improving the moderating effects of the soil on root cellar temperatures by reducing the insulation value of the walls. Your cellar will be cooler in summer and warmer in winter, so it's definitely worth the trouble.

Before you start filling, cut pieces of $1/2$-inch (13 mm) steel or fiberglass reinforcing rod long enough to extend from the top of the footing to the top of the wall — one for each cavity. Fill the first cavity one-third full of concrete, then use a rented concrete vibrator to jiggle the mess down into place, allowing air bubbles to rise to the top. A vibrator is a hand-held electric tool with a flexible wand on one end. Push the end into the concrete when the cavity is one-third full, then again when it's two-thirds done and finally when it's completely full. It's essential that you use a vibrator when filling a space that's as narrow and tall as your root cellar block cavities will be. Big air pockets are almost certain to develop if you don't vibrate the concrete to consolidate it as it's poured. Once the cavity is full, use a sledge hammer to pound a length of reinforcing rod into the middle of the cavity, all the way down, then move on to the next cavity. Before the concrete starts to harden, place L-shaped anchor bolts into the top of the wall every 36 to 48 inches (900 to 1200 mm) to secure the 2x6 (150x50) rafter plates that will hold the roof to the walls. The illustration at right shows the details.

Although chances are good that water leakage won't be a problem if you've chosen a location with good drainage for your cellar, now's the time to apply two wall treatments to make absolutely sure you won't have trouble. It will never be easier to do than now, so don't skip this step.

Masonry is porous and leak-prone stuff, even when hollow concrete blocks are filled with reinforced concrete. That's

The same kind of gas-powered saw used to cut blocks is ideal for cutting rebar (reinforcing rod) to length. Just be sure to fit it with an abrasive wheel designed for metal, instead of the diamond wheel meant for masonry.

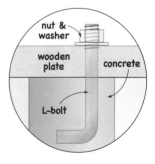

nut & washer

wooden plate

concrete

L-bolt

why it makes sense to coat the outside surfaces of your root cellar walls with a waterproof coating. This is the first part of a prudent two-part waterproofing campaign. If you've used textured blocks for the visible portion of the walls, leave them bare. They'll remain above ground after backfilling, so concentrate on those blocks destined to sit below grade. Xypex and Drylok are two brands of coating with long track records, and either will work well. Just brush it on the outside surface. Or, if you prefer, apply self-adhesive, rubberized roofing underlay to the walls instead.

Dimpled plastic drainage membrane is the second waterproofing precaution you need to take, and it works in conjunction with drainage tile. It's a tough, flexible sheet material that sits against the foundation wall, with the dimpled face pointing inwards. Besides being waterproof on its own, the membrane creates vertical drainage channels by holding soil slightly away from the wall. This eliminates the soil pressure that's usually the driving force behind water leakage through foundation walls. Drainage membrane allows water to trickle down harmlessly into the perforated pipes at the base of the footing.

Ready-Mix Concrete

There are two times during the cellar construction process when ordering poured concrete makes sense: when you're building the footings and when you're filling block wall cavities. This is especially true with a large cellar. As long as the concrete truck has easy access to your building site, it's not much more expensive to have concrete brought in, and it's much faster than mixing your own. Even if you have a portable, drum-style cement mixer, it takes a surprising amount of time to mix the quantities you'll need.

There are two things you should specify when ordering concrete: air entrainment and reinforcing fibers. "Air entrainment" is a fancy term for a small amount of tiny bubbles intentionally worked into the mix, and it's especially valuable for boosting the durability of concrete in regions with seasonal freeze-thaw cycles. Ready-mixed concrete usually has air entrainment, but ask for it just the same.

The addition of synthetic fibers to concrete while it's being mixed contributes strength and crack-resistance to the completed structure, and though it does cost a little extra, the results are worth it. The fibers look like coarse hair in the wet concrete.

You'll also be asked what "slump" you'd like for your concrete. Slump refers to how much a cone-shaped column of wet concrete sags downwards after a small test form is removed. A slump of 4 inches (100 mm) is common and works well for root cellar construction.

Step 4: Backfill the Soil

Soil moderates the air temperature in your cellar, and with walls complete and hard, now's the time to place dirt in position against them. You could do this later, after the roof is on, but continued work will be easier with the backfilling done first. A skid-steer loader is an excellent machine for this work, whether you run it yourself or hire a landscaping firm to do the job. Aim to have soil covering the full height of the side and back walls, up to the bottom of the last course of blocks (or all the way up if you're planning to build a concrete roof covered with soil), plus as much soil as you can place against the front wall on each side of the door. To maximize soil coverage of the front wall, build a retaining wall on each side of the path leading to the door. Timbers, stone or ready-made modular retaining wall systems all work well to flank a root cellar door. To reduce pressure on this structure and the cellar walls, install geogrid within the backfilled soil as it's built up (see Geogrid Eases Soil Pressure, below, for details).

If you couldn't avoid building your cellar in an area with heavy clay soil, consider bringing in some lighter, coarser fill for backfilling. It's easier to move into place and spread, and it puts less pressure on cellar walls than clay would during freezing winter temperatures.

Soil will invariably settle around your cellar over the first year after construction, especially after rains have soaked the backfilled soil. Be prepared to keep adding more soil periodically to settled areas using a shovel and wheelbarrow. You won't be moving large amounts of soil beyond the first few episodes of settling, so you won't need heavy equipment. Get some grass growing around your cellar as soon as possible. It will protect against erosion of the sloped sides and prevent weeds from gaining a foothold.

You can minimize settling around your cellar by compacting the soil in stages as you backfill it. A small, gas-powered compactor called a jumping jack, which uses a small, flat metal plate to pound the soil down, is perfect for the job. Compact after every 6 to 12 inches (150 to 300 mm) of new soil you add.

Geogrid Eases Soil Pressure

Geogrid is to soil dynamics what long, flat noodles are to lasagna. It's a coarse, synthetic, flexible mesh sheet installed on top of the layers of fill every 12 to 18 inches (300 to 450 mm) as it's pushed into place next to retaining walls and other structures that hold back soil. Geogrid gives the soil tensile strength, preventing it from applying side pressure, as it normally would. In the same way that lasagna noodles hold meat sauce and melted cheese together in a tall shape on your dinner plate, geogrid makes the mound of soil more or less self-supporting around the masonry walls and any retaining walls in the entrance area, greatly increasing the chance that your root cellar will age gracefully.

Step 5: Add the Roof and Gable Walls

Although traditional root cellars typically had soil banked up over a simple wooden framework for the roof, 21st century designs and materials offer better performance, longer life and an easier construction process.

The cellar on page 47 uses a low-slope, metal-clad roof to shelter the space, with two triangular gable walls to cover the area below the roof where it meets the back wall and the area over the door. You have a couple of options when it comes to roof and wall construction. Both involve building highly insulated, moisture-resistant structures to couple with the block walls below.

One excellent approach uses structural insulated panels (SIPs). These are factory-laminated sandwiches of wood-based sheet material glued onto each face of a thick slab of foam. The real-world energy performance of SIPs is amazing, and they function without the need for rafters or wall studs. You can learn more about SIPs on page 40.

A good alternative to SIPs involves conventional stud frame and rafter construction, sealed and insulated with spray foam applied to the inside surfaces, then covered with wood. This is far superior to the usual approach of using batt-style fiberglass or rock wool insulation, both of which are susceptible to moisture damage and offer excellent bedding material for rodents, which will always be eager to make themselves at home in your outdoor cellar. A batt-insulated frame is also prone to internal condensation in the high-humidity environment that is a necessary part of a functioning root cellar, and this condensation will promote mold growth. A SIP structure or foam-sealed wood frame, on the other hand, is impervious to internal condensation. At this point, most builders use neither spray foam nor SIPs, but don't let this sway you. These products really are the best for root cellar construction. Don't use anything else for an outdoor cellar.

Regardless of whether you use SIPs or a spray-insulated wood frame for the above-ground parts of your cellar, aim to have at least R30 (5.3 RSI) of insulation on your side to keep out summer heat and winter frost (see page 40 for information on insulation values).

For more information on SIP construction, check out *Building with Structural Insulated Panels* by Michael Morley. If you opt for studs and rafters, check out *Building a Shed* by Joseph Truini. Although it's aimed at building sheds and doesn't include information about spray foam, the framing techniques you'll need for your root cellar roof are covered very well in Truini's book. In any case, the details on spray foam in the previous chapter (page 38) are relevant to this application as well.

Structural insulated panels are light enough to be handled and installed by hand for a structure as small as a root cellar.

Make sure there are no gaps between the roof structure and walls. Extra care will yield better performance and keep rodents out.

If your site is particularly steep, or you don't like the appearance of a frame roof, you can build a concrete roof covered in soil. Building forms for a reinforced concrete roof is about as complicated as building a sloped roof, but design and construction details are more site-specific. Consult an engineer to determine required thicknesses of concrete, placement and size of reinforcing rod, and safe methods of form construction. You'll also need to take steps to waterproof the concrete to keep out rainwater trickling through the soil, either by adding Everdure Caltite while the concrete is mixing or by waiting for the concrete roof to cure long enough for a waterproof treatment such as Xypex or Drylok to be applied. Once the roof is waterproof, cover it with 24 to 30 inches (600 to 750 mm) of soil.

Step 6: Roofing, Siding, Doors and a Vent

If you've decided on an exposed sloped roof for your cellar, all the usual options for roofing a house apply. But there's good reason to go with factory-finished metal instead of asphalt shingles, wood shakes or roll roofing. Several good reasons, in fact. The first has to do with roof slope. Metal roofing comes from building supply outlets in sheets specially ordered to match the length of specific roofs. It's secured to the underlying roof structure with screws fitted with flexible neoprene washers under the heads to keep water out. A root cellar doesn't need to have a steep roof, and metal keeps out water better than any kind of shingles when used in low-slope applications. Metal also goes up fast, and the factory finish keeps looking new for at least a couple of decades.

All this is reason enough to use metal, but perhaps the best incentive of all has to do with performance. The right metal roofing used in the right way keeps out more summertime heat than any other kind of roofing, thanks to reflective radiant barrier products. The greatest source of damaging summertime heat comes from direct sunlight. The more of that heat you can reflect away, the cooler your cellar will be. That's why a growing number of metal roofing products come with factory-applied coatings meant to do just that. Ask about this when you choose a roofing product. There are also reflective radiant barrier membranes you can install on top of the roof sheathing and underneath the metal roofing before it goes down.

You can use the same kind of metal roofing to cover the gable end walls, or, for a more rustic look, you can go with wood shingles if they're produced in the region where you live and have been proven durable under local conditions. Although wood shingles sometimes have a comparatively short life on roofs (as little as 10 to 15 years), they can easily last 60 or 70 years without any kind of finish when used on walls.

Everdure Caltite is a unique ingredient that makes concrete completely waterproof. Add it while the concrete is mixing, and a concrete roof will be as waterproof as a boat hull. It doesn't make sense to use waterproof concrete to fill block walls, because the filling makes up only part of the wall structure and you'll need to take other waterproofing measures anyway. Waterproof concrete is, however, a wise option for root cellar walls made entirely of poured concrete.

Special screws are used to hold metal roofing onto the structure, and the easiest way to make holes for them is to do so when your roofing sheets are still sitting together in a pile. Drill 1/8-inch (3 mm) diameter holes every 12 to 18 inches (300 to 450 mm) through all the sheets at once, along the raised ribs that run from end to end.

If you have an SIP left over from building your cellar roof and gable end walls, use it to make an energy-efficient door. Inset lumber into the edges, then cover the exterior face with the same weatherproofing treatment you used on the gable end walls.

A root cellar needs ventilation to allow excess moisture and transpired gases to escape.

You'll get the best performance for your cellar from a door made of a structural insulated panel (see sidebar, at left) or from a prehung, insulated exterior steel door. Choose a model without a window, to keep your cellar dark. (Darkness is especially important for potatoes, as they take on a greenish tinge when exposed to light.) If your region is particularly hot or cold, consider building a dual door system. The outer door will lead into the first half of your cellar, which will store foods that can withstand warmer temperatures. A second insulated door will lead into the back half of the cellar, used for foods that need colder and more humid conditions. You'll need to build an insulated wall between the two sections to keep them separate. You'll also need to install a vent and control valve for each section, managing each section to create different conditions.

A roof vent is a key root cellar feature because it admits a small amount of fresh air and allows manual control over humidity and temperature. Four-inch (100 mm) diameter ABS or galvanized steel pipe makes an excellent vent. Add a U-shaped top to keep out water and drafts, and install a control valve inside to regulate air flow.

The best time to add a vent to a framed or SIP roof is after the structure is up but before the roofing goes down. If you're building a concrete roof, set a length of oversized ABS pipe in place while you're forming the roof. The pipe should be large enough to form a hole in the concrete that will be the right size to fit your vent duct later on. Before you begin backfilling soil over your finished roof, install and seal your vent pipe in the opening. Make sure the pipe is long enough to extend all the way up through the depth of soil you plan to backfill.

Stellar Cellar

Your cellar is now ready to stock, though it's not going to win any decor contests. At least not yet. Want a root cellar that looks great inside, kind of like a fancy wine cellar, but filled with food? Take a look at Finishing Touches for Your Root Cellar, page 74, for hands-on electricity, plumbing, flooring, wall treatment, work table and shelving ideas that make for a stunning space.

Option 4
Outdoor Root Cellaring

Not every vegetable in the garden has to come indoors when the growing season ends. Some vegetables, such as beets, cabbage and parsnips, actually taste better after a frost or two (see Using Frost to Your Advantage, page 102). Some do quite well outside for several months after a hard frost, and a few can even remain wonderfully edible throughout the winter with minimal attention. The key to outdoor root cellaring is insulation.

Storing Crops Right in the Garden
The Organic Blanket

The earth holds a surprising amount of summer heat in its mass. If you can trap this heat with some kind of fluffy organic blanket — clean straw, sawdust, leaves or even banked-up snow — it's entirely possible to keep soil from freezing for months longer than if it is left bare. In areas with mild winters, you can even keep soil soft and diggable all year round, making it possible to harvest snapping-fresh, cold-tolerant vegetables while everyone else is relying on food from the grocery store.

Vegetables that can be harvested when the soil is covered in snow include beets, Brussels sprouts, carrots, cabbages, endive root, Jerusalem artichokes, kale, leeks, parsnips and salsify. After the first hard frosts mark the end of the growing season, nestle them under an organic blanket and they'll keep reliably down to about 25°F (–4°C). They might even be okay at somewhat lower temperatures, depending on snow cover, the soil moisture level and the variety of vegetables involved. You'll know the weather has gotten too cold if the vegetables freeze — after they defrost, they will be soggy and soft, fit only for the compost pile.

The Trench Silo

Root crops come from the soil, and soil is wonderful at keeping them fresh. This is the power behind the trench silo, and a shovel is all you need to make one. Start by digging up your carrots, beets, parsnips and other long-keeping root crops, leaving the tops attached. Next, dig a trench 6 to 10 inches (150 to 250 mm) deep and 18 to 24 inches (450 to 600 mm) wide. Replant your vegetables close together in the bottom of

Fuseau is a French-Canadian variety of Jerusalem artichoke selected from wild North American stock.

Even in very cold climates, root crops accidentally left in the garden over the winter without an organic blanket often grow again the following spring, proving that they never froze solid.

this trench, replacing the soil around them and heaping it 6 to 10 inches (150 to 250 mm) above them, allowing their tops to extend just slightly above ground. A variety of crops can be kept in the same trench.

The temperature and humidity levels below ground are perfect for preservation, so you may be able to harvest crisp living produce from your trench silo right through the winter and into the spring. Since your vegetables are deeper underground once they're replanted in a trench silo, they are better protected against winter temperatures than they would be if you simply covered them with an organic blanket. How low can the temperature get? That depends on snow cover (the more the better — snow is a good insulator) and the type of soil you're working with: frost penetrates deeper into heavy, wet clays than it does into dry, sandy soil.

If you live in a region that has very cold winters during which the soil gets too hard to dig, you may have to leave your root veggies cozy in their trench until spring before harvesting them. But if your climate is mild enough to allow you to dig into the soil all winter long (perhaps with the help of an organic blanket over the trench), you can harvest as needed throughout the winter. In that case, be sure to mark the ends of your trench silo with a couple of stakes so you can find it easily once snow starts to fall. When you're ready to harvest something, simply dig down, take what you need, then replace the soil (and blanket, if you're using one) and move the stakes so you know where to dig next time.

Digging is much easier with a sharp shovel. Use a sharp file to create a 70- to 80-degree tip on the end of the shovel, holding it in a vise while you work.

Prepare to Share

Where Steve lives, white-tailed deer are everywhere, though an electric livestock fence has helped him forge an agreement with them about who gets the garden space during the growing season. The deer are quite respectful, at least until winter arrives. That's when push comes to shove over the remaining kale, beets and carrots Steve has protected for harvesting through early snows. At that point, it takes a sturdier physical barrier to keep wild herbivores away. (An electric fence doesn't work during winter because the snow acts as an insulator, preventing deer from receiving a shock.) A fence made of old lumber or snow fencing usually does the trick. Still, if you plan to keep produce in the garden for long-term winter harvests and you have wild animals in your neighborhood, prepare yourself for differing opinions about who gets what, and leave at least a little bit available for your four-legged neighbors.

The Hole-in-the-Ground Cellar Pit

The human race probably wouldn't be around today if preserving food were a technically complicated affair. The effectiveness of the root pit proves it. Nothing more than a glorified hole in the ground, a root pit offers simplicity and economy of construction in exchange for a certain amount of inconvenience. It may not be the easiest thing to pull potatoes out of a pit during a February blizzard, but at least you didn't have to invest much in building a structure to keep the spuds in good shape. And they will be in good shape! Root pits work very well, as long as they're built according to some basic but essential parameters.

The first of these parameters is a location with good drainage. Sandy soil is usually the best because the particles that make up the soil are large, allowing water to be drawn down quickly by gravity. A slightly elevated spot is perfect, as it encourages surface water to run away from your pit as it percolates downwards.

If your wintertime temperatures drop below 25°F (–4°C), build your cellar pit deep enough that your stores are entirely below ground. As you dig the hole, flare the sides to keep the soil from caving in. You'll need more flare to stabilize light soils, less for heavier ones. Line the bottom and sides of the hole with straw or dried leaves to protect your vegetables from the soil. Cover the hole with a ³⁄₄-inch (19 mm) thick wooden lid, then cover the lid with soil.

Bulgarian black carrots have a deep purple exterior covering an orange inner core.

German yellow fingerling potatoes are a long, relatively narrow heirloom variety with exceptional flavor and firm texture.

6" to 8" (150 to 200 mm) compacted soil

4" to 6" (100 to 150 mm) of straw

flat rock or heavy board to shield chimney from rain

straw chimney for ventilation

long-keeping root crops

partial burying protects against colder winter temperatures

SEMI-BURIED CELLAR PIT

If you get more than a little snow where you live, use a felt-tipped marker to label the stakes with what kind of produce is in the pit. Snow and the passage of time make it easy to forget exactly where everything is.

If your winters are milder, you can make the hole shallower, storing some of the produce above ground and protected by straw or dried leaves underneath a 6- to 8-inch (150 to 200 mm) layer of compacted soil. In this case, you won't need a lid, but you will need to create a straw chimney for ventilation (see illustration, page 63). Place a flat rock or a heavy board on top of the chimney to shield it from rain. It is easier to dig and draw produce out of a shallow pit than a fully subterranean one, but keep in mind that it's not as frost-resistant.

Regardless of whether you dig your pit deep or shallow, mark its location with stakes to make it easier to find when snow builds up. You can store potatoes, carrots, beets and parsnips in the same pit, but if you have enough produce for multiple pits, separate the vegetables. You'll find it easier to retrieve the ones you want if each kind is stored in its own pit.

The Indoor Root Pit

If you have a basement or crawl space with a dirt floor, you have the makings of a fine subterranean root pit, even if the space is too warm and dry for optimal vegetable storage. Simply dig a hole in the floor and set a wooden or sheet metal box in the hole, then make a lid that fits tightly into the opening of the box. As long as your basement doesn't flood, an indoor root pit is a simple, inexpensive way to store long-keeping produce. It's also easier and more pleasant to retrieve food from the basement than it is from an outdoor pit.

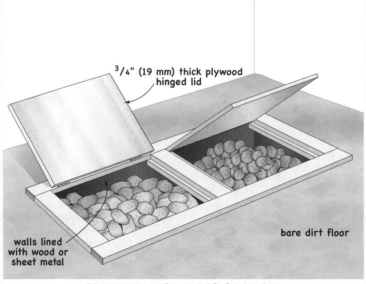

³/4" (19 mm) thick plywood hinged lid

bare dirt floor

walls lined with wood or sheet metal

BASEMENT DIRT FLOOR ROOT PIT

The Garbage Can Cellar

Keeping water out is one of the challenges of a hole-in-the-ground cellar pit, and that's where a garbage can will help. A galvanized metal can works best. Dig a hole slightly larger than the diameter of the can, and deep enough that the lid sits 6 inches (150 mm) or so below grade. Set the can inside the hole, snap the lid on, use a stick to pack soil all the way down into the gap around the outside of the can, then flare the soil out at a tidy angle around the opening. Long-keeping root vegetables will live very happily down there, even in the coldest weather. Long-keeping apple varieties will too.

Cut a couple of 2-inch (50 mm) thick pieces of extruded polystyrene foam slightly larger than the diameter of the lid and place the foam on top of the can to keep out frost. Cut another circle of ³/₄-inch (19 mm) thick exterior-grade plywood the same size and place it over the foam, with a stone on top to keep it from blowing away.

This technique also works well with other buried containers, such as an old chest freezer or a wooden barrel. Or you can line your pit with circular concrete well tiles.

The Old-Fashioned Root Clamp

The British use the word "clamp" to describe a pile of anything. A root clamp is an elongated outdoor pile of produce that's protected against frost. It's the easiest way to store large quantities of root vegetables in all temperate regions except those with very hard winters. To make a root clamp, mound

straw chimney for ventilation

flat rock or heavy board to shield chimney from rain

6" to 8" (150 to 200 mm) straw

6" to 8" (150 to 200 mm) compacted soil

straw tunnel for ventilation

slightly raised area of garden

ROOT CLAMP

If you have a choice, dig the hole for your garbage can cellar in sandy soil. It's much easier to dig than clay soil, offers better drainage and resists frost penetration better.

Periodically opening the can to examine and retrieve vegetables allows excess moisture to escape. Keep a small hygrometer inside to monitor humidity. Levels in the can should match optimum relative humidity levels for root cellars.

If you have a variety of produce to store, reserve different parts of the clamp for different types of vegetables, just to keep things organized.

your vegetables on a bed of straw, cover the pile with more straw, then cover everything with a layer of soil, shoveled on and packed down. The process is simple enough, but there are make-or-break details you must work into your clamp for it to function well.

Start by sorting your freshly dug crop — any long-keeping root vegetable can be clamped, though potatoes are the most popular — removing small and damaged specimens for immediate use. Place a 6- to 8-inch (150 to 200 mm) deep layer of straw on the soil, then heap your produce on top as steeply as you can, making the pile 32 to 40 inches (800 to 1000 mm) deep. As you work, create horizontal tunnels of straw that extend beyond the edges of the pile every few feet. These are an essential part of the ventilation system that allows excess moisture and gases to escape from the clamp.

With your vegetables mounded, cover everything with 6 to 8 inches (150 to 200 mm) of straw before grabbing your shovel and capping the pile with 6 to 8 inches (150 to 200 mm) of compacted soil. Be sure to leave the tunnels of straw exposed near the ground, and create chimneys of exposed straw every few feet along the top of the clamp. The idea is to allow a slow upward flow of air to pass through the pile, keeping things fresh, venting off excess moisture and helping the clamp retain enough of the earth's heat to prevent freezing. Place a flat rock or a heavy board on top of each chimney to shield it from the rain.

> Even after harvest, root vegetables are still alive and transpiring (which means they release water vapor). For successful storage, it is essential to vent off the gases emitted by the crops.

Straw and How to Get It

Straw — an essential ingredient in the root-clamping process — is the dried stalks of grain plants, and it's typically used for animal bedding. Don't confuse straw with hay, which is dried grasses and nutritious green fodder that's stored and used to feed livestock in the winter. Straw is definitely what you want for root clamping, and depending on where you live, the availability of straw might be the deciding factor on whether clamping makes sense. Even in farming areas, straw is often in short supply, since modern varieties of grain have been bred to grow short, sturdy stalks instead of long, floppy ones.

Straw is often gathered into large, round bales that are way too big to handle by hand and transport in the trunk of your car. Look for a friendly farmer who still puts up some straw in the old square bales. Cost is usually minimal: a couple of dollars for each small square bale. Three or four bales is all you need for a medium-sized clamp, and the organic matter can be worked back into your composting system to enrich the soil. A note of caution: Since it's virtually impossible to tell at a glance if the straw you're buying is clean or loaded with weed seeds, assume the worst and compost old clamping straw thoroughly before applying it to your garden.

Option 5
Root Cellars for Condos, Townhouses and Warm Climates

If geography or the design of your home prevents access to the natural cooling action of the soil that's necessary for a traditional root cellar, there are alternatives. Small, efficient, electrically driven units are available to create cooling action instead. They do add complication and expense to the root cellar adventure, and they do reduce the environmental advantages, but electric assistance also makes cellaring possible where it wouldn't normally be an option.

Does an electric root cellar make about as much sense to you as organic heroin? Are you concerned about the environmental implications of energy use? At first you might be puzzled by the idea of an energy-assisted root cellar. Depending on your environmental convictions, you might even be angered by the idea of electricity being used for this purpose. After all, how can anyone justify using environment-harming energy to keep food fresh when a traditional root cellar doesn't need electricity? Good question, but there's also a good answer. It springs from two facts.

- *Fact Number 1:* Many places in the world never experience the cold temperatures needed for food preservation.
- *Fact Number 2:* One way or another, food *will* be preserved in hot climates — and for people without the ability to create a naturally cool cellar, even if their region enables it.

In light of these facts, the only variables are who does the preserving and how it is accomplished. You can eat your share of factory-grown carrots pulled out of a vast, refrigerated warehouse somewhere downtown, or you can draw food from your own super-efficient, lovingly managed, personally stocked, energy-assisted root cellar. If you take care to construct an efficient electric cellar, you can even reduce the overall environmental impact of your food choices, especially if your energy-assisted cellar allows you to make use of locally grown foods in season. After all, the closer you are to the source of production, the less energy it takes to bring the food to you.

More and more electrical utility suppliers are offering green power options for customers interested in supporting sustainable technologies such as wind and hydro generation. Selecting power from these sources makes your electric root cellar that much greener.

According to the BBC, the almost 200 urban garden plots in Havana, Cuba, produce 4 million tons of produce each year; most of it is sold at nearby stands.

Help for the Basement-Deprived

If you live in a basement-free apartment or home, you're not necessarily out of the root cellar game. You might not even need to build and operate an electric cellar in order to store food. Instead, consider sharing cellar space with someone who has some to spare. Social networking options make it easier than ever to find a cellar partner in your area, and you'll gain more than just a new culinary experience. Food has brought people together since the dawn of time, and with courtesy, respect and consideration, you can make some great new friends over a wooden crate of carrots.

It takes about 0.8 calories of energy to move one pound of food one mile by truck (about 1.2 calories to move a kilogram one kilometer), and that really adds up. A 2-pound cabbage (a little less than 1 kg) can travel only 200 miles (about 320 km) from where it was grown before the energy required to move it exceeds the food energy contained in it. And a couple of hundred miles is not very far as these things go. Many foods regularly travel thousands of miles to get to your table, with huge hidden energy costs that go beyond what you pay at the grocery checkout. If an electric cellar allows you to eat locally for a longer period of time than the immediate harvest season, it still offers environmental benefit, even if it does use a bit of power.

Energy consumption in the United States increased by almost 40% between 1970 and 2000. It's expected to increase an additional 40% by the year 2020.

Location, Location, Location

Since you're not relying on the moderating action of soil to deliver cool temperatures, technically you can put an electric cellar anywhere indoors. That said, there are practical advantages to locating the installation along an exterior wall, with a window you can convert for use as a vent (see page 33), especially if you live in an area that gets cool or cold seasons.

As with any root cellar, you must vent your installation to the outdoors, though not necessarily all the time. Use the same two-vent system shown in the basement root cellar plan on page 29, along with sliding metal gates to control air inflow.

Energy efficiency is another reason to locate an electric cellar against an exterior wall. Whenever the outdoor temperature drops below the desired temperature of your cellar, you can use that cold air as a source of cooling action, reducing the need to use electricity for cooling — or even replacing it. In fact, with a properly insulated electric cellar structure, you may be able to go electricity-free for a large part of the year. With experience, you'll come to learn which vent control position is necessary to create the proper indoor temperature given various outdoor conditions.

If you divide your electric cellar so that it includes a slightly warmer area — 55°F (13°C) — you can also use it to store and age wines successfully.

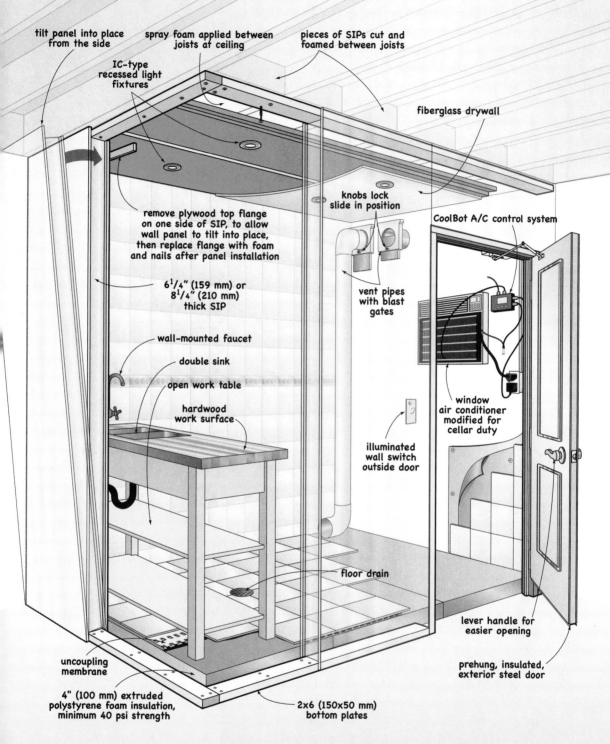

tilt panel into place from the side

spray foam applied between joists at ceiling

pieces of SIPs cut and foamed between joists

IC-type recessed light fixtures

fiberglass drywall

remove plywood top flange on one side of SIP, to allow wall panel to tilt into place, then replace flange with foam and nails after panel installation

knobs lock slide in position

CoolBot A/C control system

$6^1/4$" (159 mm) or $8^1/4$" (210 mm) thick SIP

vent pipes with blast gates

wall-mounted faucet

double sink

open work table

hardwood work surface

window air conditioner modified for cellar duty

illuminated wall switch outside door

floor drain

lever handle for easier opening

uncoupling membrane

4" (100 mm) extruded polystyrene foam insulation, minimum 40 psi strength

2x6 (150x50 mm) bottom plates

prehung, insulated, exterior steel door

ELECTRIC ROOT CELLAR DETAILS

A Little Plug-In Root Cellar

Even if your home doesn't have room for a full-fledged cellar, you might be able to find space for a root fridge. Refrigerators typically have internal humidity levels of about 30% to 40% — way too low for anything more than short-term storage. That's why produce goes soft in a fridge, though it doesn't have to. By storing roots in airtight containers filled with slightly damp sand, sawdust or peat moss, you create a high-moisture microclimate that will keep food fresh and crisp as long as any traditional root cellar. To maximize the storage capacity of your root fridge, choose a refrigerator with no built-in freezer, then take out the shelves and build stackable wooden boxes that make full use of all internal space.

If your indoor space challenges make even an extra fridge impossible and you have an electric outlet on your balcony, you can try putting your root fridge out there — just make sure your condo bylaws allow this. Success will depend on the climate you live in (seasonal temperatures should remain above freezing for the most part) and how sheltered your balcony is from the weather.

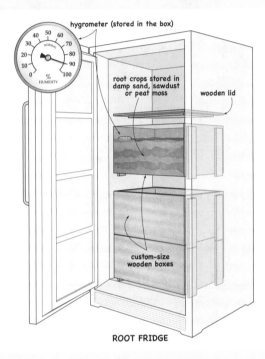

ROOT FRIDGE

Building an Electric Cellar with Structural Insulated Panels

Practically speaking, structural insulated panels (SIPs) are the fastest and most effective way to build electric cellar walls. Although the industry standard for insulation in walk-in coolers is only 4 inches (100 mm) of foam, you'll get a better cellar and more economical performance by using $5\frac{1}{2}$-inch (140 mm) or even $7\frac{1}{4}$-inch (184 mm) thick panels. The only potential difficulty may be getting the panels where you need them in your home. SIPs come in standard 4-foot (1220 mm) widths, and can be as long as required for the job at hand. If you have doubt about the practicality of carrying SIPs successfully to your cellar location, walk through the house carrying a 4- by 8-foot (1220 by 2440 mm) sheet of oriented strand board (OSB) or plywood. SIPs are thicker than this, of course, so keep that in mind as you go. If you find that you

Cutting SIPs is a messy endeavor, so plan to precut the panels outdoors. You can reduce the amount of cutting you'll need to do by designing your cellar so that its dimensions on all sides are multiples of 4 feet (1220 mm) — the width of a standard SIP.

can't get panels indoors, you can always build your cellar using 2x6 (150x50) stud frame walls (see page 35), with the internal cavities filled with spray foam (see page 38).

Whatever you do, don't insulate with fiber-based products. They work fine in houses, but the constant humidity levels in a cellar are too high for long-term success, even if the cellar is located above ground. Fiberglass batts allow the passage of air, which besides the wasted energy can also allow internal wall cavities to grow mold and mildew.

The procedure for building an electric cellar with SIPs is similar to what's described on page 40 for the interior walls of a basement cellar. The only difference is that the panels must be installed on all four sides of the cellar and on the ceiling. SIPs are physically strong and require no wood framing for structural support. All that matters is that you diligently apply expanding polyurethane foam to all joints as neighboring panels go together. As an added precaution against air leakage, apply polyurethane caulking to the joint lines between panels after they're up.

You must also insulate the floor. Extruded polystyrene foam is the best material for this job. Lay down two layers of 2-inch (50 mm) thick foam, with the sheets in the top layer oriented perpendicular to those in the bottom layer. Apply expanding polyurethane foam to the seams as you're putting each sheet in place — sealing against air leaks is vital for reducing energy use, for ensuring that your cellar can get as cold as it needs to and for maintaining a high enough level of humidity. Cover

For information on the metric conversions used in this book, see page 9.

The Easy Way Out

If you want an electric root cellar but would rather avoid the hassle of building one, consider a ready-made walk-in cooler. These are professionally built as self-contained, insulated units, complete with a compressor that's ready to go, so all you need to do is find a place to put one. Ready-made coolers with a range of compressor and coil locations are available, and you can choose either an indoor or a permanent outdoor installation.

One of two kinds of insulation materials is typically used in a walk-in cooler: extruded polystyrene foam or expanding polyurethane foam. If quality and long cellar life are your goals, choose extruded polystyrene insulation. It's more impervious to water and retains a greater proportion of its insulation value in the long term.

There are also companies that will custom-build a walk-in cooler to fit a particular location inside or outside your home. Google "walk-in coolers" to search for a supplier.

You'll probably have to compensate for lower-than-ideal humidity in a walk-in cooler, so plan on storing produce in damp sand or sawdust (see page 92) to help it retain moisture.

the foam with $\frac{5}{8}$-inch (16 mm) plywood, secured with screws driven down into the underlying floor structure. You'll need extra-long screws to make this happen, but there's no need for any support underneath the plywood other than the foam. Headlok is the leading brand of screws for this job. Their large, flat head is unique, and they come in lengths up to 18 inches (450 mm). If your underlying floor is wood, choose a screw that extends at least 1 inch (25 mm) into the floor joists. If you're anchoring into a concrete floor, predrill the plywood, mark screw locations on the concrete with the tip of the drill bit, remove the plywood and foam, then bore holes and install metal anchor plugs into the concrete before setting down the foam and plywood again. Finally, torque the screws down into the anchors.

Technology to Make Things Cold

An electric root cellar is really a walk-in cooler that's designed to handle extra humidity. There are several kinds of cooling technologies you can use, but before you choose one, you need to understand how much cooling your electric cellar needs, based on its size.

British thermal units per hour (BTU/hr) are a measurement of power commonly used in the heating and cooling business. The table opposite provides a guideline for assessing the approximate amount of cooling power needed for effective electric cellars of various sizes, assuming at least an R20 (3.5 RSI) insulation value (see page 40) in the walls, ceiling and floor, and an 8-foot (2.4 m) ceiling height.

There are two main ways to get this cooling action: you can install a conventional refrigeration unit in your insulated enclosure, or you can make innovative use of a window air conditioner to get the 33°F to 45°F (0.5°C to 7°C) temperatures you need for cellaring.

Harnessing the Sun

Photovoltaics are flat panels that convert light into electricity, and they're poised to make a big difference in how the modern world is powered. As the cost of photovoltaic production drops and the price of traditional sources of energy rises, a time will come when photovoltaics become mainstream. Right now, however, photovoltaics are still too expensive — at least without government incentives — for most people to use them to power an electrically cooled cellar that's within reach of the grid. If you still want to use the sun's power to keep your cellar cool, go ahead; from a technical perspective, it's completely possible. Photovoltaic panels can also be used in a smaller way, to charge a bank of batteries for lighting and small amounts of AC power produced by an inverter.

Cellar Size	Power Required
6 by 8 feet (1.8 by 2.4 m)	10,000 BTU/hr
8 by 8 feet (2.4 by 2.4 m)	12,000 BTU/hr
8 by 10 feet (2.4 by 3.0 m)	15,000 BTU/hr
8 by 12 feet (2.4 by 3.6 m)	18,000 BTU/hr
10 by 12 feet (3.0 by 3.6 m)	21,000 BTU/hr
10 by 14 feet (3.0 by 4.2 m)	25,000 BTU/hr

The conventional approach to cooling an electric cellar uses the same kind of electric compressors designed for walk-in commercial coolers. These are hard-wired into the circuitry in your house and require a place to vent outdoors and some plumbing to drain condensed water away. Compressor systems of the size suitable for a home root cellar cost around $2,500, plus the installation fee.

Need something simpler and cheaper? A growing number of small farms are using a residential window air conditioner to make their root cellar spaces cold, though this alone won't do the job. You also need a piece of equipment that sidesteps the air conditioner's built-in inability to cool air much lower than about 60°F (15°C), regardless of how large the BTU/hr capacity is and how small the room it's cooling. That's where something called a CoolBot comes in. This unique, inexpensive electronic control device easily connects to almost any window air conditioner, allowing it to refrigerate spaces enough for long-term vegetable storage. As long as the air conditioner model you choose has enough BTU/hr power to do the job, CoolBot makes it work. If you're handy enough to build a root cellar, you'll find it easy to wire up the unit so that a window air conditioner makes the place cold.

Thinking of using an electric wine cellar cooler as your thermal engine? They're not usually designed to produce temperatures cold enough for most produce preservation, so it's best to stay away from them for root cellar applications.

Stellar Cellar

Your electric root cellar is now ready to stock, though it's not going to win any decor contests. At least not yet. Want a cellar that looks great inside, kind of like a fancy wine cellar, but filled with food? Take a look at Finishing Touches for Your Root Cellar, page 74, for hands-on electricity, plumbing, flooring, wall treatment, work table and shelving ideas that make for a stunning space.

Finishing Touches for Your Root Cellar

The easiest way to bring power to your basement cellar is from an existing electrical box nearby, ideally one housing a plug outlet. These are almost always unswitched, allowing cellar lights to be controlled independently from their own switch. Before you make plans to tie into a particular receptacle, however, determine how many other receptacles the circuit serves. Switch off the breaker, or remove the fuse protecting the circuit, and see what doesn't work in other parts of your home. If more than eight or nine receptacles are on the circuit you have in mind, add a new circuit to serve your cellar.

Install a light switch for your indoor cellar just outside the cellar door, and choose a switch that lights up when turned on. This immediately alerts you if the light is accidentally left on.

Except perhaps in the rustic sense of the word, root cellars don't have a reputation for beauty. In fact, many are downright homely, though that needn't be the case. There's every opportunity in the world to make your root cellar a stunning example of interior design, especially if you're building indoors. The key is to enhance a technically excellent and energy-efficient structure with power outlets, running water, flooring options, wall treatments, work tables and storage features that are pleasing to look at, inviting to touch and convenient to use. But for this to work in an environment that is humid, cool and regularly filled with dirty vegetables, you need to consider more than just the usual interior design treatments.

In this chapter, you'll find all the details you need to know to make your cellar inviting and functional in a way few root cellars are. None of these added features are necessary for your cellar to work well; they simply make cellaring even more enjoyable.

Electricity

Although lights and power outlets in your root cellar aren't essential, including them in the design improves the experience of living with a cellar. Ample illumination makes it easier to sort and retrieve foods, while plug outlets allow you to use a workshop vacuum to clean, or power tools to modify shelving and other structural features. You might even find it handy to use a small appliance such as a food processor or a juicer in the cellar, completing one step of your food preparation without having to tote the produce from your cellar to your kitchen.

Because wiring is one of the first things to go in after the root cellar structure starts to take shape, you'll need to decide on the location of plug outlets, light fixtures and light switches at the earliest stages of planning. To that end, you'll find it very helpful to draw a scale floor plan of your cellar (which will also help you decide on your plumbing layout and shelving locations). Choose a scale that makes the footprint of your cellar cover most of a sheet of standard graph paper. Include the location of the doorway opening, the arc of the door as it swings, the position of any floor drains within the cellar space and the location of vent pipes and vent control gates.

The first purpose of this drawing is to act as a springboard for your imagination. What will it be like to walk into the cellar? Where is the handiest location for a light switch? Light fixtures? Plug outlets? To make it easier to answer these questions, cut out scale representations of the shelves you anticipate installing (see page 84), the floor area set aside for storage bins (see page 93) and the size and shape of the sink (see page 78) and/or work table (see page 83) you'd like to have in your cellar. Keep these scale paper cutouts loose for now, so you can move them around and play with different floor plans. Settle on positions that make sense for all these features, then add plug outlets and light fixtures where they make the most sense. The perfect wall plug configuration for most walk-in cellars is two GFCI plugs at floor level and one GFCI plug just above a work table. In most cases, two 48-inch (1220 mm) ceiling-mounted fluorescent light fixtures provide ample illumination.

Before you start building the walls, you need to finalize the path the wiring will follow through or across wall and ceiling structures. If you're building a stand-alone outdoor cellar, you'll also need to run power cables to it underground, according to local codes. This usually means protecting wires in conduit that extends from your home to the cellar. Your local electrical standards authority or a licensed electrician can tell you what's required.

The best time to install wiring in a wood or steel frame cellar is when the wall frames and ceiling structure are complete but the insulation is not yet in place. If you're building with SIPs, bury the wiring in vertical channels cut through the wooden outer surface and 2 inches (50 mm) into the foam. Either way, it's often easiest to run the wiring into the cellar area through the ceiling frame, then drop it down to switches and outlets as required. When the wires are in place, fill the channels with expanding polyurethane foam, then trim off the excess when the foam has hardened. If you're wiring an all-masonry cellar (or including an outlet or light fixture on masonry walls that are part of a framed design), you'll need to protect the cables inside conduit pipes.

Whether you're installing the wiring yourself or hiring an electrician, be sure to obtain the permits you need and follow local wiring codes. Infractions of electrical regulations can affect insurance coverage if damage or injury ever occurs because of technical deficiencies. And even if your local authority doesn't require a ground fault circuit interrupter (GFCI) on root cellar circuits, install one anyway. It will reduce the risk of electrical shocks, and that's especially important in potentially damp locations.

GFCI stands for ground fault circuit interrupter, a plug outlet or circuit breaker that's designed to prevent electricity from travelling directly to ground, which is what happens in most cases of electric shock. A GFCI can shut down a dangerous circuit within one-thirtieth of a second, protecting you from shock.

A full explanation of how to wire your root cellar for lights and outlets is beyond the scope of this book, but *Wiring a House*, by Rex Cauldwell, is an excellent resource if you want to tackle the work yourself.

Conduit protects wiring for a safer and more secure installation of wiring on hard surfaces. PVC electrical conduit is much easier to work with than metal conduit. PVC can be cut with any saw meant for wood, and it joins using a simple solvent.

Low-Profile Lighting

Recessed light fixtures (also called pot lights) sit flush with the ceiling surface, so they're perfect for cellars with a low ceiling. That said, you must choose the right kind of recessed fixtures, and there are several technical considerations you need to understand.

Since root cellar lighting works best with a wide beam of light for general illumination of the space (as opposed to spot lighting), you might want to install a high-voltage fixture that uses a standard screw-in bulb. The hardware is inexpensive, dimmer switches are cheap and replacement bulbs are available everywhere. Compact fluorescent bulbs fit into these fixtures and offer efficient lighting with minimal heat generation — an important issue if you'll be spending extended amounts of time working in your cellar with the lights on.

On the downside, high-voltage recessed fixtures are often large and visually obvious. That's why designers have created small, low-voltage lighting systems. The most popular versions use an MR16 bulb. With a face diameter of just 2 inches (50 mm), these small 12-volt bulbs are surprisingly bright and versatile, and they're available at most hardware stores.

Low-voltage fixtures do, however, need a transformer to step down the usual AC household current. They also generate a lot of heat, though that's only an issue if you'll be keeping cellar lights on for long periods. Cool-running LED bulbs meant to fit into low-voltage fixtures are gradually becoming available to replace conventional MR16 bulbs.

The most important technical issue you'll have to address involves the ability of the recessed fixture to seal against air leakage and heat transfer to surrounding materials. A fixture that bears the IC designation is an absolute must. These letters stand for "in contact," which means the fixture is safe even when completely shrouded in insulation. But even more importantly, IC fixtures prevent air movement through the fixture to the area above. Although this feature was designed to prevent warm, moist indoor air from leaking up through the fixture and condensing in cold attic spaces during winter, it also stops moist root cellar air from causing problems in surrounding ceiling structures.

Your final decision is what type of trim rings to purchase. These are the parts of a recessed fixture that are visible on the ceiling surface, but there's more to consider than just visual appeal. Some trim rings hold the bulbs fixed, while others allow the bulb to be aimed at an angle. Not all trim rings fit onto all fixtures, so ask before you buy.

Plumbing

Remodel Plumbing by Rex Cauldwell covers a lot more than just installing a new tap, but it's also an inexpensive resource that's easy to follow.

Plumbing the cellar for hot and cold running water, with a sink connected to a drain, gives you a place to wash stored produce before bringing it into the kitchen. Cellarable foods, especially root crops, are likely to carry at least a bit of soil — and sometimes quite a lot. Your kitchen will stay much cleaner if you do the initial washing of the vegetables in the root cellar.

Before you get started, refer to the scale drawing you created to help you plan your wiring. Figure out where a sink would work best for you and where it makes the most sense to tap into existing hot and cold water supply lines.

Water Supply Pipes

Even if your house has rigid water pipes (most likely copper), it makes sense to use PEX water supply lines to bring water from existing pipes in your home to a sink in a basement root cellar or indoor electric root cellar. PEX also works well for the interior supply lines in an outdoor stand-alone cellar. This synthetic piping uses fittings that connect easily, without soldering. And since PEX pipe is flexible, it's much easier to install in the tight quarters you'll find in and around a root cellar. There's no need for elbows; just bend the pipe as needed. Fittings are made to connect PEX to any kind of pipe you're likely to have in your house. Half-inch (13 mm) water supply lines work best for interior runs of pipe that feed a faucet. Install these lines through wooden wall and ceiling frames or mounted on the interior surface of masonry walls, using clips and screws.

PEX is an acronym for "cross-linked polyethylene."

The main supply line that delivers water from your home to a stand-alone outdoor cellar is different from interior water supply lines because it runs underground. It must be worked into the earliest stages of stand-alone cellar construction. A type of laminated pipe called PEX-AL-PEX makes an ideal underground water supply line for two reasons: first, the internal layer of aluminum makes this pipe much stronger than ordinary PEX; second, PEX-AL-PEX pipe can safely withstand five or six episodes of unusually deep frost penetration, whereas ordinary copper or plastic water pipe would probably crack and leak after the first. Install the main water supply line (and the main drain pipe) into a stand-alone cellar as the concrete footings go down, placing them below the level of anticipated frost penetration. Use a $3/4$-inch (19 mm) supply line to deliver water to an outdoor cellar, rather than the $1/2$-inch (13 mm) pipe you'll use inside — you need this bigger pipe to maintain adequate water pressure at a distance from your home.

It's not practical to have both hot and cold water supply lines running from your house to an outdoor cellar, so you'll need to either live with just cold running water or install a satellite water heater.

Running a year-round water line to your stand-alone cellar involves the same work as supplying water to any outbuilding. You need to extend a pipe from the existing network in your home through an exterior foundation wall into an underground trench leading to the cellar. This pipe must be protected from freezing temperatures along its entire length, which in cold climates could mean it must exit your house as much as 4 or 5 feet (1.2 or 1.5 m) underground. In situations where this is impossible, electric heating cables and insulation kits are available to keep exterior water lines without sufficient soil cover from freezing.

An easier alternative is to bring water to your stand-alone cellar seasonally, with a removable garden hose that runs along the surface of the ground from an outdoor tap at your house

Garden hoses have a threaded male fitting on one end and a female fitting on the other, but both the outdoor tap at your house and the one at your cellar will have male ends. A homemade adaptor made with two female hose ends, a short piece of garden hose and some clamps solves this connection problem.

to an outdoor tap at your cellar. This approach still supplies running water for much of the year, even in the coldest climates, and you can still enjoy the convenience of a tap inside your cellar — all for less work and disruption than a buried four-seasons system. If you decide to go this route, though, you'll need to install the water supply pipes inside your stand-alone cellar in a very specific way. First, the pipes serving the sink must begin at an outdoor garden hose tap that extends outside the root cellar wall. Unlike in a conventional plumbing installation, however, water won't come out of this tap during normal use; instead, it will go in, delivered by the garden hose. Second, since you're installing a seasonal system that will need to be drained before winter, all horizontal runs of pipe inside the cellar must slope slightly towards this outdoor tap, allowing water to drain out completely when you shut down the system in the fall. When cold weather threatens (or you need to get the hose out of the way so you can cut the lawn), remove the hose and open the faucet inside the cellar to let air into the system as water drains out.

Sinks and Drains

Choose a deep laundry sink for root cellar duty. If you have room for a double sink, so much the better: you can cover a pile of dirty vegetables with water in one side, then pull them out individually and scrub them off with a brush under slowly running water on the other side. Institutional-style wall-mounted faucets work best for a root cellar sink. They make it easier to keep the sink area clean, because there are no vertical pipes or flanges to catch dirt. They also eliminate the holes in the sink or counter surface that could allow water to leak down during a wet root-scrubbing session.

Sinks go hand in hand with work surfaces, so see page 83 for information on the best countertops for a root cellar.

Every sink needs a drain, though creating one may be easy or difficult, depending on your situation. If your cellar is in the basement, there's probably a concrete floor drain somewhere down there that's connected to the main drain leaving your house. The neatest way to connect your sink to that drain is to break a swath through the concrete floor, lay drain line in the channel, then refill the space above with concrete. If your cellar is above ground, with a floor frame underneath it, you'll need to open up the floor covering, install drain pipe, then replace the subfloor and finished floor — or, if the underside of the floor frame is open and uncovered, you may be able to install drain pipes from below. The drain for a stand-alone cellar needs to extend out from underneath the building, connecting to a large hole in the ground called a dry well that allows water to seep away in the surrounding soil. Check with local

Easy Indoor Water Supply and Drainage

If it's not possible to create a conventional drain in your basement cellar, consider having your sink empty into a 5-gallon (20 L) pail placed underneath. Though this solution is not as convenient as a built-in drain, it's not all that much trouble to periodically empty the pail outdoors or into a nearby laundry sink. Supply water to your cellar sink by running a hose from a laundry sink or hose connection somewhere else in the basement. Be sure to install a spring-loaded garden nozzle on the end of the hose that shuts off automatically when you release the lever. This will prevent you from absent-mindedly leaving the tap running, causing the pail to overflow.

authorities about the size, shape and design required for a dry well where you live. Regardless of what type of cellar you're building, use 2-inch (50 mm) drain pipe. You'll find smaller pipes, but they're more likely to clog.

There are two crucial features you must work into your drain: a trap and a vent. A trap is a curved section of pipe immediately below the sink. It retains a small amount of water that prevents sewer gases from backdrafting into your house. Less obvious, though just as important, is the need to vent your drain line. As water rushes down the drain pipe, it creates an area of suction behind it. If not relieved, this suction can pull water out of the drain trap, allowing foul gases to enter your cellar, or can cause slow or noisy drain performance. Drain lines are usually connected to a vent pipe that goes up through the roof of your house; however, this is not always convenient or even possible, especially in a basement root cellar. Most jurisdictions allow the use of a drain vent valve that sits underneath the sink. Placed as high as possible above the drain line and connected to it, the vent admits air into the drain pipe as needed, yet won't allow sewer gases to enter the room.

Does your basement lack drain pipes at floor level? You can purchase an electrically driven pump to raise wastewater up to existing drain pipes at the ceiling. (These units even work when connected to showers and toilets!)

Power-Washable Cellar

If you have a floor drain in your cellar (or have the option of installing one), consider the advantages of a completely waterproof root cellar. By making both the floor and the walls impervious to water (see pages 82–83), when it comes time to give your cellar a proper spring cleaning, you can simply hose down the walls and floor after moving out your crates and any remaining produce. It's fast, easy and highly effective. *Plumbing a House* by Peter Hemp includes information on installing drains. The guidelines for installing a shower drain most closely apply to a cellar floor drain.

Flooring

Although you could just live with the plain concrete floor usually found in a cold room or basement root cellar, or the dirt floor that has been the traditional choice for stand-alone root cellars for centuries, there are beautification options. Stamped concrete, solid wood and tiles are three worth looking at.

Stamping is a technique that imparts color and texture to fresh concrete. Best applied over solid existing concrete or dry, compacted fill, the process involves applying coloring dyes to the surface of the concrete when it's wet. Immediately thereafter, a textured rubber mat is placed over the concrete and pounded down to transfer visual details to the concrete. Texturing mats are available in a range of patterns that simulate stone or tile.

For a more rustic look that is easier on the feet than concrete, consider an unfinished wood floor. Either softwood or hardwood will work fine. Although you can't hose down a wood floor, you can keep it plenty clean with a broom. Sprinkle a little water on the surface before sweeping, to keep dust down.

Hard surface tiles such as ceramics, porcelain and stone make a durable and beautiful cellar floor, especially when they're combined with a built-in floor drain in a waterproof cellar installation. The trick to making a reliable tile floor happen involves using a modern tile setting accessory called an uncoupling membrane, which has roots going back to the Middle Ages.

In the late 1980s, the German company Schluter Systems pioneered the development of the first modern synthetic uncoupling membrane, bearing in mind lessons learned from traditional, sand-based ceramic tile installations dating back more than a thousand years. Back then, the best tiles were set in mortar laid down on beds of sand contained on all four sides to provide solid support while also allowing a tiny amount of side-to-side expansion and contraction of the tiles, grout and setting mortar they rested on. This bit of side-to-side forgiveness is key, because it dissipates shear forces and prevents tile cracking and grout failure; it's why these ancient tile installations remain crack-free, and it's why you want to incorporate the modern equivalent, now made by a handful of companies, if you plan to tile your root cellar floor.

Uncoupling membranes increase the reliability of all hard surface tile installations, regardless of whether you're putting them on a concrete floor or a wood-framed floor. The technology is also lightweight and easy to handle. A 320-square-foot (29.7 m²) roll of plastic uncoupling membrane

Small, inexpensive ceramic tile saws are effective for cutting tile during installation. These power tools use water to cool the cut and eliminate dust. If you have just a few straight cuts to complete, though, consider a snap cutter instead. It's a hand tool that scores the tile, then snaps it along the scored line. To make curved cuts, try tile nippers, a type of sharp-jawed pliers that allow you to nibble areas of tile away in small bites.

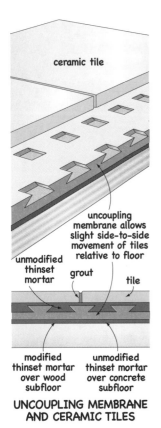

ceramic tile

uncoupling membrane allows slight side-to-side movement of tiles relative to floor

unmodified thinset mortar

grout

tile

modified thinset mortar over wood subfloor

unmodified thinset mortar over concrete subfloor

UNCOUPLING MEMBRANE AND CERAMIC TILES

weighs about 40 pounds (18 kg) and eliminates the need for 1,000 pounds (450 kg) worth of cement board. Uncoupling membranes really are a no-brainer for hard surface tiles installed anywhere.

To install uncoupling membrane, trowel a layer of thinset onto your subfloor, embed a layer of plastic uncoupling membrane on top, trowel unmodified thinset deep into the cavities on the top surface of this membrane, then press the tiles in place. Completely filling the recesses with thinset before the tiles go down is a crucial detail that's easy

A mixing paddle installed in an electric drill is the best way to prepare smooth and consistent tile setting mortar.

Root Cellar Refresh

Annual spring cleaning of your root cellar is a great idea regardless of the design, but besides taking out all the old produce and sweeping the floor (or hosing down the walls and floor if you have a washable cellar), consider the advantages of periodic ozone treatment, which not only eliminates odors, but also disinfects.

Ozone is nothing more than an ordinary oxygen molecule (O_2) with an extra oxygen atom tacked on to form O_3. In high enough concentrations, ozone has a powerful oxidizing effect that doesn't just mask existing odors but eliminates the compounds behind them via chemical reaction while also killing micro-organisms of all kinds. Afterwards, ozone turns back into ordinary, harmless oxygen, with no long-term residual presence at all.

The key to odor-busting ozone treatment is an industrial-strength ozone generator. All models use a small amount of electricity to create an output of gaseous ozone derived from oxygen in the air. Volumes of the gas are large enough to flood enclosed and evacuated spaces with high concentrations of O_3 for short-duration shock treatments. Don't confuse ozone generators with consumer-grade ozone-producing electric air fresheners or cleaners of the sort that occasionally elicit government warnings. True ozone generators are used successfully all the time by restoration crews to eliminate stubborn odors such as smoke, mustiness and other bothersome smells.

To refresh your root cellar with an ozone treatment (or your home, cottage or vehicle, for that matter), you can either buy a generator (they typically cost between $500 and $2,000) or hire a professional, if one is available in your area, to complete the treatment for you (this will cost $100 to $200). If you decide to do it yourself and your root cellar is more than 10 by 15 feet (3 by 4.5 m), set up a fan to enhance the distribution of ozone during treatment periods. The best ozone generators have built-in timers to automate the treatment. Once the generator is shut off, even if you leave the room closed, nothing can stop the eventual reversion of active O_3 back to harmless O_2. The chemical instability of ozone guarantees it. However, you will still need to buy a respirator to protect yourself as you open up a newly treated room for ventilation, just to be safe.

For those concerned about reports that industrial ozone emissions contribute to greenhouse gas concentrations, rest assured that a portable generator creates such small quantities of ozone, and for such a short period of time, that it has no wider environmental impact.

to overlook. An uncoupling membrane is not a complete substitute for diligent workmanship and good judgment. Thinset coverage under each tile must be 80% or higher for a reliable installation.

For completely waterproof performance in cellars designed to be washed down (see below), you also need to waterproof the seams between the sheets of uncoupling membrane. A 5-inch (125 mm) wide swath of KERDI (see page 83) set over the seams with thinset mortar keeps water out. Be sure to include a similar waterproofing band that extends several inches up the walls, connecting to the KERDI that covers the wall surface.

Wall Treatments

If you have finished your walls with water-resistant drywall and you're not fond of green, you can simply paint them a different color. One hundred percent acrylic latex paint offers the greatest durability. It's easy to apply, washes well, has low odor and cleans up with water.

Wood paneling or wainscoting is another option for framed or SIP cellar walls, and it offers a surface that's easy to fasten things to securely. Wood is best applied over a foundation of taped and painted drywall, because this treatment prevents air movement in and out of the cellar much better than boards alone, considering the cracks between them. Three-quarter-inch (19 mm) thick boards fastened horizontally are easiest to install on a framed wall because studs run vertically. You need to be careful when it comes to finishing the wood, though: varnishes can sometimes impart an odor to the cellar space and the food stored there. You can either leave the wood bare or finish it with a low-odor product such as water-based urethane or a food-safe oil finish.

Worried about mold growth on wood? Wooden shelves, crates and bins are a part of every root cellar in one form or another, and they won't grow mold even if left bare, and even with relative humidity levels up to 95%, because of the cold conditions in a cellar. But you do need to be watchful. Areas of stagnant air can boost humidity levels in isolated areas to the point where liquid water may appear on surfaces, allowing mold to develop. Even non-organic surfaces can grow mold as relative humidity reaches 100%. Adequate air circulation is the best way to prevent this problem (see page 85).

If you want to go fancy, and you'd also like to have the option of regularly hosing down your entire cellar to clean it, consider creating a waterproof ceramic tile installation on the walls. It's easier than ever thanks to the development of polyethylene waterproofing membranes with very low vapor permeance. They're made for showers and laundry rooms, but they're also

If your cellar has rough masonry surfaces, consider coating the inside with whitewash, a traditional, low-cost paint made of slaked lime and chalk that offers safe antimicrobial properties.

Urethane finishes tend to roughen wood surfaces as they dry. Use 180- or 220-grit sandpaper to lightly sand the wood, removing the roughness. A smooth surface is not only visually appealing, but also makes the walls easier to wipe down.

perfect for high-end root cellars. Polyethylene membranes, such as KERDI (see below) make otherwise porous ceramic tile installations completely waterproof, even when applied over conventional drywall, but just to be safe, it's best to complete this work over water-resistant or fiberglass drywall. The best systems come with waterproof grommets that seal areas where water supply pipes enter water-prone areas. Secure membranes with thinset tile adhesive, let it dry, then apply tiles on top with more thinset.

Want to add insulation value and create a tiling substrate all at once? KERDI-BOARD (see below) can be fastened to metal or wood studs with special anchoring washers, and is ready to tile as soon as it goes up.

Remember that you need to leave exterior masonry walls uninsulated wherever they are in contact with soil. This is the source of cooling action for most cellar designs, so you need to avoid anything that will add insulating value there. You can, however, use 100% acrylic latex exterior paint to improve the appearance of brick, block, concrete or stone.

Setting Tile by Michael Byrne offers excellent advice on all aspects of installing ceramic tiles.

Durable Waterproof Tiling Made Easy

A product called KERDI, made by Schluter Systems, is the leading example of waterproof tiling membrane, an orange fabric made to cover and waterproof drywalled surfaces before the installation of tiles. It doesn't look like it could possibly keep water out, but it does, and you can prove it to yourself. Use scissors to cut out a circle of KERDI about 12 inches (300 mm) in diameter, then make one cut from the outside edge to the center. Fold the circle into an inverted cone, then fill it with water. Even though the seam is just overlapped, not sealed, no water will leak out.

Schluter's KERDI-BOARD is a multifunctional foam substrate and building panel that supports ceramic, porcelain and stone tiles secured with thinset mortar. It comes in thicknesses ranging from $7/_{32}$ to 2 inches (5 to 50 mm) and in several configurations: as flat sheets, as L- or U-shaped segments and in a factory-slotted format that can be bent into curves. The board itself is impervious to water and forms the basis for completely waterproof walls and ceilings when used with KERDI applied to the joints. KERDI-BOARD is strong enough to use without additional support when you're building benches and countertops, and can even serve as self-supporting partition walls when used with proprietary metal caps on exposed edges. In all cases, pieces of KERDI-BOARD join with the same kind of thinset adhesive used to set the tiles.

KERDI-BOARD is also the easiest way to insulate poured concrete or block walls and prepare them for tiling (a situation you'll often encounter when creating an electric cellar in an apartment or condominium). Simply trowel thinset onto the walls, then press the boards in place against them; no further anchoring is required.

KERDI-BOARD can also serve as the foundation for a tiled root cellar work surface. It cuts like drywall: simply slice through the surface membrane on one side with a utility knife, snap the board over your knee, then slice the membrane on the other side.

Work Tables

When it comes time to sort or process cellared food, you'll be glad to have a surface to work on. You can build a small workbench on-site, using construction-grade lumber, or you can buy an open kitchen island table. Either can be fitted with a sink and taps or installed without running water.

The top of your work table should be solid, waterproof and easy to clean. You could use a standard plastic laminate countertop, but it's not the best choice. Water can (and eventually does) sneak underneath the laminate covering, making a mess of the particleboard below. Instead, try a solid surface material such as Avian or Corian. These synthetic options are both waterproof and attractive, and can be cut, drilled and shaped with conventional woodworking tools. Although access to solid surface material was restricted to professionals for many years, a growing number of manufacturers are now making it available at the retail level for do-it-yourself use. Google "DIY solid surface countertop" to find a local source.

Stone and ceramic tiles also make durable, waterproof work surfaces, especially when installed over KERDI-BOARD (see page 83). Fasten KERDI-BOARD to the underlying support frame with construction adhesive, then cap the edges with metal trim. Use thinset mortar to secure the tiles to the substrate.

Despite what you might think, hardwood makes one of the best root cellar work surfaces. Besides offering a knife-friendly cutting surface, wood is also less likely to harbor bacteria than plastic. Studies completed by Dr. Dean O. Cliver of the University of California show that wood has a natural ability to kill microbes that extends beyond any specific cleaning procedures. The best wooden countertop surfaces are manufactured with waterproof, food-safe adhesives. They should be maintained regularly with applications of finishing oil made especially for the job.

If space is limited and you can't fit a stationary work surface next to your sink, consider building a fold-down work surface. Hinged to the wall, with pivoting support legs, this design tilts up against the wall like a Murphy bed, out of the way, when you're not using it. When you need to sort, cut or process cellared foods, simply fold the work surface down.

Shelving
Shelving Systems

Your cellar will almost certainly evolve over time as your household food habits change and as you learn more about the art of root cellaring, so you need a flexible shelving system you can adapt and re-adapt. And since root cellar space is always at a premium, you want that shelving to hold as much stuff as possible, while also allowing maximum accessibility. The items you're going to store are almost always heavy, so the shelves must be strong and corrosion-proof; root cellars can sometimes get damp enough to cause bare or painted steel to rust.

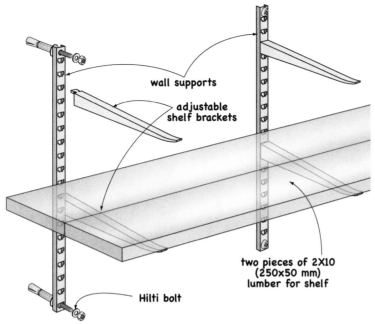

wall supports

adjustable
shelf brackets

two pieces of 2X10
(250x50 mm)
lumber for shelf

Hilti bolt

HEAVY-DUTY WALL-MOUNTED SHELF INSTALLATION

Steve uses three store-bought options in his cellar: hanging wire frame shelving, hanging platform shelving and a wall-mounted support arm system. All are galvanized, rust-proof, easily installed and easily reconfigured. None of them touches the floor, making it easier to sweep up the inevitable onion skins and shriveled carrots that find their way out of storage and underfoot.

Begin with hanging wire frame shelving, with shelves made of ordinary 2x12 (300x50) lumber. It's the cheapest and easiest to install (just a couple of heavy screw eyes torqued into overhead joists or metal anchors set in a masonry ceiling for the frames to hang from). Small jars of dried nuts, fruit destined for short-term use and containers of fermenting sauerkraut or flats of growing mushrooms are some of the items you can store on hanging wire shelves. You'll also find it handy to keep knives, brushes and your thermometer/hygrometer on these small shelves. Taller, heavier objects can be stored here too, if you have enough vertical space (just omit one of the 2x12s to create higher storage zones where needed).

Platform shelving hangs from the ceiling as well, but it's designed for wider shelves. Because it has angled braces fitted onto the support arms, you can use $3/4$-inch (19 mm) thick plywood up to 4 feet (1220 mm) wide to create shelves big enough to support fully loaded wooden crates, as well as crops such as winter squash, pumpkins and zucchini that are best stored up near the ceiling, where the air is warmer and drier.

If you want to store fully loaded produce crates on the walls, go for a wall-mounted support arm system. The best use heavy

Use large screw eyes with $3/8$-inch (10 mm) diameter shanks to support hanging wire frame shelving. If you're attaching the shelves to wood, predrill $1/4$-inch (6 mm) diameter holes to ensure that the threads enter the wood straight and easily.

galvanized steel arms that fit into slotted vertical anchor strips bolted to the wall, and are rated to safely support hundreds of pounds per arm. Crates can also be stacked on the floor.

Plan your shelf layout to allow as much top-to-bottom air movement through the cellar as possible. Instead of installing continuous shelving across all walls, leave 4- to 6-inch (100 to 150 mm) gaps between columns of shelves and keep them an inch or two (25 to 50 mm) away from walls. This will eliminate the stagnant pockets of air that can lead to excessive humidity in small areas, causing mold growth.

Anchoring Shelves to Masonry

Most root cellars have exterior walls made of brick, block, concrete or stone. Anchoring shelving hardware into masonry like this requires unique tools, hardware and techniques. All but the lightest shelves should be secured with expanding masonry anchors. Also called Hilti bolts after the company that made them famous, all expanding anchors operate on similar principles. Imagine a bolt without a head, and with sliding metal wings along the sides. Drill a hole that's just wide enough to accept the bolt, hammer it into place so that the threaded end extends about $1/2$ inch (13 mm) beyond the surface of the item you're anchoring, then place a flat washer over the threaded portion of the anchor and tighten on a nut with your fingers. As the nut is torqued down with a wrench, it pulls the entire anchor forward slightly in the hole, causing the metal wings to expand, jam and grip against the sides of the hole. What you get is a firmly secured metal bolt sticking out of the wall, an arrangement that can safely support hundreds of pounds (or kilograms).

To anchor lightweight objects such as electrical conduit and water pipes, you have two options: ordinary screws driven into plastic or metal anchor sleeves set into holes in the wall, or special screws that thread into the masonry, gripping directly into precisely predrilled holes.

Always drill holes for expanding masonry anchors at least $1/2$ inch (13 mm) deeper than required. This allows room for masonry dust, which might otherwise prevent the anchor from being driven completely into the hole.

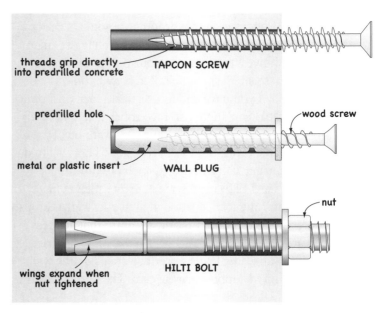

threads grip directly into predrilled concrete — TAPCON SCREW

predrilled hole — wood screw

metal or plastic insert — WALL PLUG

nut

wings expand when nut tightened — HILTI BOLT

Making Holes in Concrete

All masonry anchoring hardware needs some kind of hole to fit into. Depending on the size of the hole involved, you'll need one of two tools. For holes up to $\frac{3}{8}$ inch (10 mm) in diameter, a hammer drill is the implement of choice. Many seemingly ordinary corded or cordless drills also sport hammer capabilities. If you see a little hammer icon embossed in the adjustment ring just behind the end of the drill that holds bits (called the "chuck"), then you have a hammer drill. They get their name from the back-and-forth pounding action imparted to the chuck while it's spinning. Coupled with a carbide-tipped masonry bit, hammer drills bore holes in masonry at least three or four times faster than the same size of non-hammer drill. Hammer drills are ideal for making holes that accept plastic or metal screw anchors, as well as Tapcon screws (which thread directly into masonry).

For holes larger than $\frac{3}{8}$ inch (10 mm), rent a rotary hammer. This plug-in electric tool is really just a much larger hammer drill that also uses percussion and rotation to bore holes up to $1\frac{1}{2}$ inches (38 mm) in diameter. A rotary hammer is what you need when you're installing expanding masonry anchors that will support medium-weight and heavy-duty wall shelf systems.

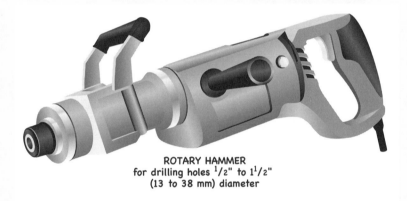

ROTARY HAMMER
for drilling holes $\frac{1}{2}$" to $1\frac{1}{2}$"
(13 to 38 mm) diameter

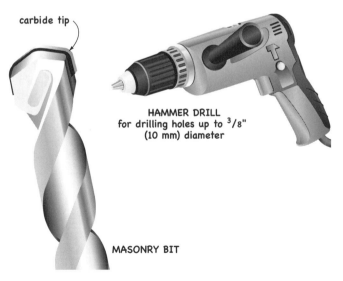

carbide tip

HAMMER DRILL
for drilling holes up to $\frac{3}{8}$"
(10 mm) diameter

MASONRY BIT

POWER TOOLS FOR DRILLING HOLES IN MASONRY

Part 2

Storing Food in Your Root Cellar

Every kind of root cellar, whether it's a fancy urban set-up or a humble potato pit, has the same purpose: to preserve food for as long as possible. But preservation is about more than just having the right kind of space. It's also about management. In the same way that successful driving involves more than just owning an automobile, successful root cellaring is about more than just having a cool, humid, dark storage space. You also need to stock and steer your root cellar with skill, and exactly how you do that depends on what you're storing and the design of your cellar.

Graded Storage

While it's important to learn how different kinds of produce vary in their ability to stay fresh in a cellar, there's more to effective cellar management than just this. You also need to understand something more fundamental, beginning with an appreciation of the importance of skin.

Every fruit and vegetable on the planet has a skin — some thick, some thin. Skin forms an essential barrier for keeping out organisms of decay, and any break, blemish or injury offers an entry point for deterioration, which will spread. That's why it's important to choose only the cream of the crop for long-term storage. Dented, scratched, broken and bruised produce won't last long, no matter how good a cellar you have, but there are strategies for including the misfits from your garden or local farmers' market in your cellaring system.

There's always the option of canning or freezing less-than-perfect produce instead of cellaring it, but there are limits to how much of this you can reasonably do. That's where a technique called graded storage comes in. It works well for all root crops and for many kinds of fruits, too.

When you're digging, say, carrots or potatoes from the garden, it's not unusual for some of the roots to get damaged by the shovel or digging fork. And some specimens will be smaller than others, which makes them more susceptible to drying out and shriveling over time. There's a wide range of potential storage lifespans in any given pile of produce — a range that can work in your favor or against you, depending on how you deal with it.

With graded storage, you separate the larger and better items for longer-term storage and arrange the damaged and smaller produce separately, available for immediate use. When grading produce, don't keep any that shows signs of decay. If you ignore

You can minimize damage to root crops from your garden by digging them up from the side of each row. Insert the shovel or digging fork 3 to 6 inches (75 to 150 mm) away from the potato vine or carrot and beet tops you're working on, then lean back on the handle to loosen the soil. Even in heavy clay, the roots should pull right out of the soil, without getting anywhere close to damaging contact with a shovel blade or fork tine.

this advice, that decayed item will probably cause premature deterioration of perfectly good neighboring produce, too. That old saying about one bad apple spoiling the barrel really is true.

Graded storage works best with a portable bin system (see page 93) or other small containers rather than permanently installed bins. Because portable bins are smaller, you can have many more of them, allowing the large, perfect, long keepers to be completely separated from the use-right-away misfits. Small bins also allow easier and more thorough weekly patrols for that one bad potato, parsnip, onion or beet that could spread decay to neighbors if not plucked out in time. Since the depth of produce stored in each portable bin is only about 10 to 12 inches (250 to 300 mm), it's possible to spot rot that would otherwise be hidden in the middle of a bin two or three times deeper.

Use cut, dented or runt produce first and for as long as you can. This takes willpower (don't we all want to use the best produce first?), but restraint is a virtue, and it's also the best way to extend the storage life of cellared foods.

Separation

Separation is another essential root cellar management technique, because it extends produce storage life. Different foods have different optimal storage conditions — some cooler, some warmer, some drier, some moister (see page 114). You will never be able to satisfy all these conditions perfectly in one open-concept root cellar — especially when it comes to humidity — but there are technical ways around the challenge.

Many cellars average around 70% to 80% relative humidity without intervention, and that's a little too dry to keep some types of produce crisp long-term. You can boost humidity somewhat in the whole cellar by placing moist burlap sacks on the floor or hanging them up. If your root cellar has a dirt floor, you can also sprinkle water on it as required to raise humidity. But you might still need to create high humidity just where you

You can't reliably guess the temperature and humidity of your root cellar and expect things to work out. Don't even try. You need to know the numbers. Invest in at least one high-quality thermometer/hygrometer. Two or three are better. Place one at floor level, one halfway up one of the walls and another at the ceiling. Temperature and humidity vary a lot with height, offering small microclimates you can use to your advantage.

Controlled Atmosphere Storage

Commercial fruit producers and packing houses sometimes use a system of controlled atmosphere (CA) storage to keep specific varieties of fruit (most often apples and pears) in good condition longer than is normally possible, even in ideal root cellar conditions. CA storage involves temperatures at or very near freezing, with regulated concentrations of carbon dioxide to modify the atmosphere in sealed storage environments. Long-lasting varieties that are picked at just the right stage of ripeness, cooled quickly and handled carefully can last almost from one growing season to another in CA storage vaults. This explains how grocery stores are able to stock local fruit so long after the growing season — far beyond what's possible in even a well-kept cellar.

Transipration is the loss of moisture from living plants, and the process continues even after produce has been harvested. Root cellars preserve food by reducing the rate of transpiration as much as possible with high humidity, though you do need to be careful. Transpiration can raise humidity too high, especially when produce is sealed in closed containers.

To prevent ethylene from spreading from apples to other produce, you can store apples in sealed plastic bags, with one pinhole in the bag per pound of fruit inside (two or three pinholes per kilogram).

need it. Sealable containers such as sand cans (see page 98) and wooden boxes with lids (see page 99) allow you to achieve the high-humidity (90% to 95%) storage conditions required for the best preservation of beets, carrots and other root crops. Layer the produce with damp sand, sawdust or peat moss as you pack it away, then either close the lids or leave them partially open to control humidity. The damp packing and the transpiration of the fruit or vegetables themselves create a moist microclimate inside the container, even in a cellar that is considerably drier than ideal.

If your cellar gets too humid, boost ventilation if the outdoor air is cool and dry enough. After increased ventilation, if the ambient air is too moist to lower relative humidity, place open containers of hydrated lime in the cellar. This white powder absorbs many times its weight in moisture. When the lime stops working, or you don't need it anymore, sprinkle it on soil or compost piles — it contains a lot of calcium and reduces soil acidity.

Another good reason to store each type of crop separately is the issue of produce personality. Some fruits and vegetables simply don't sit well next to each other. In some cases, this is a matter of flavor transfer (who wants apples that taste like onions?), but it's also a chemical thing. Some ripening fruits, including apples, avocados, bananas, melons, peaches, pears and tomatoes, give off a colorless, odorless gas called ethylene, which causes neighboring produce to ripen and spoil prematurely. Broccoli, cabbage, cauliflower and leafy vegetables all go bad much more quickly in the presence of ethylene, because it signals them to drop their leaves in a process called abscission — just one of nearly two dozen different plant responses to ethylene. Ripe apples, a prolific producer of ethylene, also cause potatoes to sprout and get soft. Depending

Cellar Division

Since the range of ideal temperature and humidity conditions for various foods is wider than you can expect to achieve in a single cellar space, dividing your cellar into two or three sections makes sense. This allows you to store things like avocados, bananas, garlic and onions in cool and dry conditions, while giving beets, carrots, eggplants, potatoes and turnips the cold and very moist conditions they need. The process is simple: create an insulated wall and door to divide one section from the next. Make sure each section has a separate controllable vent to the outdoors. If your floor plan allows it, it's nice to have a door from the basement into each section so you don't have to walk through one zone to get to another. Before building your cellar, consider its layout and location, then orient it so that the part you want to be coldest has the most exposure to subterranean wall surfaces.

on the size of your cellar, how much fruit you are storing in it and how much ventilation you have, it may be enough to keep ethylene producers on the other side of the cellar from ethylene-sensitive foods. If not, you'll need to find a separate place to store ripe fruit.

An 85% ethylene, 15% oxygen mix was historically used as an anesthetic for surgery. In concentrations as low as one part in 10 million, ethylene acts as a fruit-ripening hormone.

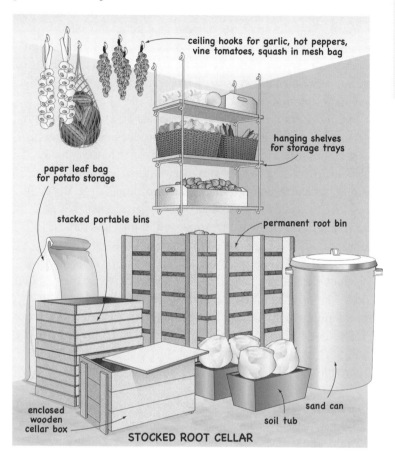

STOCKED ROOT CELLAR

ceiling hooks for garlic, hot peppers, vine tomatoes, squash in mesh bag

hanging shelves for storage trays

paper leaf bag for potato storage

stacked portable bins

permanent root bin

enclosed wooden cellar box

soil tub

sand can

Crop-Specific Storage Containers

Regardless of what foods you are cellaring, you will need containers to keep them organized and in good condition. The type of containers you choose will have a huge effect on your experience of root cellaring.

Portable Bins

The bulk of root cellar storage happens in some kind of bin, and most traditional bin designs are permanently installed in the cellar (see Permanent Bins, page 94). While this approach works, in 1991 Steve developed a system of interlocking, build-it-yourself portable wooden crates. He calls them win-win storage bins, and the instructions for building one are on page 96. The design includes short legs that interlock with the bin below, making stacks more stable. As many as four bins can be safely stacked on a hard, flat floor.

This system offers three advantages. First, since the bins are portable, you can take them to the garden or market, fill them on the spot, then carry them to your cellar in a wheelbarrow or the trunk of your car. There's no need for fancy packing — just place your produce in the bin gently to avoid damaging the skin.

Besides giving you something to transport the produce in, portable bins eliminate the damage that invariably occurs when you dump bucketloads of potatoes, beets or carrots into a big stationary bin. Cuts, bruising and dents shorten the life of stored vegetables unnecessarily by creating footholds of decay for micro-organisms.

Finally, portable bins allow much easier and more thorough periodic examinations of your stored produce. Since the total depth of produce in each portable bin is less than 12 inches (300 mm), it's easy to spot and pick out the "bad apples" that would wreak havoc undetected in a traditional large, deep bin.

All root vegetables, as well as onions, garlic, small squash, hard fruits and citrus fruits, store well in portable bins, assuming the bins are placed in an area of the cellar that provides the ideal temperature and humidity level for the produce within (see page 114). The spaces between the wooden slats that form the sides and ends of the bin allow lots of air circulation, which is great for ventilation in an area of optimum storage conditions, but not so great if you are trying to raise the humidity level inside the container to create a high-humidity microclimate.

Permanent Bins

Large capacity is the advantage permanent bins offer over portable ones. If you need to pack the greatest amount of food into a specific space, permanent, site-built wooden bins are the way to go. Because the pressure at the bottom of a fully loaded bin is so great, they are best used to hold strong, damage-resistant root crops such as potatoes, beets, carrots and parsnips. Do your best to place produce in the bins gently, rather than just dumping it in hastily.

To build a permanent bin, use construction lumber to create a bottom and sides that will fit snugly into your available space, then fasten these parts together into a bin that's open at the top. Wooden shipping pallets can often be used to make permanent bins, but you will still need to custom-build an installation that makes use of every square inch of cellar floor space.

Like portable bins, permanent bins work best in a cellar that already satisfies the optimal storage conditions for the produce you are storing (see page 114). If you need to create a high-humidity microclimate for your vegetables, sand cans or wooden boxes with lids will prove a better option.

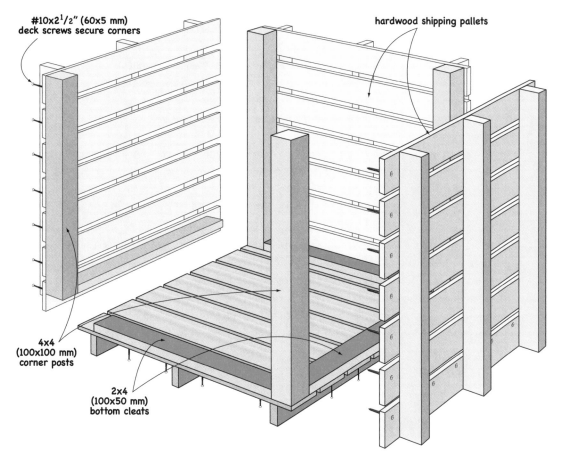

#10x2$^{1}/_{2}$" (60x5 mm)
deck screws secure corners

hardwood shipping pallets

4x4
(100x100 mm)
corner posts

2x4
(100x50 mm)
bottom cleats

SHIPPING PALLET STORAGE BIN

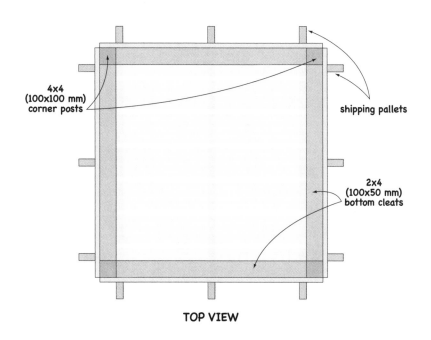

4x4
(100x100 mm)
corner posts

shipping pallets

2x4
(100x50 mm)
bottom cleats

TOP VIEW

How to Build a Win-Win Storage Bin

To keep things as simple as possible, these crates are made with only two thicknesses of wood: $\frac{5}{16}$-inch (8 mm) and $\frac{5}{8}$-inch (15 mm) stock. Neither of these are standard thicknesses, but Steve chose them because they make the lightest possible crate that's also strong enough to work reliably. It's easy to use a table saw or thickness planer to cut or plane standard $\frac{3}{4}$-inch (19 mm) lumber to the right thickness after cutting the parts to width. If you don't have this equipment or the necessary experience, a woodworker near you certainly does.

Start by crosscutting the parts to length (see the table below), using either a handsaw or an electric chopsaw. Next, lay two corner posts on your work surface, with one thick end slat at the top, another at the bottom and three thin end slats in between (see construction plans, opposite). Leave a $\frac{1}{2}$-inch (13 mm) gap (or wider if you want) between the top thick end slat and the upper thin end slat to create a place for your fingers to grip the box. Make sure the corner posts extend $\frac{1}{2}$ inch (13 mm) below the bottom edge of the crate to create short legs that interlock with the crate below when they're stacked.

Bring all these parts together on the corner of a piece of plywood, or use a metal framing square to make sure the corner posts and slats are square. When all looks good, secure the joints permanently using a couple of dabs of weatherproof carpenter's glue and $\frac{3}{4}$-inch (19 mm) long box nails — two nails per joint. Complete the second crate end the same way, then connect the two ends using the thick and thin side slats. Finish up by fastening the bottom cleats and the bottom slats, then get ready for the handiest harvest and storage season ever.

Part	Material	Size	Quantity
Thick side slats	softwood	$\frac{5}{8}$" x $2\frac{1}{8}$" x 32" (15 x 53 x 800 mm)	4
Thin side slats	softwood	$\frac{5}{16}$" x $2\frac{1}{8}$" x 32" (8 x 53 x 800 mm)	6
Corner posts	softwood	$\frac{5}{8}$" x $2\frac{1}{8}$" x $11\frac{1}{2}$" (15 x 53 x 288 mm)	4
Thick end slats	softwood	$\frac{5}{8}$" x $2\frac{1}{8}$" x $14\frac{1}{2}$" (15 x 53 x 363 mm)	4
Thin end slats	softwood	$\frac{5}{16}$" x $2\frac{1}{8}$" x $14\frac{1}{2}$" (8 x 53 x 363 mm)	6
Bottom slats	softwood	$\frac{5}{16}$" x $2\frac{1}{8}$" x $14\frac{1}{2}$" (8 x 53 x 363 mm)	13
Bottom cleats	softwood	$\frac{5}{8}$" x $\frac{5}{8}$" x 29" (15 x 15 x 725 mm)	2

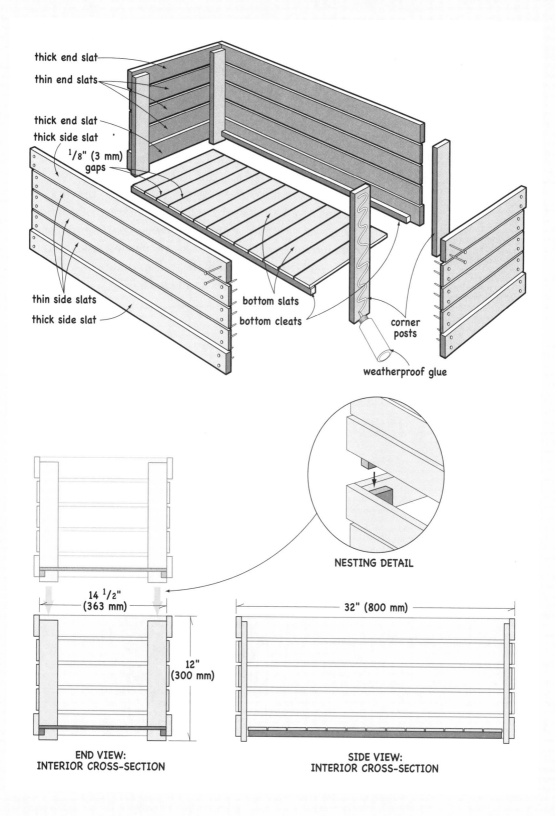

thick end slat

thin end slats

thick end slat

thick side slat

$^1/_8$" (3 mm) gaps

thin side slats

thick side slat

bottom slats

bottom cleats

corner posts

weatherproof glue

NESTING DETAIL

14 $^1/_2$"
(363 mm)

12"
(300 mm)

END VIEW:
INTERIOR CROSS-SECTION

32" (800 mm)

SIDE VIEW:
INTERIOR CROSS-SECTION

Sand Cans

One of Steve's favorite ways to store root vegetables long-term is what he calls the sand can. Buy a new metal garbage can with a lid, lay down several inches of slightly damp sand (or sawdust or peat moss) on the bottom, add a layer of vegetables on top — each specimen blemish-free and separated slightly from its neighbor — then add another couple of inches of damp sand to cover the food. Repeat the layers until the can is full, ending with a layer of sand, then cover the can with its lid. A sand can is a perfect way to create a high-humidity microclimate for beets, carrots, celery root, gingerroot, parsnips, potatoes, rutabagas and turnips. Dig down to retrieve your stores as needed. If transpired moisture isn't enough to keep humidity in the 90% to 95% range within the can, sprinkle a little water on the top layer of sand before closing the lid.

You can also use smaller sealable plastic or metal containers to create a high-humidity microclimate around foods that need it.

In her 1837 book *Direction for Cookery*, Eliza Leslie explains that "potatoes keep best buried in sand or earth. They should never be wetted till they are washed for cooking."

If you have the room, keep a second can in your cellar and move sand into it as you work your way down through stored vegetables.

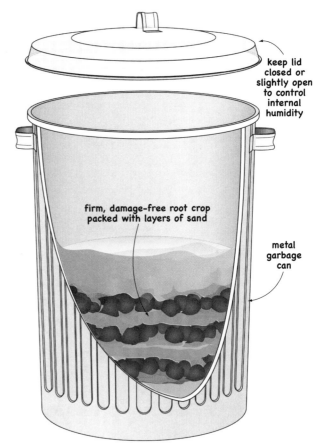

keep lid closed or slightly open to control internal humidity

firm, damage-free root crop packed with layers of sand

metal garbage can

SAND CAN STORAGE

Marathon Beets

As an experiment, Steve decided to see how long he could store his favorite root vegetable — beets — in the limestone root cellar of his house. He grew a long-keeping heirloom variety called Cylindra in his organic garden, chose the biggest and best specimens for storage, then nestled them in slightly damp sand in a brand-new garbage can bought especially for the job (see Sand Cans, opposite). In the end, he pulled the last of these beets out of their dark, sandy home 18 months after they went in. Though they lacked the usual intense beet flavor, his ancient beets were almost as firm and crunchy as the day he harvested them from the garden.

Wooden Boxes with Lids

Unlike portable bins, these wooden boxes are constructed to be airtight (see illustration below), with tight-fitting lids, so they offer a compact way to create a high-humidity microclimate. It's best to use solid lumber to make them, as plywood and other sheet goods contain glues that can affect the flavor of stored produce. You can make the boxes whatever size is convenient.

Place a small hygrometer inside each sand can or wooden box to measure the relative humidity of the microclimate inside. Transpiration can easily raise humidity too high in a completely sealed container. To manage individual containers, open lids incrementally until you achieve a steady ideal moisture content.

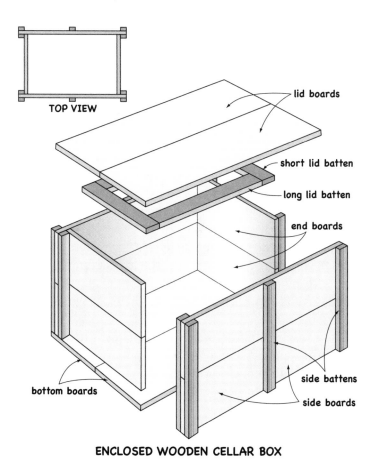

TOP VIEW

lid boards

short lid batten

long lid batten

end boards

side battens

bottom boards

side boards

ENCLOSED WOODEN CELLAR BOX

COMBINATION TEMPERATURE AND HUMIDITY METER

Line the bottom of the box with 2 to 3 inches (50 to 75 mm) of slightly damp sand, sawdust or peat moss, add a layer of vegetables on top, then add another couple of inches of damp sand to cover the food. Repeat the layers until the box is full, ending with a layer of sand, then cover the box with its lid.

Other Useful Storage Options

Not all produce needs to be stored in bins, cans or boxes. Small quantities of most kinds of produce gathered near the beginning of the harvest season keep well for several weeks in 5-gallon (20 L) food-grade plastic storage pails. Many fruits and vegetables can simply be placed individually on shelves (cauliflower, celery root, cucumbers, eggplants, kale, pumpkins and winter squash) or in baskets (bell peppers, figs, garlic and gingerroot). Broccoli is best stored in sealed plastic bags to preserve moisture, while apples and Brussels sprouts do well in perforated plastic bags.

A great way to maximize all the available space in your cellar is to hang stuff from the ceiling or the underside of shelves, and many types of produce benefit from this treatment.

- Onions and soft-necked garlic can be braided together to hang from the ceiling.
- Hot peppers can be tied together, then hung from a nail or hook in a warm, dry part of the cellar to dry. Once dry, they can be stored, still hanging, for up to 6 months.
- Overripe shell peas and shell beans can be pulled from the garden, stalk and all, and hung in a dry part of the cellar until hard and dry. When you have some time, separate the peas and beans by hand for cooking — they usually come out of the husks easily. Make sure they are completely dry through the center, then store them in a jar in a dry location.
- Green tomatoes do well hanging upside down on their vines. Bring them indoors after the threat of autumn frosts begins, then pick ripening tomatoes for the next month.
- Pumpkins and winter squash keep well in hanging mesh bags.
- Cabbages and cauliflower store well hanging by their roots. Tie a string tightly to the root, then loop it over a hook in the ceiling or the underside of a shelf.

Tubs of soil offer another way to enhance the storage life of certain cellared foods, including leeks, cauliflower, celery and Chinese cabbage. In the fall, transplant leeks from the garden into containers of soil, then harvest them throughout the winter, moistening the soil every 3 or 4 weeks. Although

Paper bags offer one of the best and easiest ways to preserve potatoes in your root cellar. The secret is paper's ability to breathe. Those large paper leaf disposal bags do an especially good job. They're strong enough to contain quite a few potatoes, and they're cheap, too.

You can force the growth of container-planted asparagus and Belgian endive by bringing them into warmer conditions after cold cellar storage, harvesting fresh growth for winter meals.

cauliflower, celery and Chinese cabbage won't continue to grow once replanted in tubs of soil, they do keep longer that way than in open storage. Regardless of what you plant in your cellar, make sure not to overwater. Since it's cold and humid in the cellar, overwatering can lead to waterlogged soil and rot. It is usually sufficient to water once a month.

Botanically, pumpkins are a fruit, not a vegetable.

Forcing Rhubarb

You may have seen bright pink stalks of rhubarb with small, pale yellow leaves in grocery stores and produce markets long before your garden rhubarb has broken through the ground. It's not imported from some tropical locale; rather, it's indoor, or "forced," rhubarb and you can grow it in your root cellar.

To force rhubarb, you need to start the preparation in the fall, when your rhubarb plant has finished producing and the leaves have died down, but before the frost — or at least while the ground is still workable. Choose large-diameter roots of a garden rhubarb plant that is at least 3 years old. Carefully dig up the rhizome and root (leaving enough of the plant in the garden to ensure that it will continue producing next year) and place root end down in a pot of soil, removing any dead stalks or leaves and leaving the top of the root uncovered. Each root requires its own pot of about 12 inches (300 mm) in diameter. Leave the pot(s) outside until they've been exposed to temperatures below 32°F (0°C) but above 10°F (–12°C) for at least 1 week. (Temperatures below freezing break the dormancy, but temperatures below 10°F/–12°C can damage the roots.)

At this point, you can decide when you want to start harvesting your rhubarb. It will take 8 to 12 weeks from the time you bring it into your cellar until it has grown enough for harvest, so proceed with the next step accordingly. (If you don't want to grow the rhubarb yet, move it to a location that is protected from the deep freeze but still below 32°F/0°C.) Sprinkle a thin layer of soil or compost over the top of the pot and place it in the root cellar in an area with a temperature of 50°F to 65°F (10°C to 18°C), and with maximum ventilation to prevent mold. Keep the plant moist but not soggy. Constant dark is optimal, so that the energy from the roots goes into producing the edible stalks rather than into photosynthesis to feed and grow the leaves.

Each root may produce only a few stalks. When the stalks are the desired size, grasp at the base of each and pull gently with a slight twisting motion to remove just the stalk from the plant, leaving the root intact. If conditions are good, more stalks may grow from the plant — you'll see them popping through the soil within a week or two.

Once the plants are dormant again, replant them in the garden. This is when chance kicks in: the plants may rejuvenate and start to produce more stalks in a year or two, or they may not.

Selecting and Preparing Foods for Storage

While understanding and managing temperature and humidity conditions in your root cellar is crucial for successful storage, you also need to select and handle foods properly. Even with perfect cellar conditions on your side, you won't get the longest possible storage times unless you choose suitable varieties of top-quality produce. How you handle that produce, whether before or after harvest, can also affect its quality and its storage life: some crops benefit from staying in the ground until after a frost, for example, while others need to be cured before storage. Whether you're harvesting your own produce or purchasing tip-top specimens from a farmers' market or grocery store, you will benefit from an understanding of the qualities that make foods good candidates for root cellar storage.

Using Frost to Your Advantage

About 75% of the earth's land mass experiences some kind of frost during the course of a typical year, and while this brings its own set of gardening challenges, frost also makes certain varieties of produce taste better. Slightly freezing temperatures cause stored starches to convert into sugars, which, of course, makes more than just the medicine go down. You'll enjoy tastier produce from your cellar or outdoor storage campaign if you follow these harvesting guidelines.

Supermarkets don't usually offer produce that has been touched by just the right amount of frost, but farmers' market vendors sometimes do. It's worth asking.

- *Apples:* One or two light frosts boost sweetness considerably, especially in thick-skinned varieties that store well, such as Arlet, Crispin (Mutsu), Ida Red, Fuji, Granny Smith, Jonathan and Northern Spy, and the more obscure Allen's Everlasting, Arkansas Black and Baldwin. Once apples freeze completely, however, they quickly turn brown and rot in the cellar, proving once again that too much of a good thing can be a bad thing.
- *Beets:* A marked improvement in flavor is noticeable in beets after several hard frosts. It's difficult to overdo frost when it comes to beets, as most of the root sits below ground.

- *Brussels sprouts:* Many people dislike this vegetable, and that just might be because the Brussels sprouts available in stores almost never get the chance to develop optimal flavor. Two solid frosts are absolutely essential for the best taste, and even after the first few snowfalls, a harvest will still yield great produce.
- *Cabbage and Chinese cabbage:* Light frosts improve flavor. Just be sure to harvest cabbage before a heavy frost.
- *Carrots:* Frost improves flavor, especially in non-hybrid varieties, though the difference is less noticeable than with other produce.
- *Celery root (celeriac):* The best flavor develops after the first frost.
- *Horseradish:* Light fall frosts improve flavor.
- *Kale:* The flavor of this winter-hardy vegetable improves a lot after heavy frosts. Kale can be harvested all winter, even when buried in snow.
- *Kohlrabi:* Because kohlrabi is a member of the cabbage family, light frosts improve flavor.
- *Parsnips:* These root vegetables are similar to their relative the carrot, but their flavor is frost-dependent. Don't even consider digging up parsnips until at least one good frost has hit. Over-wintered parsnips can also be dug up after they start growing again the next season.
- *Pumpkins and winter squash:* A very light frost improves flavor moderately.
- *Rutabaga:* Both cool growing weather and light to moderate frosts improve flavor.
- *Salsify:* Also known as the "oyster plant," salsify needs a cracking good frost to develop full flavor.
- *Turnips:* A moderate frost improves flavor noticeably.

Even in cold climates, carrots can often be left in the ground all winter, mulched with lots of straw. In the spring, you'll probably find a few hollow, cone-shaped depressions in the soil — evidence of the wintertime root cellaring activity of a mouse.

A Winter Home for Your Plants

A good root cellar can improve your ornamental gardens as well as your culinary life, because it allows you to winter over plants — especially container-grown plants — that would otherwise die during cold weather. Steve and his wife, Mary, keep ferns and ivies alive for 5 or 6 years in a climate where they'd normally need to be treated like annuals. The luxuriant growth of a 5-year-old Boston ivy in a hanging basket wouldn't be possible without the steady 34°F to 36°F (1°C to 2°C) temperature of their root cellar in winter. The only thing to remember is to keep the soil moist. A good soaking every 3 to 4 weeks is essential to keep wintering plants from drying out and dying.

Harvesting or Purchasing Produce

To stay fresh as long as possible, the produce you harvest or purchase must be in top condition. Damaged specimens won't last long, no matter how good your cellar is. Root crops keep the longest of any produce in a root cellar, but they're also the most likely to get damaged during harvest.

When you're digging up your own root vegetables, you can maximize the number of undamaged pieces by working from one side of the row, not the middle. Sink a round-mouthed shovel or a digging fork into the dirt just outside the zone where you expect roots to be hidden, then push the handle partway back to lever up the soil and loosen it. There's no need to dig anything up; just loosen the dirt. Even in the heaviest soils, this allows you to grab the plant tops and pull the roots out with their skin intact. You may need to hunt around a bit more to find potatoes, since their stalks often break off at the roots. And you may damage the odd root that ventured out beyond where you thought it would be, but just eat those outliers for dinner that night.

If you're buying harvested produce, look for items that received careful handling during harvest, packing and shipping to preserve the all-important skin integrity. Remember, you're making a sizeable investment by buying, hauling, storing and retrieving this food over the next several months. You don't want your efforts to fail just because the food you chose wasn't up to the challenge. Get to know local farmers or vendors at the farmers' market and place a request ahead of time for items you want to store. They will likely be happy to leave the produce in a more natural state (unwashed, untrimmed) for you, and you'll get produce that's better for storage.

While unblemished skin is the most important quality to look for when you're choosing produce for storage, there are other criteria that will affect storage life, such as variety, degree of ripeness and how much of the plant is harvested. In addition, some produce benefits from certain preparations, such as curing or salting, before it is stored.

- *Apples:* Choose tart, thick-skinned, late-harvest varieties, such as Arlet, Crispin (Mutsu), Ida Red, Fuji, Granny Smith, Jonathan and Northern Spy. Mid-fall varieties such as Cortland, Empire and McIntosh also store well, though not quite as long as varieties that are harvested later. Summer and early fall varieties don't store as well and are best used soon after harvest. Apples should be heavy for their size, with taut skin and no signs of wrinkling, bruising or sponginess. Keep the complete stem intact for optimal storage quality.

How long you can store food in a root cellar varies with the food you're dealing with and how close your conditions come to ideal. Soft fruits and leafy produce have the shortest lifespan, while root vegetables last the longest.

Never wash produce before putting it into storage — washing damages the skin and greatly reduces storage life. Root crops are especially vulnerable.

Salting Green Beans

After harvesting young, tender green beans, thinly slice them lengthwise. Place 1 inch (25 mm) of dry salt in the bottom of a ceramic crock, then pack down a couple of inches (about 50 mm) of beans on top. Cover the container with a lid and store in a cool, moist area of your cellar. Layer with more salt and more packed sliced beans as the harvest goes on. Water from the beans dissolves the salt, preserving the vegetables. Remove the beans as you need them, rinse them in fresh water, then soak for an additional 30 to 60 minutes before boiling.

- *Avocados:* Select very firm, unripe avocados.
- *Bananas:* Choose green, firm, unripe fruit.
- *Beans, green:* Choose young, tender green beans. Prepare them for storage by packing them in dry salt in a ceramic crock (see Salting Green Beans, above).
- *Beets:* Choose varieties bred for long keeping, such as Cylindra, Lutz Winter Keeper and Bull's Blood. The beets should be firm and feel heavy for their size. Leave 1 inch (25 mm) of stem on each beet.
- *Broccoli:* Store only those with buds that are still tight.
- *Brussels sprouts:* Harvest after the first fall frosts for best flavor. Select sprouts with tight leaves and minimal browning of edges. For optimal storage, leave the sprouts on the stalk, if space allows.
- *Cabbage:* Harvest heads with the roots attached for longest storage life. Light frost improves flavor. Cabbage heads should be firm and compact and feel heavy for their size.
- *Carrots:* Choose varieties bred for long storage, such as Kingston, Oxheart and Saint Valery. When harvesting, use your hands to break off the tops, flush with the carrot body. Store only firm roots with unbroken skin. Carrots grown in coarse, sandy soil often have minute scratches on the skin, which greatly reduce their keeping quality. If you're not growing them yourself, ask the grower or vendor about the soil type they were grown in; only buy those grown in heavier, less sandy soils.
- *Cauliflower:* Harvest before frost. For optimal storage, leave roots attached. If you're purchasing heads without roots, cut stems just below the head. Store only fully firm heads.
- *Celery:* Choose firm stalks with leaves and a good portion of the base intact.
- *Celery root (celeriac):* Harvest with the long roots intact and leave 1 inch (25 mm) of stem attached. Choose roots that are firm with no signs of wrinkling or mold.
- *Chinese cabbage:* Harvest after first mild frosts but before a hard frost. Harvest with roots attached for longest storage. Choose heads that feel heavy for their size.

Edible varieties of burdock root taste similar to globe artichokes; they are popular in Japan.

Chervil root is a rare heirloom vegetable with a mild licorice taste. It is a different variety than the more common chervil plant we use as an herb.

Even the slightest frost exposure ruins cauliflower's keeping qualities.

- *Cucumbers:* Thick-skinned varieties store best, and even they can only be kept for short periods. Avoid English-style or seedless cucumbers and small pickling cucumbers — these need to be used as soon after harvest as possible. Choose just-ripe cucumbers that feel heavy for their size. Make sure there are no yellow spots, which are a sign of overmaturity.
- *Eggplant:* Harvest at first sign of glossy skin. Choose firm, plump eggplants that feel heavy for their size. The skin should be shiny and the leaves fresh and green.
- *Fennel bulb:* Choose firm bulbs without any browning or bruises and with a good portion of the stalks intact.
- *Figs:* Choose firm fresh figs with no bruising or signs of mold.
- *Garlic:* Choose tightly closed bulbs with no signs of sprouting or mold. If harvesting fresh garlic, cure the bulbs before hanging them in the cellar (see Curing Vegetables for Storage, below).
- *Gingerroot:* Choose gingerroot with taut, shiny skin and no signs of shriveling or mold.
- *Grapefruit:* Choose firm fruit that feels heavy for its size.
- *Grapes:* Choose grapes with firm, green pliable stems. The grapes should cling tightly to the stems.
- *Horseradish:* Harvest after light fall frosts. Choose large, firm roots with no signs of shriveling or mold.
- *Jerusalem artichokes:* Best harvested as needed, but firm artichokes with taut, somewhat shiny skin can be stored for 2 to 4 weeks.
- *Kale:* Best harvested as needed, but fresh-cut stalks with crisp-firm leaves can be stored for 5 to 10 days.

Figs have a short shelf life (5 to 7 days). If you don't know when they were harvested, it may not be worth trying to store them.

Soft-neck garlic varieties last longer than hard-neck varieties.

Curing Vegetables for Storage

You can boost the cellar life of garlic, onions, potatoes, sweet potatoes and winter squash you've harvested by letting them sit in a dry, well-ventilated spot for a while before storage. This process, called curing, enhances the toughness of the skin. Cure onions and garlic at room temperature for 2 to 4 weeks, or let them dry in dappled sunlight for a week of dry weather (protected from frost and rain). Cure potatoes at 50°F to 60°F (10°C to 15°C) for 2 weeks, in the shade or on a shed floor — sunlight causes potatoes to turn green. Cure sweet potatoes and winter squash (except acorn squash) in a warm spot for 10 to 14 days.

Don't cure other vegetables before storage, as it may actually reduce cellar life.

- *Kohlrabi:* Only late-harvest will remain tender during storage. Choose small- to medium-size firm bulbs with no signs of wrinkling and leave about 1 inch (25 mm) of leaves intact.
- *Leeks:* Harvest before soil freezes, leaving plenty of soil attached.
- *Lemons and limes:* Choose firm fruit that feels heavy for its size. Varieties with thick skin will store the longest.
- *Melons:* Select firm but not hard, just-ripe honeydew or cantaloupe that feel heavy for their size. Don't cellar watermelons.
- *Onions:* Before harvest, shock onions into dormancy (see Shocking Onions, below). Choose only very fresh onions with no signs of mold, softening or shriveling. Leave as much of the papery skin and root intact as possible. Cure onions before cellaring (see Curing Vegetables for Storage, page 106).
- *Oranges:* Choose firm fruit that feels heavy for its size.
- *Parsnips:* Choose firm roots that feel heavy for their size. Leave the entire taproot and about 1 inch (25 mm) of the stem intact.
- *Peaches:* Select firm fruit that yields slightly to finger pressure and that feels heavy for its size. Avoid very green peaches or any that show signs of shriveling.
- *Pears:* Choose slightly green pears that feel very firm when gently squeezed at the top of the neck, just below the stem. You shouldn't feel any yield to the pressure.
- *Peppers, bell (sweet) and hot:* Harvest before any frosts. Hot peppers should be fully ripe when picked. Choose firm peppers with shiny skins and green, pliable stems.
- *Plums:* Choose late-season hardy varieties with thick skins, such as Late Santa Rosa, Empress, President and Stanley. Firm fruit that feels heavy for its size stores best.
- *Potatoes:* Late-maturing varieties, such as russets (many varieties), Yukon gold, Chieftan, Shepody, Kennebec and Red Pontiac, store best. For best results, cure for 2 weeks before storage (see Curing Vegetables for Storage, page 106).

Many leeks that are left in the ground will grow again in spring.

Although dahlias are typically grown for their flowers, the roots of edible heirloom varieties, such as Yellow Gem, first introduced in 1914, are also prized as a crunchy, flavorful food.

Shocking Onions

If you grow your own onions, they'll never keep for more than a few weeks unless you do something brutal: you need to step on them a month or so before harvest, as the tops begin to die back naturally. Breaking each and every green stalk underfoot or with a garden rake is essential, to shock the bulbs into dormancy. Without this essential step, your onions will just keep on growing in the cellar, quickly using up their internal stores of moisture and getting soft and green.

- *Pumpkins:* Harvest after the first light frost. Choose pumpkins that have tight, somewhat shiny skin, with no signs of wrinkling or soft spots. They should feel heavy for their size. Leave as much of the stem intact as possible for the best storage life.
- *Quinces:* Choose pale green fruit that is firm and shows no signs of shriveling. Leave any fuzz on the skin until just before use.
- *Radishes, winter:* Choose roots that have firm skin and feel heavy for their size. Leave about 1 inch (25 mm) of the stem intact for longest storage.
- *Rutabagas:* Harvest after a moderate frost. Choose rutabagas with firm skin and that feel heavy for their size. Leave about 1 inch (25 mm) of the stem on, if possible.
- *Salsify:* Choose firm roots that feel heavy for their size, with no signs of shriveling. Leave about 1 inch (25 mm) of the stem intact for longest storage.
- *Squash, acorn:* Choose squash that have tight, somewhat shiny skin, with no signs of wrinkling or soft spots. Avoid those with orange or yellow spots on the skin, a sign of overmaturity. They should feel heavy for their size. Leave as much of the stem intact as possible for the best storage life. Acorn squash have thinner skins than other winter squash; therefore, they don't store as long and need more humidity. Do not cure acorn squash before cellaring.
- *Squash, winter:* Choose squash that have tight, somewhat shiny skin, with no signs of wrinkling or soft spots. They should feel heavy for their size. For the best storage life, leave as much of the stem intact as possible. Cure for 10 to 14 days (see Curing Vegetables for Storage, page 106) before cellaring.
- *Sweet potatoes:* Choose potatoes that have taut skin, with no signs of shriveling or soft spots. Cure for 10 to 14 days (see Curing Vegetables for Storage, page 106) before storage.
- *Tomatoes:* Bring unripe tomatoes in on vines for after-season ripening in the cellar. Cherry tomatoes cellar especially well this way.
- *Turnips:* Harvest after a moderate frost. Choose turnips with taut skin and firm flesh, with no signs of shriveling. They should feel heavy for their size. Leave the long taproot and about 1 inch (25 mm) of the stem intact for longest storage.
- *Zucchini:* Choose just-ripe, firm zucchini with taut skin and no scratches. They should feel heavy for their size and have no yellow spots, which are a sign of overmaturity.

Many commercially grown rutabagas are waxed after harvest to help them retain internal moisture and extend storage life.

Some tomato cultivars are now being produced with the specific intention that they be harvested green and ripened slowly. Check your favorite seed catalog or nursery to see if they are available in your area.

Small zucchini can only be stored for 1 to 2 weeks, but large zucchini, with their thicker skins, will keep for up to 3 months.

Organic Produce

How produce is grown has at least as much effect on cellar life as the variety of produce involved. Maybe even more. Although there has been no close scientific study of the link between growing practices and longevity, experienced root cellar users know that foods fertilized with compost, seaweed or other organic materials keep many months longer than even the freshest equivalents grown using a highly soluble fertilizer. And when compost-grown produce does finally "go bad," it often just shrivels up from loss of moisture. Nothing gross. By contrast, store-bought, non-organic produce tends to be more likely to develop mold and rot before it ever gets to the dried-out phase.

So once you have a root cellar, you'll probably develop an interest in stocking it with organically produced food as often as possible. Trouble is, the word "organic" doesn't necessarily mean very much. You need to look past the label to discover how organic a particular item of "organic" food really is.

Ideally, organic food is produced using practices that replenish and maintain soil fertility in a way that enhances biological activity in the soil. Most truly organic food has also been audited and approved by a recognized third-party certification program that tracks the movement of that food from farm to store shelf, beginning with land that has been under continuous organic management practices for at least 3 years before harvest.

Depending on where you live, specific government standards for the word "organic" may be in place, but you'd still be wise to do your homework. Look for the name of the third-party certification body, then check it out. See exactly what their idea of an organic soil fertility program or pest control program is, and if it matches what you have in mind. Due diligence becomes even more important when you're looking at foods that carry more nebulous terms such as "ecological," "regenerative" and "LISA" (low-input sustainable agriculture).

Corning Meat in the Root Cellar

Corning is the pickling process used to create cured meats, such as corned beef. It tenderizes the toughest cuts and eliminates the gamey flavor of wild meats. A temperature of 38°F (3°C) is ideal for corning, so if your root cellar is consistently cold enough, you can try making your own deli-style meats at home.

Many small growers follow impeccable growing standards but simply can't afford the expensive organic certification process. Develop a one-on-one relationship with the people who grow your food, or who sell food locally. This doesn't guarantee you'll be purchasing organic produce, but it's a good start.

Sir Albert Howard (1873–1947) is considered the founder and pioneer of today's organic food movement. His book *An Agricultural Testament*, published in 1943, is based in part on his 26 years directing agricultural research in India.

Aromatic vegetables, such as onions and cabbage, have been known to impart undesirable flavors to wine, so make sure to store your bottles well away from this type of produce.

You might want to consider purchasing an outdoor cook stove that operates from a self-contained fuel supply and keeping it on hand in case of an emergency situation where you are without power. It will save you from having to eat your potatoes raw.

Recipes vary, but all include the use of salt, spices, sugar and sodium nitrate, combined with water to form a brine. The meat is soaked in the brine, completely submerged under a weight, for a total of 15 days, and is turned on day 5 and again on day 10. For optimum food safety, be sure to seek out a tested recipe from a reliable source and follow it carefully.

Storing Wine in the Root Cellar

Ideally, wine needs a stable temperature in the 50°F to 55°F (10°C to 13°C) range and 70% relative humidity. Root cellars tend to be colder and moister than the ideal, but that's not a problem. Somewhat colder temperatures simply slow the maturation process, and moister air won't do any harm, beyond the slight risk of label deterioration. Whatever you do, avoid storing wine in an area warmer than 55°F (13°C), an area where the temperature fluctuates more than a few degrees, or an area prone to vibrations caused by machinery. All of these factors will make wine age poorly. Humidity levels lower than 70% can cause corks to dry out.

Emergency Preparedness

Most of us have lived for so long with a steady, assured supply of grocery store food that we've learned to buy in small quantities for the short term. But you may not want to bet your next weeks' meals entirely on this practice. Catastrophic weather events can disrupt commercial food supplies, and even if you've never lived through anything like this and severe weather is uncommon in your region, you may well find a well-stocked root cellar very useful one day.

Managing your cellar for emergency preparedness is different from ordinary food storage, and it begins with asking yourself a simple question: What would my life be like if my cellar was my family's only source of food for a week?

The first thing you'd miss is drinking water. That's why it makes sense to keep a couple of 5-gallon (20 L) casks in cellar storage. You'll also need to supplement your seasonal stores of fresh food with canned and dry goods, especially in the spring and summer months, when produce supplies in the cellar are low. Make sure to keep canned goods in an area with less than 50% relative humidity to prevent rusting (see Canned Goods and Root Cellars, page 111). Dry goods should also be kept in a dry area of the cellar.

Emergency food supplies do not have to be lavish, but the stock does need to be rotated. Acquire new supplies of food and water three or four times a year and consume older stock to keep your emergency supplies fresh.

Canned Goods and Root Cellars

A root cellar may seem like a logical place to store jars of home-canned preserves and store-bought canned goods; however, it does not necessarily provide optimal storage conditions for cans of food or jars with metal storage lids. Metal will rust if exposed to humid conditions. The rust can break the seal of the lid and expose the contents to air and microbes, causing the food inside to spoil.

To keep your preserves and cans sealed tight, they must be kept away from areas with humidity higher than 50%. Ideally, they should be stored at 35% relative humidity or lower. If your cellar has a dry area (less than 50% humidity) that stays at a constant temperature, this is a good place to store canned goods, particularly at times when the humidity in the rest of your house is high. Otherwise, it is best to store your canned goods in a dry, cool, dark place elsewhere in the house.

Storing Fruits and Vegetables

This chapter provides you with a quick guide to the ideal storage conditions for cellarable fruits and vegetables. It's not essential that all these conditions be met perfectly all the time, just that you get as close to them as you can. Seasonal variations in cellar temperature and humidity are inevitable.

You'll also want to take a look at Harvesting or Purchasing Produce (page 104) for advice on how to choose the best fruits and vegetables for long-term storage, and at Outdoor Root Cellaring (page 61) and Crop-Specific Storage Containers (page 93) for information on the different storage options mentioned in this guide.

Visit www. therootcellarbook.com for a printable wall chart showing optimal storage conditions for more than two dozen of the most popular produce items.

How to Achieve Ideal Cellar Conditions
Cold and Very Moist

To achieve temperatures this cold, an underground cellar must be protected by a high soil level on the exterior walls and high insulation values on exposed exterior wall surfaces, interior walls and the ceiling. Electric cooling assistance may also be necessary in warm climates (see Technology to Make Things Cold, page 72). To raise humidity levels this high, you may need to scatter damp burlap sacks or sprinkle water on the floor. You can also create high-humidity microclimates within sealed or semi-sealed containers (see page 98 and 99). The coldest, moistest conditions are found at floor level.

Avoid raising overall cellar humidity higher than 95%; otherwise, water may condense on interior surfaces.

Cool It

With the exceptions of garlic, onions, potatoes, sweet potatoes and winter squash, which benefit from a period of drying out in warm temperatures (see Curing Vegetables for Storage on page 106), all produce needs to be cooled as quickly as possible after harvest for maximum storage life. The quality of leafy produce begins to decline noticeably after just 2 hours at 70°F (21°C), and even hard, tough produce is the worse for wear after a couple of days of room temperature storage. So get your produce into the cellar as quickly as possible. If you are storing large quantities of produce in big bins, consider using a fan to speed up the cooling process. It's not the temperature of the air that counts, but the temperature of the produce itself.

Cold and Moist

The same insulation levels and soil conditions discussed above will be required to achieve cold temperatures, but you will need less added water to maintain the lower humidity. In a cold, very moist cellar, a storage position just above floor level will provide these conditions.

Use an accurate hygrometer to guide humidity control.

Cool and Moist

Most well-constructed underground cellars offer these conditions year-round with little or no intervention. In a cold, very moist cellar, a storage position 3 to 4 feet (1 to 1.2 m) above the floor will provide these conditions. A small supplemental heat source, such as a shaded 40- or 60-watt incandescent light bulb, can be useful for maintaining these temperatures in regions with cold winters.

In the summer, increased ventilation helps increase humidity, but don't open the vents so much that the temperature of the cellar rises.

Cool and Dry

Locations in the top 25% of the cellar are the most likely to offer these conditions. In cold climates, a small supplemental heat source, such as a shaded 40- or 60-watt incandescent light bulb, can help keep temperatures this high during the winter. However, to achieve both higher temperatures and lower humidity, you may need to build a separate cellar area and use hydrated lime (see page 92) to reduce humidity in this area.

If you're using a light bulb to raise cellar temperatures, cover it with a metal bucket to prevent it from illuminating the cellar. Produce, especially potatoes, keeps better in complete darkness.

Warm and Dry

To achieve temperatures this high, a separate cellar area is almost certainly required, especially during cold seasons. You may need to use hydrated lime (see page 92) to reduce humidity in this area of the cellar. Alternatively, an area near the ceiling of an unheated basement often delivers these conditions in both summer and winter.

COLD / **VERY MOIST**	**COLD** / **MOIST**	**COOL** / **MOIST**	**COOL** / **DRY**	**WARM** / **DRY**
Cold and very moist 33°F to 40°F (0.5°C to 4.5°C) and 90% to 95% relative humidity	**Cold and moist** 33°F to 40°F (0.5°C to 4.5°C) and 80% to 90% relative humidity	**Cool and moist** 40°F to 50°F (4.5°C to 10°C) and 80% to 90% relative humidity	**Cool and dry** 40°F to 50°F (4.5°C to 10°C) and 60% to 70% relative humidity	**Warm and dry** 50°F to 60°F (10°C to 15.5°C) and 60% to 70% relative humidity

Optimal Storage Conditions

Apples

COLD MOIST

Outdoor storage: straw-lined hole-in-the-ground cellar pit or garbage can cellar (for long-keeping varieties)

Indoor storage: portable bin, perforated plastic bags

Special instructions: store away from vegetables; wrap individually in dry newsprint to maximize cellar life

Storage life in cellar: 4 to 6 months

Asparagus

COLD VERY MOIST

Indoor storage: tub of soil (roots only)

Special instructions: in the fall, replant large, mature roots in containers of soil; store in the root cellar, then bring to room temperature to force growth for winter harvest

Storage life in cellar: 3 to 5 months

Avocados

COOL DRY

Indoor storage: on shelves or in shallow containers

Storage life in cellar: up to 10 days

> To ripen avocados before use, place them in a paper bag with a ripe banana. To test for ripeness, gently squeeze the avocado; once ripe, it will yield slightly to the pressure.

Bananas

COOL DRY

Indoor storage: on shelves or in shallow containers

Special instructions: store away from vegetables and ripe fruits

Storage life in cellar: up to 7 days

Beans, Green

COOL MOIST

Indoor storage: salted in a ceramic crock (see page 105)

Storage life in cellar: 4 to 6 months

Beans, Shell

WARM DRY

Indoor storage: hang plants until beans are hard and dry

Special instructions: once beans are completely dry through the center, separate from the husks by hand, then store in a jar in a dry location

Drying time in cellar: 1 to 2 weeks, depending on variety and conditions

Beets

Outdoor storage: organic blanket, trench silo, hole-in-the-ground cellar pit, garbage can cellar or root clamp

Indoor storage: portable bin, permanent bin, sand can or wooden box with lid

Special instructions: sort beets and store in groups according to size; use the smallest first, as they deteriorate more quickly

Storage life in cellar: 4 to 6 months

COLD
VERY MOIST

> Beets that have gone soft during storage are still good to eat after they are boiled.

Belgian Endive

Outdoor storage: organic blanket

Indoor storage: tub of soil (roots only)

Special instructions: in the fall, replant roots in containers of soil; store in the root cellar, then bring to temperatures above 50°F (10°C) to force leafy growth for winter harvest

Storage life in cellar: 4 to 6 months

COOL
MOIST

Broccoli

Indoor storage: sealed plastic bags

Storage life in cellar: 1 to 2 weeks

COLD
VERY MOIST

Brussels Sprouts

Outdoor storage: organic blanket

Indoor storage: perforated plastic bags

Special instructions: leave sprouts on the stalk, if space allows

Storage life in cellar: 3 to 5 weeks

COLD
VERY MOIST

Cabbage

Outdoor storage: organic blanket

Indoor storage: individually on shelves or hanging by the roots

Special instructions: if stored in a basement cellar, lots of ventilation required to prevent odor from spreading to building above

Storage life in cellar: 4 to 6 months

COLD
VERY MOIST

> The cellar is the perfect location for making sauerkraut (see recipe, page 236).

Carrots

Outdoor storage: organic blanket, trench silo, hole-in-the-ground cellar pit, garbage can cellar or root clamp
Indoor storage: portable bin, permanent bin, sand can or wooden box with lid
Special instructions: sort carrots and store in groups according to size; use the smallest first, as they deteriorate more quickly
Storage life in cellar: 4 to 6 months

Cauliflower

COLD
VERY MOIST

Indoor storage: individually on shelves, hanging by the roots or planted in tub of soil
Storage life in cellar: 2 to 4 weeks

Celery

COLD
VERY MOIST

Outdoor storage: trench silo
Indoor storage: planted in tub of soil
Storage life in cellar: 5 to 8 weeks

Celery Root (Celeriac)

COLD
VERY MOIST

Outdoor storage: hole-in-the-ground cellar pit
Indoor storage: portable bin, sand can or wooden box with lid or, in a very moist cellar, on open shelves
Storage life in cellar: 3 to 6 months

Chinese Cabbage

COLD
VERY MOIST

Indoor storage: planted in tub of soil
Storage life in cellar: 3 to 5 months

> Chinese cabbage does not emit the same pungent odor as common cabbage, but it has a shorter cellar life.

Cucumbers

COOL
MOIST

Indoor storage: individually on shelves
Storage life in cellar: 1 to 3 weeks

Eggplant

Indoor storage: individually on shelves
Storage life in cellar: 1 to 2 weeks

COLD
VERY MOIST

Fennel Bulb

Indoor storage: portable bin, sand can or wooden box with lid
Storage life in cellar: up to 6 months

COLD
MOIST

Figs (Fresh)

Indoor storage: shallow baskets
Special instructions: figs have thin skin that requires gentle handling; store them in a single layer in baskets
Storage life in cellar: 5 to 7 days

COLD
MOIST

Garlic

Indoor storage: portable bin, baskets or hanging from ceiling
Special instructions: cure before storing (see page 106)
Storage life in cellar: 2 to 3 months for hard-neck varieties; 4 to 5 months for soft-neck

COOL
DRY

Gingerroot

Indoor storage: sand can, wooden box with lid or baskets
Storage life in cellar: up to 6 months

COOL
MOIST

Grapefruit

Indoor storage: portable bin
Storage life in cellar: 4 to 6 weeks

COLD
MOIST

Grapes

Indoor storage: hanging by individual bunches
Storage life in cellar: 4 to 6 weeks

COOL
MOIST

Horseradish

Indoor storage: sand can or wooden box with lid
Storage life in cellar: 4 to 6 months

COLD
VERY MOIST

Jerusalem Artichokes

`COLD`
`VERY MOIST`

Outdoor storage: organic blanket
Indoor storage: portable bin
Storage life in cellar: 2 to 4 weeks

> Jerusalem artichokes keep best in garden soil; once harvested, their thin skin makes them dry up and shrivel quickly. Dig them up as needed in early winter or spring.

Kale

`COLD`
`VERY MOIST`

Outdoor storage: organic blanket
Indoor storage: individually on shelves
Special instructions: leafy produce remains edible right out of the garden, even during hard winters, so best harvested as needed
Storage life in cellar: 5 to 10 days

Kohlrabi

`COLD`
`VERY MOIST`

Indoor storage: sand can, wooden box with lid or layered with straw in portable bin
Storage life in cellar: 3 to 4 months

Leeks

`COLD`
`MOIST`

Outdoor storage: organic blanket
Indoor storage: tub of soil
Special instructions: in the fall, transplant leeks into containers of soil; harvest throughout the winter, moistening the soil every 3 or 4 weeks
Storage life in cellar: 2 to 3 months

Lemons and Limes

Indoor storage: portable bin
Storage life in cellar: 1 to 3 weeks

Growing Mushrooms in Your Cellar

It has always been possible to grow your own mushrooms, but the current availability of mushroom kits makes it easier than ever. Many mushroom plants will produce abundantly in a section of your cellar that is 50°F to 60°F (10°C to 15.5°C) and 70% to 80% relative humidity, or in an unfinished basement area immediately outside the cellar. Light may be an issue, though. Shiitake mushrooms, for instance, require a daily cycle of light and dark; other species grow better if given a small amount of light.

Melons (Honeydew or Cantaloupe)

Indoor storage: individually on shelves
Storage life in cellar: 1 to 2 weeks

COLD
MOIST

> Handle melons gently when you're placing them on shelves.

Onions

Indoor storage: portable bin or hanging from ceiling
Special instructions: cure before storing (see page 106)
Storage life in cellar: 4 to 6 months

COOL
DRY

Oranges

Indoor storage: portable bin
Storage life in cellar: 4 to 6 weeks

COLD
MOIST

Parsnips

Outdoor storage: organic blanket, trench silo, hole-in-the-ground cellar pit, garbage can cellar or root clamp
Indoor storage: portable bin, permanent bin, sand can or wooden box with lid
Special instructions: sort parsnips and store in groups according to size; use the smallest first, as they deteriorate more quickly
Storage life in cellar: 4 to 6 months

COLD
VERY
MOIST

Pears

Indoor storage: portable bin
Special instructions: store away from vegetables
Storage life in cellar: 2 to 3 months

COLD
MOIST

> About 3 days before you plan to use pears, bring them into a cool room to ripen fully. Pears ripen from the inside out, so test by squeezing gently; in a perfectly ripe pear, the flesh at the top of the neck should yield slightly to gentle pressure. If you let your pears ripen to the point where the widest part is soft on the outside, the inside is likely overripe and mushy.

Peas, Shell

Indoor storage: hang plants until peas are hard and dry
Special instructions: once peas are completely dry through the center, separate from the husks by hand, then store in a jar in a dry location
Drying time in cellar: 1 to 2 weeks, depending on variety and conditions

WARM
DRY

Peppers, Bell (Sweet)

Indoor storage: shallow baskets
Special instructions: temperatures below 45°F (7°C) speed spoiling
Storage life in cellar: 1 to 3 weeks

COOL
MOIST

Peppers, Hot

Indoor storage: hanging from ceiling (see page 100)
Storage life in cellar: 4 to 6 months once dry

WARM
DRY

Plums

Indoor storage: wooden box with lid
Special instructions: store in a single layer in a box no deeper than 4 inches
(100 mm)
Storage life in cellar: 2 to 4 weeks

COLD
VERY
MOIST

Potatoes

Outdoor storage: trench silo, hole-in-the-ground cellar pit, garbage can cellar
or root clamp
Indoor storage: portable bin, permanent bin, sand can, wooden box with lid
or paper bag
Special instructions: store in complete darkness
Storage life in cellar: 4 to 6 months

COLD
MOIST

> Store potatoes at least 6 feet (1.8 m) away from apples to prevent premature sprouting.

Pumpkins

Indoor storage: individually on shelves or hanging in mesh bags
Storage life in cellar: 5 to 6 months

WARM
DRY

Quinces

Indoor storage: portable bin
Storage life in cellar: 4 to 6 months

COLD
MOIST

Radishes, Winter

Indoor storage: sand can or wooden box with lid
Storage life in cellar: 5 to 8 weeks

COLD
VERY
MOIST

> Winter radishes will shrivel unless they are packed in damp sand, sawdust or peat moss.

Rhubarb

Indoor storage: tub of soil

Special instructions: see page 101 for instructions on how to store and force rhubarb

Storage life in cellar: 3 to 4 months

> **COLD**
> ___
> **MOIST**

Rutabagas

Outdoor storage: organic blanket, trench silo, hole-in-the-ground cellar pit, garbage can cellar or root clamp

Indoor storage: sand can or wooden box with lid

Storage life in cellar: 5 to 6 months

> **COLD**
> **VERY MOIST**

Dipping rutabagas in melted food-grade wax greatly reduces moisture loss, thereby extending their storage life. Beeswax is the safest type to use.

Salsify

Outdoor storage: organic blanket

Indoor storage: sand can or wooden box with lid

Special instructions: sort roots and store in groups according to size; use the smallest first, as they deteriorate more quickly

Storage life in cellar: 3 to 5 months

> **COLD**
> **VERY MOIST**

Squash, Acorn

Indoor storage: portable bin or individually on shelves

Special instructions: do *not* cure before storing

Storage life in cellar: 2 to 4 months

> **COOL**
> ___
> **DRY**

Squash, Winter

Indoor storage: individually on shelves or hanging in mesh bags (or in portable bins if squash are small)

Special instructions: cure before storing (see page 106); leave space between each squash and its neighbor

Storage life in cellar: 4 to 6 months

> **WARM**
> ___
> **DRY**

Rubbing vegetable oil on the outside of pumpkins and squash extends their storage life.

Sweet Potatoes

Indoor storage: individually wrapped in paper and placed on shelves or in shallow crates

Special instructions: cure before storing (see page 106); temperatures below 50°F (10°C) promote rot; avoid handling before use — movement promotes decay

Storage life in cellar: 2 to 3 months

Tomatoes, Green

Indoor storage: hang vines from ceiling

Cellar ripening season: 20 to 30 days

> Green tomatoes should be kept at temperatures above 55°F (13°C); lower temperatures destroy the enzymes necessary for them to ripen properly. Once tomatoes are ripe, a storage temperature of 40°F (5°C) is ideal.

Tomatoes, Ripe

COOL / DRY

Indoor storage: individually on shelves

Storage life in cellar: 5 to 10 days

Turnips

COLD / VERY MOIST

Outdoor storage: organic blanket, trench silo, hole-in-the-ground cellar pit, garbage can cellar or root clamp

Indoor storage: portable bin, sand can or wooden box with lid

Storage life in cellar: 4 to 5 months

Zucchini

Indoor storage: portable bin or individually on shelves

Storage life in cellar: 1 to 2 weeks for small zucchini; up to 3 months for large zucchini

Storing Nuts in the Root Cellar

Fresh nuts in the shell must be dried before storage. Spread them out in a single layer on mesh trays or newspaper-lined shelf racks, with as much space between nuts as possible. Leave them in a dry, well-ventilated spot (such as shelves in an attic, a warm, dry shed or any dry room) for 3 to 6 weeks. To check for dryness, shake the nuts near your ear — you should hear the nut meat rattling inside the shell. Crack a few shells open and break the nuts to make sure they are dry throughout. If nuts aren't completely dry before storage, they will mold, and any moldy nuts must be discarded. Transfer dry nuts to a jar with several holes poked in the lid for ventilation. Store in a cool, dry area of the cellar for up to 1 year.

Pest Contol

While it's true that money makes most of the human world go around, food is the universal currency of the animal kingdom. Creatures everywhere spend most of their time seeking out food and eating it, and a root cellar will certainly attract the attention of rodents and insects if you let it. The key to keeping pests at bay begins with an understanding of which creatures are likely to be interested in your cellar and how to design and manage your installation so pests are a non-issue.

Rodents

You're not the only one who likes cellared foods. Rodents do too, and they have an uncanny ability to get what they want. No matter where you live and where you have your root cellar, rodents will test the integrity of your installation. They can crawl through tiny gaps and chew small spaces to make them wider, and if they do get into your cellar, they'll leave behind chewed food and droppings that will take all the appeal out of cellaring.

Traditional cellar structures offered virtually no impediment to rodents. Sharing food with them was part of the deal in years gone by. These days, we're pickier about such things, and we can afford to be because we have building materials and strategies that make rodent infiltration much less likely.

The first step is to do everything you can when building your cellar to make it rodent-proof. They may be sneaky, but rodents aren't ghosts. They can't pass through walls. Gap-free construction is what it's all about, especially around the door. Fortunately, energy-efficient construction techniques also yield rodent-resistant results. The weatherstripping and sweep on an insulated steel door, for instance, keep mice out. SIP construction and spray foam insulation strategies virtually eliminate the risk of rodents getting in through walls or ceilings.

People are sometimes reluctant to make a root cellar part of their home because they fear an invasion of pests, but in reality pests are rarely a big problem in cellars, especially those that have been built tightly and are managed well.

There's no way to prevent mice from snacking on produce stored in a root clamp or an unlined root pit, but rodent prevention measures are definitely worth the effort for any kind of structure-based cellar you're building from scratch.

Hantavirus Facts

Rodents in various parts of the world are carriers for hantaviruses. Fortunately, although these viruses can be transmitted directly to humans, hantavirus infections in people are rare. Humans contract the disease by inhaling microscopic particles from rodent droppings and urine, and its symptoms include fever, aches, cough and headache. If you find rodent droppings, you can remove them safely by airing out the space for 30 minutes, soaking the droppings with a solution of 1 part bleach to 9 parts water for 5 minutes, then picking them up with paper towels, using gloved hands. Mop down the area with the bleach solution, then allow it to dry before closing the room again.

Critters love to tunnel in and around batt-style insulation in wall and ceiling cavities — yet another reason to avoid this material when building your cellar.

If you have a hole-in-the-ground cellar pit, and you visit it less often than every couple of days, don't put a trap inside. A live mouse is less trouble than a dead one when you're not there to take it out right away.

Root cellar vents offer the most likely point of entry for rodents, so it's essential to incorporate screens over the ends of your vents (see page 35) and use expanding polyurethane foam and caulking to seal around pipes where they go through holes in the walls to the outdoors. The bottom edges of wooden doors are also especially tempting for rodents. They can chew and tunnel through wood, so if you must use a wooden door, fasten strips of sheet metal around the bottom and 3 inches (75 mm) up both faces as a preventative measure.

If you want to store produce in a hole-in-the-ground cellar pit but don't want mice to take a share of your food and leave behind their calling cards, consider having a concrete well tile installed in your yard. Designed to line the sides of shallow water wells and typically 36 inches (900 mm) in diameter, these concrete pipes sit in a vertical position underground, with a removable concrete lid on top. They come in lengths from 12 to 36 inches (300 to 900 mm). Place alternating layers of straw and produce inside the tile, then close the lid until you need to make a withdrawal from your stash.

Regardless of the steps you take to make your cellar rodent-proof when you're building it, you'll need a plan B, just in case. Rodents are sneaky, and a particularly daring individual might just steal in unnoticed while you have the door open. Or you might miss sealing a tiny crack somewhere. Snap traps offer a safe and inexpensive plan B. Keep two or three baited and set at all times in out-of-the-way places, behind crates or bins, for instance. Peanut butter is an exceptionally effective, long-lasting bait. It works best with the type of trap that has a wide, yellow plastic trigger pad. Smear $1/4$ teaspoon (1 mL) on the top of the trigger and it will remain attractive to rodents for months. Raisins work well too. A single raisin pressed onto the pointed spike on a metal trap trigger often works for multiple catches.

Some people set out poison rodent bait in their cellars, either in conjunction with traps or alone. Opinions vary on how safe this

Keep It Clean

To keep your root cellar sanitary, inviting and less likely to harbor rodents should they get in, you'll need to thoroughly clean it every once in a while. Summer is the best time to do this maintenance work. Empty the cellar completely, move the old produce to the compost pile, then sweep the walls and floor (or hose them down if your cellar is completely waterproof; see page 79). If your cellar has rough masonry surfaces, consider coating the inside with whitewash, a traditional, low-cost paint made of slaked lime and chalk that offers safe antimicrobial properties. Ozone treatments offer another safe and effective way to sterilize root cellars, kill bugs and eliminate odors; see page 81 for more information.

is, but if in doubt, use traps alone. They work very well without help, especially when used in a generally rodent-tight cellar.

If you're cellaring in an existing space that's not rodent-tight, and the little critters are damaging your food stores before they reach your traps, consider storing produce in plastic containers with lids. Bore ¼-inch (6 mm) holes through the containers in a 1-inch (25 mm) grid pattern to increase ventilation if internal humidity gets too high. The holes let in air, but are too small for even the tiniest rodents to enter.

Insects

Because of the low storage temperatures that are ideal for most cellared foods, and because cellars are built tight and kept dark, insects are rarely an issue in root cellars. Even if some bugs were to make a more-than-casual appearance in the cellar, your regular patrols for rotting produce would alert you to the problem. If by some strange chance produce does become infested, remove it.

Grains are susceptible to insect infestation when stored at room temperature, but they shouldn't be kept in the humid conditions provided by a typical root cellar anyway. Store grains in the freezer to eliminate all chances of insect infestation.

Freedom from Fruit Flies

Small, usually numerous and always prolific breeders, fruit flies are made to sense ripe fruit, hover around it and lay eggs in it. And though fruit flies almost certainly won't make an appearance in the dark, cool conditions of your root cellar, they may show up as soon as you bring ripe fruit out of storage and into your kitchen. If you'd rather not have them in your home, a small, safe, homemade fruit fly trap can make all the difference.

Put a few chunks of sweet, ripe fruit (apple, peach or strawberry work well) and a tablespoon (15 mL) of cider vinegar in the bottom of an 8-ounce (250 mL) mason jar. This is the aromatic bait. Next, make a paper cone with a large end that's slightly larger than the mouth of the jar and a small end that tapers down to a ⅛-inch (3 mm) opening. The cone should extend three-quarters of the way to the bottom of the jar. Use tape to hold the seam of the cone together. Set the cone in the mouth of the jar, tip down, then fold the excess paper over the edges of the opening before tightening on the screw band to hold the cone in place.

The paper cone funnels the flies down toward the small opening near the bottom of the jar as they seek the bait. The cider vinegar mimics the smell of fermenting fruit (which the flies love), luring them away from your fruit bowl and towards confinement. Once they travel past the end of the cone and into the jar, they rarely make their way back out through the tiny hole.

fruit flies travel down the open cone into jar

paper cone folded over jar mouth, with ring tightened over paper

8-oz (250 mL) mason jar

1 tbsp (15 mL) cider vinegar

ripe fruit pieces

few flies make it back out the ⅛" (3 mm) diameter hole in the bottom of the cone

HOMEMADE FRUIT FLY TRAP

Part 3

Root Cellar Recipes

Soups

Vegetable Stock

Use those vegetables that have slight physical damage and aren't good for root cellar storage to fill your freezer with this multipurpose stock. Be sure not to use any that are spoiled, though — only use quality vegetables you still want to eat.

Tips

Some people don't peel vegetables for stock, or they include peels along with the vegetables, and that's fine, but you do get a fresher, cleaner vegetable flavor when you discard the peels. Be sure to clean or scrub vegetables regardless of whether you're peeling them.

Portion cooled stock into 2- or 4-cup (500 mL or 1 L) airtight containers, leaving at least $1/2$ inch (1 cm) at the top for expansion, and freeze for up to 6 months.

6	carrots, chopped	6
4	stalks celery, chopped	4
3	onions, cut into quarters	3
3	leeks, halved lengthwise and cut into chunks	3
1 cup	packed parsley sprigs (including stems)	250 mL
4	bay leaves	4
1 tbsp	whole black peppercorns	15 mL
12 cups	water	3 L
	Salt	

1. In a large pot, combine carrots, celery, onions, leeks, parsley, bay leaves, peppercorns and water. Bring to a boil over medium heat. Reduce heat and simmer gently for about 1 hour or until liquid is flavorful.

2. Set a fine-mesh sieve over another large pot or bowl; ladle in stock, emptying solids from sieve as necessary. Strain again, if necessary, to remove any solids from the stock. Season to taste with salt.

> Autumn Giant is a productive, cold-hardy variety of leek that cellars well in tubs of soil.

Chicken Stock

Makes about 8 cups (2 L)

Homemade stock gives a terrific, pure flavor to soups, risottos and sauces that is difficult to replicate with commercial products.

Tips

When you're preparing chicken, put any trimmings, such as backs, rib bones and wing tips, in a sealable freezer bag and keep it in the freezer. Add to the bag as you have more trimmings.

Portion cooled stock into 2- or 4-cup (500 mL or 1 L) airtight containers, leaving at least $1/2$ inch (1 cm) at the top for expansion, and freeze for up to 6 months.

Variation

Replace the chicken pieces with a carcass from a roasted chicken. Pick off the usable meat and discard the excess skin before adding it to the pot. Just be sure to add enough water to cover the bones.

3 lbs	chicken pieces (backs, necks, wing tips)	1.5 kg
4	carrots, chopped	4
3	stalks celery, chopped	3
2	onions, cut into quarters	2
2	leeks, halved lengthwise and cut into chunks	2
1 cup	packed parsley sprigs (including stems)	250 mL
4	bay leaves	4
1 tbsp	whole black peppercorns	15 mL
14 cups	water	3.5 L
	Salt	

1. In a large pot, combine chicken, carrots, celery, onions, leeks, parsley, bay leaves, peppercorns and water. Bring to a boil over medium heat. Reduce heat and simmer gently for about 2 hours or until liquid is flavorful.

2. Set a fine-mesh sieve over another large pot or bowl; ladle in stock, emptying solids from sieve as necessary. Strain again, if necessary, to remove any solids from the stock.

3. Let stock cool, then cover and refrigerate until chilled. Skim off any fat that floats to the top. Reheat over medium heat until steaming. Season to taste with salt.

> In 1941, Disney cartoonist Hank Porter created a family of carrot characters to promote carrot consumption in war-torn Britain.

Classic Leek and Potato Soup

Makes 6 servings

This soup is delicious in its classic version, using leeks, garlic and potatoes at any time of year. You can also use it as a base for even more fabulous soups. Or add in any other seasonal vegetables you like.

Tip

If you plan to freeze this soup, the puréed version works best. After puréeing the soup, transfer it to containers and let cool. Freeze for up to 3 months. Let thaw overnight in the refrigerator, then reheat until steaming.

Variation

Potato Tomato Herb Soup: Omit the lemon juice. Add 1 can (28 oz/796 mL) diced tomatoes and purée with the soup *or* purée tomatoes separately and add after the milk. Stir in ½ cup (125 mL) chopped fresh herbs (basil, oregano and/ or dill).

2 tbsp	butter	30 mL
3	leeks, white and light green parts only, chopped	3
3	cloves garlic, minced	3
2 tbsp	all-purpose flour	30 mL
4 cups	Vegetable Stock (page 130) or reduced-sodium ready-to-use vegetable broth	1 L
3 cups	diced peeled all-purpose potatoes (about 1 lb/500 g)	750 mL
½ cup	milk	125 mL
1 tbsp	freshly squeezed lemon juice	15 mL
	Salt and freshly ground black pepper	

1. In a large pot, melt butter over medium heat. Add leeks and garlic; reduce heat to medium-low and sauté for about 20 minutes or until soft and starting to turn golden. Stir in flour and cook, stirring, for 1 minute, without browning. Gradually stir in stock.

2. Add potatoes; increase heat to medium and bring to a boil, stirring occasionally. Reduce heat and simmer, stirring occasionally, for about 20 minutes or until potatoes are tender. If desired, use an immersion blender in pot or transfer to an upright blender in batches and purée until smooth.

3. Return to medium heat, if necessary. Stir in milk and lemon juice; heat until steaming, stirring occasionally (do not let boil). Season to taste with salt and pepper.

Chili Potato Soup

Tomatoes, beans and a touch of spice turn leek and potato soup into a whole new taste experience.

Tip

Avoid new potatoes or any other round, waxy potato for the puréed version of this soup, as they tend to cause a gluey texture rather than a smooth, velvety one.

2 tbsp	butter	30 mL
3	leeks, white and light green parts only, chopped	3
3	cloves garlic, minced	3
4 tsp	chili powder	20 mL
1 tsp	dried oregano	5 mL
2 tbsp	all-purpose flour	30 mL
3½ cups	Vegetable Stock (page 130) or reduced-sodium ready-to-use vegetable broth	875 mL
1	can (28 oz/796 mL) diced tomatoes, with juice	1
3 cups	diced peeled all-purpose potatoes (about 1 lb/500 g)	750 mL
1	can (14 to 19 oz/398 to 540 mL) red kidney beans, drained and rinsed	1
	Salt and freshly ground black pepper	
	Shredded sharp (old) Cheddar cheese	
	Sour cream	

1. In a large pot, melt butter over medium heat. Add leeks, garlic, chili powder and oregano; reduce heat to medium-low and sauté for about 20 minutes or until soft and starting to turn golden. Stir in flour and cook, stirring, for 1 minute, without browning. Gradually stir in stock. Stir in tomatoes.

2. Add potatoes; increase heat to medium and bring to a boil, stirring occasionally. Reduce heat and simmer, stirring occasionally, for about 20 minutes or until potatoes are tender. If desired, use an immersion blender in pot or transfer to an upright blender in batches and purée until smooth.

3. Return to medium heat, if necessary. Stir in beans and heat until steaming, stirring occasionally. Season to taste with salt and pepper.

4. Ladle into warmed bowls and top each with cheese and a dollop of sour cream.

Roasted Butternut Squash and Apple Soup with Sunflower Ravioli

Makes 8 servings

With treasures from your root cellar, you can capture the bounty of the fall harvest any time in a velvety soup with a surprisingly decadent filled ravioli. The soup is also lovely without the ravioli, for a more casual meal.

Tips

The soup can be prepared through step 3, cooled, covered and refrigerated for up to 2 days. Reheat over medium heat until steaming, stirring often just before serving.

The ravioli can be prepared through step 5, wrapped and refrigerated for up to 4 hours.

- Preheat oven to 450°F (230°C)
- Rimmed baking sheet
- Baking sheet, lined with a damp towel

2	cloves garlic	2
1	stalk celery, coarsely chopped	1
1	small butternut squash, peeled and diced	1
1	small onion, chopped	1
1	carrot, chopped	1
1	tart apple, peeled and chopped	1
2 tbsp	vegetable oil	30 mL
	Salt and freshly ground black pepper	
½ tsp	ground cumin	2 mL
¼ tsp	ground cinnamon	1 mL
2 cups	unsweetened apple juice	500 mL
2 cups	water	500 mL
	Fresh thyme sprigs	

Sunflower Ravioli

½ cup	roasted sunflower seeds, divided	125 mL
¼ cup	dried apricots	60 mL
¼ cup	heavy or whipping (35%) cream	60 mL
¼ tsp	dried thyme	1 mL
Pinch	hot pepper flakes	Pinch
16	wonton wrappers	16
1	egg, beaten	1

1. On rimmed baking sheet, toss garlic, celery, squash, onion, carrot and apple with oil. Season to taste with salt and pepper. Roast in preheated oven, stirring once, for about 40 minutes or until soft and golden brown.

2. Transfer roasted vegetables to a large pot. Add cumin, cinnamon, apple juice and water. Bring to a boil over medium heat. Reduce heat and simmer for about 30 minutes or until vegetables are very soft and soup is slightly reduced and flavorful.

Tips

Butternut squash is easy to peel and gives a smooth, buttery texture to soup. You can use other varieties of winter squash in this soup; you'll need about 5 cups (1.25 L) diced.

For an even more velvety texture, sieve the soup as directed in step 3, then purée and sieve it again. If you're making the soup ahead, do this extra puréeing and sieving after reheating, just before you plan to serve it.

3. Using an immersion blender in pot or transferring soup in batches to an upright blender, purée until very smooth. Pass through a fine sieve, if desired. Return to pot, if necessary. Season to taste with salt and pepper.

4. *For the ravioli:* Set 2 tsp (10 mL) sunflower seeds aside. In a food processor fitted with a metal blade, pulse the remaining sunflower seeds, dried apricots, cream, thyme, and hot pepper flakes until mixture is chopped and sticking together.

5. Brush the edges of 1 wonton wrapper with egg. Place one-eighth of the filling in the center of the square and top with a second wrapper, squeezing out air and pinching edges shut. Place on towel-lined baking sheet and cover loosely with damp towel while working. Repeat with the remaining filling and wonton wrappers.

6. In a shallow pan of simmering water, gently poach ravioli, in batches as necessary, for about 4 minutes or until tender.

7. *To serve:* Using a slotted spoon, lift ravioli from pan, draining well, and place in the bottom of a warmed soup bowl. Ladle hot soup over ravioli and garnish with remaining sunflower seeds and fresh thyme sprigs or leaves.

> Waltham Butternut is an open-pollinated squash with rich orange flesh. It won the All-American Selections Award in 1970.

Curried Sweet Potato and Lime Soup

Makes 4 to 6 servings

This soup is always popular when it's featured at Nuttshell Next Door, the café in Lakefield, Ontario that Jennifer co-owns with her husband, Jay. The curry, lime and coconut milk enhance the sweet potatoes wonderfully.

Tips

If using store-bought broth, reduced-sodium broth works best for this recipe. If it is not available, use 3 cups (750 mL) regular broth and 1 cup (250 mL) water.

Lime leaves are available frozen at Asian grocery stores. They have a texture similar to bay leaves and a deep lime flavor. If you can't find them, substitute $1/2$ tsp (2 mL) grated lime zest and add it with the juice in step 3.

This soup can be prepared through step 2, cooled, covered and refrigerated for up to 2 days.

Variation

Substitute 1 small pie pumpkin or butternut squash (about $2^1/_2$ lbs/1.25 kg) for the sweet potatoes.

6 cups	cubed peeled sweet potatoes (about 2 large)	1.5 L
1	all-purpose potato, peeled and diced	1
4 cups	Vegetable Stock (page 130), Chicken Stock (page 131) or reduced-sodium ready-to-use vegetable or chicken broth	1 L
3	thin slices gingerroot	3
2	lime leaves (see tip, at left)	2
$3/4$ cup	coconut milk	175 mL
$1/2$ cup	water or additional stock	125 mL
2 tbsp	freshly squeezed lime juice	30 mL
1 tsp	salt, or to taste	5 mL
$1/4$ tsp	freshly ground black pepper, or to taste	1 mL
	Granulated sugar (optional)	
	Coconut milk	
	Chopped fresh parsley	

1. In a large pot, combine sweet potatoes, all-purpose potato, stock, ginger and lime leaves. Bring to a boil over medium-high heat. Reduce heat to medium-low, cover and simmer for about 20 minutes or until sweet potato is very soft and ginger and lime are infused. Discard ginger and lime leaves. Stir in coconut milk and water.

2. Using an immersion blender in pot or transferring soup in batches to an upright blender, purée until very smooth. Return to pot, if necessary.

3. Reheat over medium heat until steaming, stirring often. Stir in lime juice. Season with salt and pepper. Season to taste with sugar (if using).

4. Ladle into warmed bowls and serve drizzled with coconut milk and sprinkled with parsley.

Wild Mushroom and Barley Soup

Start a wintry meal with a light but warming bowl of soup. Use a homemade or good-quality prepared beef stock for the best flavor.

Tips

If you don't have fresh thyme, add $1/2$ tsp (2 mL) dried thyme with the celery and carrots to bring out the flavor.

This soup can be made a day ahead, cooled, covered and refrigerated, then reheated over medium heat just before serving.

Variation

If you prefer a lighter soup, use Chicken Stock (page 131), Vegetable Stock (page 130) or reduced-sodium ready-to-use chicken or vegetable broth instead of the beef.

2	packages (each $1/2$ oz/14 g) mixed dried mushrooms (porcini, morels, shiitake, oyster)	2
2 tbsp	butter	30 mL
1	onion, finely chopped	1
1	stalk celery, finely diced	1
1	carrot, finely diced	1
$1/4$ cup	dry sherry	60 mL
2 cups	ready-to-use beef broth	500 mL
$1/4$ cup	pearl or pot barley	60 mL
2 tsp	chopped fresh thyme	10 mL
	Salt and freshly ground black pepper	

1. In a saucepan over high heat or in a microwave-safe bowl in the microwave, heat 4 cups (1 L) water until steaming; stir in mushrooms. Cover and let stand for at least 20 minutes or until soft. Strain through a paper towel– or coffee filter–lined sieve set over a bowl, reserving broth and mushrooms. Rinse mushrooms to remove any grit and pat dry. Chop finely and set aside.

2. In a large pot, melt butter over medium heat. Add onion and sauté for 2 minutes. Reduce heat to low and cook, stirring often, for about 15 minutes or until caramelized. Increase heat to medium and stir in celery and carrot; sauté for about 5 minutes or until almost tender.

3. Add reserved chopped mushrooms and cook, stirring, for 2 minutes. Add sherry and stir to scrape up any brown bits stuck to pan. Boil until almost evaporated. Stir in reserved mushroom broth, beef broth and barley; bring to a boil. Reduce heat to low, cover and simmer for about 30 minutes or until barley is almost tender. Stir in thyme and season to taste with salt and pepper. Simmer, uncovered, for 5 to 10 minutes or until barley is tender. Ladle into warmed bowls.

Cauliflower Soup with Spiced Pear Crisps

Makes 8 servings

Dressed up with a touch of orange and snappy, spiced pear crisps, cauliflower is fit for company in this easy soup.

Tips

The pear crisps can be made 5 days ahead of time and stored in a cookie tin, but you might need to hide them so they don't disappear before it's time to serve the soup.

You can prepare the soup through step 5, let it cool, cover and refrigerate for up to 2 days.

- Preheat oven to 275°F (140°C)
- Large baking sheet, lined with parchment paper

Spiced Pear Crisps

1	firm ripe Bartlett or Bosc pear	1
½ tsp	sweet paprika	2 mL
⅛ tsp	ground cinnamon	0.5 mL
	Salt and freshly ground black pepper	

Cauliflower Soup

2 tbsp	butter or vegetable oil	30 mL
1	onion, chopped	1
3	cloves garlic, chopped	3
1	bay leaf	1
½ tsp	salt	2 mL
¼ tsp	freshly ground black pepper	1 mL
1	all-purpose potato, peeled and diced	1
4 cups	Vegetable Stock (page 130), Chicken Stock (page 131) or reduced-sodium ready-to-use vegetable or chicken broth (approx.)	1 L
2 cups	water	500 mL
7 cups	chopped cauliflower (1 head)	1.75 L
½ tsp	grated orange zest	2 mL
1 tbsp	freshly squeezed orange juice	15 mL

1. *For the pear crisps:* Cut pear lengthwise into paper-thin slices. In a bowl, combine paprika, cinnamon and salt and pepper to taste. Lightly sprinkle over both sides of pear slices. Place on prepared baking sheet in a single layer. Place another sheet of parchment paper on top and set another baking sheet on top of paper to keep pears flat.

2. Bake for 45 minutes or until pears are very soft and starting to dry around the edges. Remove top baking sheet and carefully peel off top piece of parchment. Bake for 15 to 30 minutes, checking often, until pears are dry and firm. (They will crisp more upon cooling.) Carefully peel pears from parchment while still warm and place on a wire rack to cool completely.

Variation

Curried Cauliflower Soup:
Add 2 tsp (10 mL) curry
powder, 1 tsp (5 mL)
ground coriander and
$\frac{1}{2}$ tsp (2 mL) ground
cumin with the garlic. Omit
the orange zest and replace
the orange juice with lime
or lemon juice. Dollop each
bowl with plain yogurt
and sprinkle with chopped
fresh cilantro instead of or
in addition to the Spiced
Pear Crisps.

3. *For the soup:* In a large pot, melt butter over medium heat. Add onion and sauté for about 5 minutes or until softened but not browned. Add garlic, bay leaf, salt and pepper; sauté for 1 minute or until garlic is softened and fragrant.

4. Add potato, stock and water; increase heat to high and bring to a boil, scraping up bits stuck to pot. Stir in cauliflower. Reduce heat to medium-low, cover and boil gently for about 15 minutes or until cauliflower and potatoes are soft. Remove from heat.

5. Discard bay leaf. Using an immersion blender in pot or transferring soup in batches to an upright blender, purée soup until very smooth. Return to pot, if necessary.

6. Reheat over medium heat until steaming, stirring often. Stir in orange zest and juice and season to taste with salt and pepper.

7. *To serve:* Ladle into warmed bowls and float a pear crisp on top of each. Serve extra pear crisps on the side.

> Violetta Italia is an old European variety of cauliflower with large purple heads and a subdued broccoli flavor.

Root Cellar Medley Soup

You can change up the vegetables you use in this soup to suit your tastes or what's left in your stores.

Tip

When chopping or dicing vegetables for soup that won't be puréed, keep in mind that the pieces should fit nicely on a spoon, allowing room for at least two pieces per spoonful, to keep each bite flavorful.

1 tbsp	vegetable oil	15 mL
1	small onion or leek (white and light green part only), chopped	1
1 cup	diced carrots	250 mL
1 cup	diced peeled potatoes	250 mL
1 cup	diced rutabaga or turnip	250 mL
½ cup	sliced celery	125 mL
½ tsp	dried thyme	2 mL
4 cups	Vegetable Stock (page 130), Chicken Stock (page 131) or reduced-sodium ready-to-use vegetable or chicken broth (approx.)	1 L
2 tbsp	tomato paste (optional)	30 mL
2 tbsp	white wine vinegar or cider vinegar	30 mL
1 tsp	salt, or to taste	5 mL
¼ tsp	freshly ground black pepper, or to taste	1 mL
	Chopped fresh parsley	

1. In a large pot, heat oil over medium heat. Add onion and sauté for about 3 minutes or until starting to soften. Add carrots, potatoes, rutabaga, celery and thyme; sauté for 5 minutes or until carrots start to soften.

2. Add stock and bring to a boil over medium-high heat. Reduce heat to medium-low, cover and simmer for about 20 minutes or until vegetables are very soft.

3. Whisk in tomato paste (if using) and vinegar. Simmer, uncovered, stirring occasionally, for 5 minutes. Season with salt and pepper. Ladle into warmed bowls and garnish with parsley.

French Onion Soup

Jennifer has fond memories of family celebrations that often started with piping hot, gooey, cheese-topped, onion-laden soup. Dig out those '70s pottery soup bowls for the full experience.

Tips

If you have homemade beef stock, it does add a wonderful flavor to this soup in place of the store-bought broth.

This soup can be prepared through step 2, cooled, covered and refrigerated for up to 2 days. Reheat soup over medium heat while preheating the broiler.

- Ovenproof soup bowls

2 tbsp	butter	30 mL
3	onions, halved and thinly sliced	3
½ tsp	dried thyme	2 mL
¼ tsp	salt	1 mL
¼ tsp	freshly ground black pepper	1 mL
2	cloves garlic, minced	2
¼ cup	brandy	60 mL
4 cups	reduced-sodium ready-to-use beef broth (see tip, at left)	1 L
1½ cups	water	375 mL
4 to 6	slices (½-inch/1 cm thick) baguette	4 to 6
1 cup	shredded Emmental, Gruyère or Swiss cheese	250 mL

1. In a large pot, melt butter over medium heat. Add onions, thyme, salt and pepper; sauté for 2 minutes or until onions are starting to soften. Reduce heat to medium-low, cover and cook, stirring often, for about 20 minutes or until onions are very soft. Uncover and cook, stirring often, for about 20 minutes or until caramelized. Increase heat to medium-high; add garlic and sauté for 1 minute.

2. Add brandy and bring to a boil, scraping up bits stuck to pot. Add broth and water; bring to a boil. Reduce heat and boil gently for about 10 minutes or until flavors are blended. Season to taste with salt and pepper.

3. Meanwhile, preheat broiler. Arrange baguette slices on a baking sheet and lightly toast both sides. Ladle soup into ovenproof soup bowls. Float one baguette slice in each bowl and sprinkle with cheese. Place bowls on baking sheet and broil for about 2 minutes or until cheese is melted. Serve immediately.

Roasted Onion and Potato Soup

Makes 4 to 6 servings

A few simple ingredients and oven-roasting combine to make a deep, flavorful soup.

Tip

Avoid new potatoes or any other round, waxy potato in this soup, as they tend to cause a gluey texture rather than a smooth, velvety one.

- Preheat oven to 425°F (220°C)
- Rimmed baking sheet

4	cloves garlic	4
3	large onions, chopped	3
2 tbsp	olive oil	30 mL
2 tbsp	balsamic vinegar	30 mL
	Salt and freshly ground black pepper	
3 cups	diced peeled yellow-flesh or all-purpose potatoes (about 1 lb/500 g)	750 mL
1	bay leaf	1
2 cups	Vegetable Stock (page 130) or ready-to-use vegetable broth (approx.)	500 mL
2 cups	water	500 mL
	Chopped fresh parsley, basil or dill	

1. On rimmed baking sheet, toss garlic and onions with oil and vinegar. Season to taste with salt and pepper. Roast in preheated oven, stirring often, for about 30 minutes or until soft and golden brown.

2. Transfer roasted vegetables to a large pot. Add potatoes, bay leaf, stock and water. Bring to a boil over medium-high heat. Reduce heat to medium-low, cover and simmer for about 20 minutes or until potatoes are very soft.

3. Using an immersion blender in pot or transferring soup in batches to an upright blender, purée until very smooth. Return to pot, if necessary.

4. Add more stock to thin to desired consistency. Reheat over medium heat until steaming, stirring often. Season to taste with salt and pepper.

5. Ladle into warmed bowls and serve sprinkled with parsley.

Carrot and Ginger Soup

Makes 4 to 6 servings

The zing of ginger and the slight sweetness of carrots are a delightful combination. The small amount of rice gives body to the soup while keeping it light.

Tips

If using store-bought broth, reduced-sodium vegetable or chicken broth works best for this recipe. If it is not available, use 3 cups (750 mL) regular broth and 1 cup (250 mL) water.

This soup can be prepared through step 2, cooled, covered and refrigerated for up to 2 days.

Variation

To give this soup a Thai flair, add ¼ tsp (1 mL) hot pepper flakes with the ginger, stir in ¾ cup (175 mL) coconut milk with the lemon juice and garnish each bowl with chopped Thai basil instead of parsley.

1 tbsp	vegetable oil	15 mL
1	onion, chopped	1
6 cups	chopped carrots (8 to 12)	1.5 L
2 tbsp	minced gingerroot	30 mL
¼ cup	white rice (any type)	60 mL
4 cups	Vegetable Stock (page 130), Chicken Stock (page 131) or reduced-sodium ready-to-use vegetable or chicken broth (approx.)	1 L
2 tbsp	freshly squeezed lemon or lime juice	30 mL
1 tsp	salt, or to taste	5 mL
¼ tsp	freshly ground black pepper, or to taste	1 mL
	Chopped fresh parsley	

1. In a large pot, heat oil over medium heat. Add onion and sauté for about 3 minutes or until starting to soften. Add carrots and ginger; sauté for 5 minutes or until carrots start to soften. Stir in rice.

2. Add stock and bring to a boil over medium-high heat. Reduce heat to medium-low, cover and simmer for about 20 minutes or until carrots and rice are very soft.

3. Using an immersion blender in pot or transferring soup in batches to an upright blender, purée until very smooth. Return to pot, if necessary.

4. Add water or more stock to thin to desired consistency. Reheat over medium heat until steaming, stirring often. Stir in lemon juice. Season with salt and pepper.

5. Ladle into warmed bowls and serve sprinkled with parsley.

Classic Borscht

There's nothing more warming than a steaming bowl of borscht on a chilly day. "Classic" is a tricky word when it comes to borscht, since there are so many versions, but this one has the hallmark beets, cabbage and sour cream garnish.

Tip

If you have homemade beef stock, it does add a wonderful flavor to this soup in place of the store-bought broth.

Variation

If desired, add 1 tsp (5 mL) caraway seeds with the cabbage.

4	beets, peeled and finely diced	4
2	carrots, finely diced	2
2	cloves garlic, minced	2
1	onion, finely chopped	1
1	bay leaf	1
½ tsp	freshly ground black pepper	2 mL
2 cups	ready-to-use beef or vegetable broth, or Vegetable Stock (page 130)	500 mL
2 cups	water	500 mL
1	can (28 oz/796 mL) diced tomatoes, with juice	1
2 cups	finely shredded cabbage	500 mL
2 tbsp	freshly squeezed lemon juice	30 mL
	Salt	
	Sour cream	
	Chopped fresh dill	

1. In a large pot, combine beets, carrots, garlic, onion, bay leaf, pepper, broth and water. Bring to a boil over medium-high heat. Reduce heat to medium-low, cover and simmer for about 30 minutes or until beets are very soft.

2. Add tomatoes and cabbage; increase heat to high and bring to a boil. Reduce heat and simmer, stirring occasionally, for about 15 minutes or until cabbage is softened and soup is slightly reduced. Discard bay leaf. Stir in lemon juice and season to taste with salt.

3. Ladle into warmed bowls and garnish each with a dollop of sour cream and a sprinkling of dill.

> Detroit Dark Red, an excellent borscht beet, was introduced in the United States in 1892 and remains the most popular beet in North America.

Jerusalem Artichoke Soup

Makes 4 to 6 servings

Jennifer's first experience with Jerusalem artichokes was in a soup at a cooking class with Chef Neil Baxter at Rundles Restaurant in Stratford, Ontario. The velvety texture and unique flavor that these tubers add to this soup can't be matched by any other vegetable.

Tips

Jerusalem artichokes are also known as sunchokes. They are tubers with a thin, pale brown skin and creamy white flesh, similar in texture to a potato. They are native to North America and are a member of the sunflower family. They do brown when exposed to air. Use a small paring knife to remove the brown peel, adding the slices to a bowl of 4 cups (1 L) water combined with 2 tbsp (30 mL) lemon juice; let soak until you are ready to use them. Drain well before adding to the pot.

For a 5-star velvety texture, purée the soup in an upright blender until smooth, strain through a fine-mesh sieve, then purée again. Return to the clean pot and reheat until steaming.

2 tbsp	butter	30 mL
1	small onion, chopped	1
1 cup	diced peeled celery root	250 mL
3 cups	sliced peeled Jerusalem artichokes	750 mL
4 cups	Vegetable Stock (page 130), Chicken Stock (page 131) or reduced-sodium ready-to-use vegetable or chicken broth (approx.)	1 L
	Salt and freshly ground black pepper	
1 to 2 tbsp	freshly squeezed lemon juice	15 to 30 mL
	Chopped fresh chives or green onions	

1. In a large pot, melt butter over medium heat. Reduce heat to medium-low; add onion and celery root and sauté for about 5 minutes or until onion is softened but not browned.

2. Add Jerusalem artichokes and stock; bring to a boil over medium-high heat. Reduce heat to medium-low and simmer for about 15 minutes or until artichokes are very soft.

3. Using an immersion blender in pot or transferring soup in batches to an upright blender, purée until very smooth (see tip, at left). Return to pot, if necessary.

4. Add water or more stock to thin to desired consistency. Reheat over medium heat until steaming, stirring often. Stir in lemon juice to taste. Season to taste with salt and pepper.

5. Ladle into warmed bowls and serve sprinkled with chives.

> The yellow flowers of the Jerusalem artichoke, also known as helianthus, follow the sun's path across the sky each day.

Parsnip and Pear Soup

Makes 4 to 6 servings

The sweet, floral flavor of pears tames the stronger flavor of parsnips in this light and velvety soup.

Tips

If your parsnips have tough, woody cores, trim them away when chopping; they'll cause your soup to be stringy.

To dress up this soup for entertaining, float a Spiced Pear Crisp (page 138) on each serving.

1 tbsp	vegetable oil	15 mL
½ cup	chopped shallots	125 mL
2	pears, peeled and chopped	2
1	small all-purpose potato, peeled and chopped	1
4 cups	chopped parsnips (6 to 10)	1 L
4 cups	Vegetable Stock (page 130), Chicken Stock (page 131) or reduced-sodium ready-to-use vegetable or chicken broth (approx.)	1 L
1 tbsp	white wine vinegar	15 mL
1 tsp	salt, or to taste	5 mL
¼ tsp	freshly ground black pepper, or to taste Chopped fresh parsley	1 mL

1. In a large pot, heat oil over medium heat. Add shallots and sauté for about 3 minutes or until starting to soften. Add pears, potato and parsnips; sauté for 5 minutes or until parsnips start to soften.

2. Add stock and bring to a boil over medium-high heat. Reduce heat to medium-low, cover and simmer for about 20 minutes or until vegetables are very soft.

3. Using an immersion blender in pot or transferring soup in batches to an upright blender, purée until very smooth. Return to pot, if necessary.

4. Add water or more stock to thin to desired consistency. Reheat over medium heat until steaming, stirring often. Stir in vinegar. Season with salt and pepper.

5. Ladle into warmed bowls and serve sprinkled with parsley.

Salads and Appetizers

Coleslaw for a Crowd

This is Jennifer's favorite coleslaw for a number of reasons. It keeps well in the refrigerator, it's easy to make, and it's not rich and creamy like so many coleslaws, making it perfect alongside burgers or deli-style sandwiches.

Tips

To make quick work of preparing this coleslaw, use a food processor fitted with a slicing blade for the cabbage and a shredding blade for the carrots. Alternatively, you can use a mandoline slicer.

Green and red cabbage both work well in this recipe, or you can mix them, using 1 small head of each.

¾ cup	granulated sugar	175 mL
2 tsp	celery seeds	10 mL
1 tsp	dry or Dijon mustard	5 mL
½ tsp	salt	2 mL
½ tsp	freshly ground black pepper	2 mL
1 cup	cider vinegar	250 mL
½ cup	vegetable oil	125 mL
1	head cabbage, shredded (about 12 cups/3 L)	1
4	large carrots, shredded	4

1. In a saucepan, combine sugar, celery seeds, mustard, salt, pepper and vinegar. Heat over medium heat, stirring until sugar is dissolved. Remove from heat and let cool slightly. Gradually whisk in oil.

2. In a large bowl, combine cabbage and carrots. Pour in dressing while still warm and toss to coat. Let cool at room temperature. Cover and refrigerate for at least 4 hours, until chilled, or for up to 2 weeks.

> The Dutch cabbage variety Glory of Enkhuizen, which was introduced in the late 1800s, produces dark blue-green heads that make a vibrant coleslaw.

Broccoli and Apple Slaw

Broccoli stems often get discarded when the tender florets are used, but they can add great flavor and crunch to salads. They'll store in the root cellar a little longer than the crowns, so put them back into storage after cutting off the florets and save them for this twist on coleslaw.

Tips

Use a sharp vegetable peeler to peel off the tough outer layer of the broccoli stalks (you may need a paring knife for the lumpier bits). Cut the stalks crosswise into 2-inch (5 cm) chunks, thinly slice each chunk lengthwise, then stack the slices and cut lengthwise into julienne (matchsticks).

Toast sliced almonds in a dry skillet over medium heat, stirring constantly, for 3 to 5 minutes or until golden and fragrant. Immediately transfer to a bowl to cool.

1/2 cup	plain yogurt	125 mL
1 tbsp	vegetable oil	15 mL
1 tbsp	liquid honey	15 mL
1 tsp	chopped fresh thyme	5 mL
2 cups	julienned peeled broccoli stalks (about 4)	500 mL
2	tart apples, julienned	2
	Salt and freshly ground black pepper	
1/2 cup	sliced almonds, toasted	125 mL

1. In a large bowl, whisk together yogurt, oil, honey and thyme. Add broccoli and apples; toss to coat. Season to taste with salt and pepper.

2. Serve immediately or cover and refrigerate for up to 1 hour. Sprinkle with almonds just before serving.

> Di Ciccio broccoli was introduced in 1890 and is still considered one of the most flavorful varieties. It keeps producing new heads as mature ones are cut.

Warm Bulgur and Red Cabbage Salad

With its bright color and hearty flavors, this makes a lovely winter salad. Serve it on the side of pork chops or roasted chicken.

Tip

If you don't have coarse bulgur, you can use medium bulgur, but instead of cooking it, simply stir it into the boiling stock, remove from the heat and let stand for 15 minutes.

2 cups	Vegetable Stock (page 130) or ready-to-use vegetable broth	500 mL
1 cup	coarse bulgur	250 mL
1/4 cup	olive oil, divided	60 mL
1	small onion, halved lengthwise and thinly sliced	1
1/2 tsp	dried thyme	2 mL
1/2 tsp	salt	2 mL
1/4 tsp	freshly ground black pepper	1 mL
4 cups	shredded red cabbage	1 L
1/4 cup	red wine vinegar or cider vinegar	60 mL

1. In a saucepan with a tight-fitting lid, bring stock to a boil over high heat. Gradually pour in bulgur in a thin stream, stirring constantly. Reduce heat to low, cover and simmer for 15 minutes or until bulgur is tender and liquid is absorbed. Transfer to a bowl, fluff gently with a fork and let cool slightly.

2. Meanwhile, in a large skillet, heat 1 tbsp (15 mL) of the oil over medium-high heat. Add onion, thyme, salt and pepper; sauté for about 3 minutes or until onion starts to brown. Add cabbage and sauté for about 3 minutes or just until wilted. Pour in vinegar and boil, scraping up any bits stuck to pan.

3. Add onion mixture to bulgur and pour in the remaining oil. Toss gently to combine. Season to taste with salt and pepper.

Sweet and Tangy Beet and Carrot Salad

Makes 4 to 6 servings

The natural sweetness of beets and carrots is accented by honey in this slightly tangy vinaigrette.

Tips

To cook the beets, use your favorite method or follow step 1 of Steve's Balsamic Beets (page 153).

For a more elegant presentation (that is, to keep the beets from turning the carrots purple), divide the vinaigrette in half and marinate the beets and carrots separately. Combine just before serving or arrange separately on greens.

¼ cup	cider vinegar	60 mL
1 tbsp	liquid honey	15 mL
1½ tsp	Dijon mustard	7 mL
¼ tsp	salt	1 mL
¼ tsp	freshly ground black pepper	1 mL
⅓ cup	vegetable oil	75 mL
4	beets, cooked, cooled and peeled (see tip, at left)	4
4	carrots	4
1 tbsp	chopped fresh mint (optional)	15 mL
6 cups	mixed salad greens	1.5 L

1. In a large bowl, whisk together vinegar, honey, mustard, salt and pepper. Gradually whisk in oil until blended.

2. Cut beets into thin slices; stack a few slices at a time and cut into julienne (matchsticks). Add to vinaigrette in bowl.

3. Cut carrots crosswise into 2-inch (5 cm) chunks; thinly slice each chunk lengthwise, then stack the slices and cut lengthwise into julienne. Add to beets and toss to coat. Cover and let stand for 30 minutes at room temperature or refrigerate for up to 1 day.

4. Season beet mixture with salt and pepper to taste; stir in mint (if using). Divide greens among serving plates and top with beet mixture, drizzling with vinaigrette from bowl.

Beet and Mixed Grain Salad

Makes 4 to 6 servings

There are so many varieties of mixed grain blends available now, you can make this salad a bit different each time. It's nice packed for lunch or alongside steak or grilled sausages.

Tips

To cook the beets, use your favorite method or follow step 1 of Steve's Balsamic Beets (opposite).

Check the package of your mixed grain blend to determine if a different amount of water or cooking time is required.

This salad can be made with leftover cooked grains, rice or even pasta. Use about 3 cups (750 mL) cooked.

1 cup	mixed grain blend	250 mL
1¾ cups	water	425 mL
	Salt	
½ tsp	grated orange zest	2 mL
¼ cup	freshly squeezed orange juice	60 mL
1 tsp	Dijon mustard	5 mL
1 tsp	liquid honey or packed brown sugar	5 mL
	Freshly ground black pepper	
¼ cup	vegetable oil	60 mL
4	large beets, cooked, cooled and peeled (see tip, at left)	4
2	green onions, sliced	2
2	oranges, segmented	2

1. In a saucepan with a tight-fitting lid, combine grains, water and ½ tsp (2 mL) salt. Bring to a boil over high heat. Reduce heat to low, cover and simmer for 30 minutes or until grains are tender and liquid is absorbed. (Or cook according to package directions; see tip, at left). Remove from heat and let stand, covered, for 5 minutes. Fluff with a fork and let cool completely.

2. In a large bowl, whisk together orange zest, orange juice, mustard, honey and ¼ tsp (1 mL) each salt and pepper; gradually whisk in oil until blended. Add grains and toss with a fork to coat.

3. Cut beets lengthwise into thin wedges and add to bowl. Add green onions and oranges; toss gently to combine. Serve immediately or cover and refrigerate for up to 2 days. Season to taste with salt and pepper.

> Until the late 1880s, beets were called blood turnips.

Steve's Balsamic Beets

This is Steve's favorite way to cook his favorite root vegetable. They're wonderful on their own or incorporated into other dishes that call for cooked beets. Steve has even been known to eat them for breakfast.

> Whole beets
> Balsamic vinegar
> Salt and freshly ground black pepper (optional)

1. Cut off most of the root and all except about ¾ inch (2 cm) of greens on the top of each beet (leaving some of the greens preserves the most flavor). Place beets in a large pot and cover with cold water. Bring to a boil over medium-high heat. Reduce heat and boil gently for about 30 minutes or until fork-tender. Drain and let cool completely.

2. Peel off skins and use immediately or place in an airtight container and refrigerate for up to 1 week. Slice beets as desired, drizzle with a generous amount of balsamic vinegar and season to taste with salt and pepper, if desired.

Tip
For the best flavor, be sure to use the highest-quality Italian balsamic vinegar — the kind where each bottle has its own serial number.

Warm Fennel and Shiitake Mushroom Salad

Makes 4 to 6 servings

The flavors of fennel bulb and fennel seeds combined with mushrooms are terrific in this sautéed salad. Serve it on a bed of bitter greens, such as arugula, radicchio or a mix, if desired.

Tip

The stems of shiitake mushrooms are usually too tough to eat, but they do have good flavor. Trim off the ends, rinse well and use to add a woodsy mushroom flavor to Vegetable Stock (page 130).

1	bulb fennel	1
2 tbsp	olive oil	30 mL
2 cups	shiitake mushroom caps, sliced (about 8 oz/250 g)	500 mL
2	cloves garlic, minced	2
½ tsp	fennel seeds	2 mL
¼ cup	red wine vinegar	60 mL
	Salt and freshly ground black pepper	
	Shaved Parmesan cheese	

1. Trim feathery fronds from fennel; chop 1 tbsp (15 mL) and set aside. Trim off long stalks and outer layer of bulb (if tough and/or bruised) and discard. Cut fennel bulb in half lengthwise and trim out root with a paring knife. Place each half cut side down and thinly slice lengthwise; set aside.

2. In a large skillet, heat oil over medium-high heat. Add mushrooms and sauté for about 3 minutes or until wilted. Add fennel, garlic and fennel seeds; sauté for 5 to 10 minutes or until fennel is tender and mushrooms are browned. Add vinegar and scrape up brown bits stuck to pan. Transfer to a shallow serving bowl and let cool slightly.

3. Season to taste with salt and pepper. Sprinkle with Parmesan and reserved chopped fennel fronds. Serve warm.

Marinated Celery Root Salad

On the outside, celery root is probably one of the least attractive vegetables, but the taste and texture inside are lovely. Its mild celery flavor and firm texture work well in this marinated salad.

Tip

This salad can easily be doubled or tripled to feed a crowd. It makes a nice addition to a buffet table or contribution for a potluck. Odds are there won't be another salad the same.

¼ cup	freshly squeezed lemon juice, divided	60 mL
1	celery root	1
1	red bell pepper, halved crosswise and cut into thin strips	1
1	yellow bell pepper, halved crosswise and cut into thin strips	1
½	English cucumber, halved lengthwise and cut into thin slices	½
1 cup	crumbled feta cheese (optional)	250 mL
¼ cup	olive oil	60 mL
1 cup	grape or cherry tomatoes, halved	250 mL
¼ cup	chopped fresh basil	60 mL
1 tbsp	chopped fresh oregano	15 mL
	Salt and freshly ground black pepper	

1. Place 1 tbsp (15 mL) of the lemon juice in a large bowl. Using a sharp vegetable peeler or a paring knife, trim off the outer skin and small roots of the celery root. Rinse well. Cut root in half; place each half cut side down and cut into ¼-inch (0.5 cm) thick slices. Cut slices into ¼-inch (0.5 cm) sticks, adding to the lemon juice in the bowl and tossing to coat as you work, to prevent browning.

2. Add red pepper, yellow pepper, cucumber and feta (if using). Add the remaining lemon juice and oil; toss to combine. Cover and refrigerate for at least 1 hour, until flavors are blended, or for up to 1 day.

3. Just before serving, add tomatoes, basil and oregano; toss to combine. Season to taste with salt and pepper.

Dilled Cucumber and Belgian Endive Salad

Makes 4 servings

Belgian endive is sweet and mild when it has been stored properly in the dark. If the leaves are exposed to light, they turn green and can become bitter. This salad is refreshingly crunchy, particularly welcome for a winter meal.

Tips

The bright green dressing will lose a little of its vibrant color if made a day ahead, but it still tastes delicious.

The salad keeps its crispness for about an hour with the dressing on it, so you can get it ready and have it waiting in the fridge a little ahead of serving time.

1/4 cup	packed fresh dill sprigs	60 mL
1/4 cup	canola or light olive oil	60 mL
2 tbsp	rice vinegar or white wine vinegar	30 mL
1/2 tsp	granulated sugar	2 mL
1/2 tsp	Dijon mustard	2 mL
	Salt and freshly ground black pepper	
3	Belgian endives	3
1/2	English cucumber	1/2
4	radishes, thinly sliced	4
	Butter lettuce leaves	

1. In a blender, combine dill, oil, vinegar, sugar and mustard; purée until smooth. Transfer to a large bowl and season to taste with salt and pepper.

2. Trim off bottom of endives and separate 12 outer leaves. Wrap separated leaves in damp paper towels and refrigerate until serving. Cut the remaining heads of endive in half lengthwise and cut out cores. Cut crosswise into slices and add to dressing in bowl.

3. Cut cucumber in half lengthwise, then cut crosswise into thin slices. Add to the bowl, along with radishes, and toss to coat.

4. Place butter lettuce leaves and reserved whole endive leaves on serving plates. Top with cucumber mixture, drizzling with any dressing left in the bowl.

> There are three kinds of endive in the world: Belgian endive, curly endive and escarole. Belgian endive has tightly packed leaves grown in complete darkness to keep the color light and the flavor mild.

Spinach Salad with Apples, Celery and Coriander Seed Vinaigrette

Spinach has a taste and texture that pair well with fruit. Here, crispy apples and celery are featured with a zippy vinaigrette that Jennifer's husband, Jay, created for the menu at their café, Nuttshell Next Door.

Tip

Extra vinaigrette can be stored in an airtight container in the refrigerator for up to 2 weeks.

½ cup	vegetable oil	125 mL
2 tbsp	cider vinegar	30 mL
2 tbsp	unsweetened applesauce	30 mL
1½ tsp	coriander seeds	7 mL
½ tsp	granulated sugar	2 mL
½ tsp	Dijon mustard	2 mL
	Salt and freshly ground black pepper	
1	bag (10 oz/300 g) baby spinach (about 10 cups/2.5 L)	1
4	stalks celery, thinly sliced on the diagonal	4
2	apples, thinly sliced	2

1. In a blender or in a tall measuring cup using an immersion blender, combine oil, vinegar, applesauce, coriander seeds, sugar and mustard; blend until well combined and seeds are cracked. Season to taste with salt and pepper.

2. In a large bowl, toss spinach with just enough of the dressing to coat the leaves lightly. Divide among individual serving plates or transfer to a large serving bowl.

3. In a small bowl, combine celery, apples and about ¼ cup (60 mL) of the remaining dressing. Arrange on top of spinach and season to taste with salt and pepper. Serve extra dressing to drizzle over top, if desired, or reserve for another use.

> Spinach seeds planted in early fall will survive moderately harsh winters, offering fresh greens as soon as the soil warms up.

Roasted Squash Salad with Dried Cranberries

Makes 8 servings

Combine traditional autumn ingredients, squash and cranberries, in this non-traditional salad. Serve family-style in a large bowl or, for a fancier presentation, on individual plates on a bed of mixed greens.

Variation

For a different twist and a more substantial salad, mix in 3 cups (750 mL) cooled cooked grains (rice, barley, wheat berries, wild rice, quinoa or a mixture) and add an extra 2 tbsp (30 mL) each oil and vinegar before chilling.

• Preheat oven to 425°F (220°C)

2	plum (Roma) tomatoes, chopped	2
1	butternut squash, diced (about 6 cups/1.5 L)	1
1	zucchini, diced	1
1	red bell pepper, finely chopped	1
1	small red onion, finely chopped	1
½ tsp	dried basil	2 mL
½ tsp	dried thyme	2 mL
½ tsp	salt	2 mL
¼ tsp	freshly ground black pepper	1 mL
⅓ cup	olive oil, divided	75 mL
¼ cup	sherry or red wine vinegar, divided	60 mL
½ cup	dried cranberries	125 mL

1. In a large bowl, combine tomatoes, squash, zucchini, red pepper, red onion, basil, thyme, salt and pepper. Drizzle with half each of the oil and vinegar, tossing to coat.

2. Spread out on a rimmed baking sheet and roast in preheated oven, stirring often, for about 45 minutes or until tender and golden.

3. Transfer to a bowl and toss in cranberries. Let cool at room temperature. Cover and refrigerate for at least 2 hours, until chilled, or for up to 2 days.

4. Transfer to a serving dish and drizzle with the remaining oil and vinegar. Season to taste with salt and pepper.

Caramel-Roasted Apple and Blue Cheese Salad

Makes 8 servings

The vinegar-based caramel gives a unique sweet, tangy and savory flavor to the apples, which glisten on top of colorful salad greens. The addition of blue cheese elevates this salad to the sublime.

Tips

When cooking the syrup in step 2, watch carefully once you hear the bubbles get louder and see them get larger and slower — this means the color is about to change. Make sure the syrup caramelizes, but be careful it doesn't burn.

The apples and dressing can be covered separately and refrigerated for up to 2 days. Let warm to room temperature before serving.

- Preheat oven to 425°F (220°C)
- 8-inch (20 cm) square glass baking dish, buttered

2	large tart cooking apples	2
½ cup	granulated sugar	125 mL
¾ cup	cider vinegar, divided	175 mL
2 tsp	Dijon mustard	10 mL
½ cup	light olive oil	125 mL
	Salt and freshly ground black pepper	
12 cups	lightly packed mixed salad greens (about 12 oz/375 g)	3 L
4 oz	blue cheese, crumbled	125 g
½ cup	chopped toasted walnuts or almonds	125 mL

1. Peel apples, cut in half lengthwise and trim out cores. Cut into ½-inch (1 cm) thick wedges. Arrange in a single layer in prepared baking dish.

2. In a small saucepan, combine sugar and ½ cup (125 mL) of the vinegar. Bring to a boil over medium-high heat, stirring until sugar is dissolved. Boil, without stirring, for about 8 minutes or until syrup turns a golden caramel color. Remove from heat. While whisking, pour in remaining vinegar, then quickly pour over apples in dish.

3. Roast apples in preheated oven for about 15 minutes or until easily pierced with the tip of a knife. Let cool to lukewarm.

4. Carefully drain syrup from apples into a measuring cup; set apples aside. Whisk mustard into syrup; gradually whisk in oil until blended. If dressing is too thick, whisk in up to 2 tbsp (30 mL) hot water. Season to taste with salt and pepper.

5. In a large bowl, toss salad greens with half of the dressing. Divide greens among serving plates. Arrange apple wedges on each salad. Sprinkle with cheese and walnuts and drizzle with the remaining dressing to taste. Season with salt and pepper.

Pear, Blue Cheese and Belgian Endive Canapés

Makes about 24 canapés

When you need an elegant appetizer, head to your root cellar and your cheese drawer, and you can have these whipped up quickly.

Tip

After assembling, you can cover canapés with damp paper towels and plastic wrap and refrigerate for up to 1 hour. Let warm at room temperature for about 15 minutes before serving, to bring out the flavors.

- Piping bag fitted with a star tip (optional)
- Baking sheet or tray, lined with paper towels

6 oz	spreadable cream cheese, at room temperature	175 g
3 oz	blue cheese, at room temperature	90 g
1 tbsp	finely chopped fresh basil (or $3/4$ tsp/3 mL chopped fresh thyme)	15 mL
$1/4$ tsp	freshly ground black pepper	1 mL
	Juice of $1/2$ lemon	
$1/2$ cup	water	125 mL
2	Belgian endives	2
1	pear	1
	Fresh basil leaves	

1. In a bowl, mash together cream cheese, blue cheese, basil and pepper until blended. Fill piping bag (if using) with cheese mixture.

2. In another bowl, combine lemon juice and water. Trim off bottom and outer layer of endives. Carefully separate leaves, dip the cut end of each into lemon water and place on prepared baking sheet.

3. Cut pear lengthwise into quarters and trim out core and stem. Cut lengthwise into thin slices, trying to cut about the same number as you have endive leaves. Add to the lemon water and set aside for up to 30 minutes.

4. Drain pears and pat dry. Pipe or spoon a thin line of cheese mixture along each endive leaf; top with a slice of pear. Arrange on a serving platter and garnish with basil leaves.

Herbed Mushroom and Garlic Pâté

Makes about 2 cups (500 mL)

This vegetarian pâté gets even better after a couple of days in the fridge, so make it ahead for the best flavor. Along with the grilled flatbreads or crackers, serve some marinated artichokes, grilled bell peppers and pickles for a satisfying antipasto platter.

Tip

Beyond canapés, you can use the mushroom pâté as a topping for baked potatoes or grilled steak or fish. Or mix it with shredded mozzarella cheese and use it instead of tomato sauce on pizzas.

2 tbsp	butter	30 mL
3	cloves garlic, minced	3
1	onion, chopped	1
8 oz	shiitake mushrooms, stems removed, caps sliced	250 g
8 oz	button mushrooms, sliced	250 g
2 tbsp	dry white wine	30 mL
8 oz	brick-style cream cheese, at room temperature	250 g
1/2 tsp	salt	2 mL
1/4 tsp	freshly ground black pepper	1 mL
2 tsp	chopped fresh savory or thyme	10 mL
1 tsp	chopped fresh rosemary	5 mL
	Grilled soft flatbreads, crisp flatbreads or crackers	

1. In a skillet, melt butter over medium-high heat. Add garlic, onion, shiitake mushrooms and button mushrooms; sauté for about 8 minutes or until liquid is evaporated and mushrooms are browned. Add wine and cook, scraping up brown bits stuck to pan, until evaporated. Let cool slightly.

2. In a food processor fitted with a metal blade, purée mushroom mixture, cream cheese, salt and pepper until smooth. Check seasoning and stir in savory and rosemary. Pack into a pâté crock or ramekins. Cover and refrigerate for about 4 hours, until chilled, or for up to 5 days.

3. Let pâté stand at room temperature for about 15 minutes. Place flatbreads on a platter with pâté and a spreader.

Roasted Squash and Onion Hummus

Makes 2½ cups (625 mL)

Traditional chickpea spread gets a new twist from the caramelized flavors of roasted squash, onions and garlic, all highlighted by the zing of fresh lemon. Serve it as an appetizer with fresh veggie sticks and crisp flatbreads, or as a scrumptious sandwich spread.

Tips

Butternut squash has a creamy texture and a rich flavor and is perfect for this recipe, but you can use other winter squash instead.

A 19-oz (540 mL) can of chickpeas, drained and rinsed, yields 2 cups (500 mL). If you use smaller or larger cans, drain and rinse the chickpeas, then measure them. Any extra can be refrigerated in an airtight container for up to 2 days or frozen for up to 3 months. If using dried chickpeas, soak and cook 1 cup (250 mL).

- Preheat oven to 425°F (220°C)
- Rimmed baking sheet, lined with parchment paper

3 cups	diced butternut squash	750 mL
4	cloves garlic	4
1	small onion, chopped	1
⅓ cup	olive oil, divided	75 mL
2 tbsp	cider vinegar	30 mL
	Salt and freshly ground black pepper	
2 cups	drained rinsed canned or cooked chickpeas (see tip, at left)	500 mL
3 tbsp	freshly squeezed lemon juice	45 mL

1. On prepared baking sheet, combine squash, garlic, onion, 2 tbsp (30 mL) of the oil and the vinegar. Season to taste with salt and pepper. Toss to coat and spread out in a single layer. Roast in preheated oven, stirring twice, for about 45 minutes or until very soft and golden brown. Let cool on baking sheet on a wire rack.

2. In a food processor, combine squash mixture and chickpeas; pulse until finely chopped, stopping two or three times to scrape down the sides of the bowl. With the motor running, through the feed tube, gradually add the remaining oil and the lemon juice; process until smooth, adding enough water to thin to desired consistency. Season to taste with salt and pepper.

3. Transfer to a bowl and serve immediately, or cover and refrigerate for up to 2 days.

Side Dishes

Barley and Beet Risotto

While this isn't a true risotto, as there is no rice, the barley is cooked in a similar way to produce a creamy, risotto-like dish. Barley has a slightly nutty flavor and a tender-firm bite that makes it particularly satisfying. Once it's combined with earthy beets and tangy cheese, this side dish might just take over the starring role on the plate.

Tips

Pot barley is less refined than pearl barley, making it more nutritious, but you can substitute pearl barley if you wish.

Serve this risotto alongside pan-seared mild white fish, roast chicken or a veal chop.

1 cup	pot barley	250 mL
3 cups	Vegetable Stock (page 130), Chicken Stock (page 131) or reduced-sodium ready-to-use vegetable or chicken broth	750 mL
1 tbsp	butter or olive oil	15 mL
1	onion, chopped	1
2	cloves garlic, minced	2
1 tsp	dried basil	5 mL
¼ tsp	salt	1 mL
¼ tsp	freshly ground black pepper	1 mL
½ cup	dry white wine	125 mL
2 cups	diced peeled beets (about 3 medium)	500 mL
2 tbsp	freshly squeezed lemon juice	30 mL
¼ cup	crumbled soft goat cheese or feta cheese	60 mL

1. Rinse barley in a sieve under running water, stirring to make sure it is well rinsed, until water runs clear. Drain well and set aside.

2. In a saucepan over high heat or in the microwave, heat stock and 1 cup (250 mL) water until almost boiling. Cover and keep hot.

3. In a large saucepan, melt butter over medium heat. Add onion and sauté for about 3 minutes or until starting to soften. Add garlic, basil, salt and pepper; sauté for 2 minutes. Add barley and stir to coat well. Add wine and cook, scraping up any bits stuck to pan, until liquid is almost evaporated.

4. Stir in 2 cups (500 mL) of the stock mixture and the beets. Cover, reduce heat to medium-low and boil gently, stirring occasionally, for 25 minutes or until beets are almost tender. Add a little more of the stock, if necessary, to keep mixture moist.

5. Uncover and simmer, stirring often and adding stock, a ladleful at a time as the previous addition is absorbed, for about 20 minutes or until barley is tender with a slight bite and beets are tender. Adjust the heat as necessary to keep the pot at a steady simmer. You may need to add a little more hot water if the mixture gets too thick before the barley is tender. Stir in lemon juice. Season to taste with salt and pepper. Serve sprinkled with cheese.

Roasted Squash Risotto

Roasting the squash brings out its flavor and adds body and depth to a simple risotto. This makes a lovely side dish for roasted meats or poultry, yet it's hearty enough that it could be a main course.

Tips

If you're using store-bought broth, reduced-sodium works best for this recipe. If it is not available, use 3$\frac{1}{2}$ cups (875 mL) regular broth and 1$\frac{1}{2}$ cups (375 mL) water.

The squash mixture can be roasted ahead of time. Transfer to an airtight container or bowl, let cool, then cover and refrigerate for up to 1 day. Let warm to room temperature before adding to the risotto.

When cooking the risotto in Step 5, if your other dishes aren't ready to serve, remove the risotto from the heat, cover and let stand for up to 10 minutes. Stir in more hot stock or a little hot water to loosen.

- Preheat oven to 400°F (200°C)
- Rimmed baking sheet, lined with foil

3 cups	cubed peeled winter squash	750 mL
3	cloves garlic, minced	3
3 tbsp	olive oil, divided	45 mL
2 tbsp	white wine vinegar	30 mL
	Salt and freshly ground black pepper	
5 cups	Vegetable Stock (page 130) or ready-to-use vegetable broth (approx.)	1.25 L
1	onion, chopped	1
1$\frac{1}{2}$ cups	Arborio rice	375 mL
$\frac{1}{4}$ cup	dry white wine	60 mL
1	can (14 to 19 oz/398 to 540 mL) chickpeas, drained and rinsed (optional)	1
2 cups	baby spinach leaves	500 mL
$\frac{1}{2}$ cup	freshly grated Parmesan cheese	125 mL

1. In a bowl, combine squash and garlic; sprinkle with 1 tbsp (15 mL) of the olive oil and the vinegar and season to taste with salt and pepper. Toss to coat and spread in a single layer on prepared baking sheet. Roast in preheated oven, stirring occasionally, for 30 minutes or until soft and golden.

2. In a saucepan over high heat or in the microwave, heat stock until almost boiling. Cover and keep hot.

3. In a large saucepan, heat the remaining oil over medium heat. Add onion and sauté for about 5 minutes or until softened. Stir in rice and sauté for 1 minute. Add wine and cook, scraping up any bits stuck to pan, until evaporated.

4. Stir in 1 cup (250 mL) of the hot stock. Reduce heat and simmer, stirring, until stock is absorbed. Add more stock, $\frac{1}{2}$ cup (125 mL) at a time, stirring until stock is absorbed before making the next addition, until you have added 3 cups (750 mL) stock, have cooked for about 25 minutes and rice is almost tender.

5. Stir in roasted squash mixture, chickpeas (if using) and another $\frac{1}{2}$ cup (125 mL) stock and simmer, stirring, until rice is tender yet still firm to the bite and risotto is somewhat loose. Stir in spinach and Parmesan. Season to taste with salt and pepper.

Wild Rice Gratin

Makes 8 servings

The toothsome texture of wild rice mixed with brown rice adds interest to this side dish. It's perfect for a holiday meal, a potluck or any time you want something just a little different from plain rice.

Tips

If using store-bought broth, reduced-sodium vegetable broth works best for this recipe. If it is not available, use $1\frac{1}{2}$ cups (375 mL) regular broth and $\frac{1}{2}$ cup (125 mL) water.

To make ahead, complete through step 3, let cool, cover and refrigerate for up to 2 days. Let stand at room temperature for 30 minutes to remove the chill. Drizzle $\frac{1}{2}$ cup (125 mL) additional stock evenly over rice mixture. Cover dish with foil and bake in a 350°F (180°C) oven for about 30 minutes or until heated through, then proceed with step 4.

● 12-cup (3 L) shallow baking dish, buttered

$\frac{2}{3}$ cup	wild rice	150 mL
$1\frac{1}{2}$ cups	long-grain brown rice	375 mL
2 cups	Vegetable Stock (page 130) or ready-to-use vegetable broth	500 mL
$1\frac{1}{2}$ tsp	salt, divided	7 mL
2 tbsp	vegetable oil	30 mL
4	stalks celery, finely chopped	4
2	cloves garlic, minced	2
1	onion, finely chopped	1
$\frac{1}{2}$ tsp	dried thyme	2 mL
$\frac{1}{2}$ tsp	dried rosemary, crumbled	2 mL
3	apples, diced	3
	Freshly ground black pepper	
1 cup	fresh bread crumbs	250 mL
1 cup	shredded Swiss cheese	250 mL

1. Rinse wild rice in a sieve under running water, stirring to make sure it is well rinsed. Drain and set aside. Rinse brown rice, stirring to make sure it is well rinsed, until water runs clear. Drain well and set aside separately.

2. In a large pot with a tight-fitting lid, bring stock and 4 cups (1 L) water to a boil over high heat. Add wild rice and 1 tsp (5 mL) of the salt. Reduce heat and boil gently for 15 minutes. Stir in brown rice, reduce heat to low, cover and simmer for about 45 minutes or until wild rice kernels begin to burst open, brown rice is tender and most of the liquid is absorbed. Cover and let stand for 5 minutes. Fluff rice with a fork.

3. Meanwhile, in a large skillet, heat oil over medium heat. Add celery, garlic, onion, thyme, rosemary and the remaining salt; sauté for about 7 minutes or until soft. Add apples and sauté for about 3 minutes or until tender. Season to taste with pepper. Gently fold into rice mixture. Spread into prepared baking dish.

4. Preheat the broiler.

5. In a bowl, combine bread crumbs and cheese; season to taste with pepper. Sprinkle over rice mixture.

6. Broil for about 3 minutes or until cheese is melted and bread crumbs are toasted.

Golden Potato and Roasted Red Pepper Dauphinois

Makes 4 to 6 servings

With thin layers of golden potatoes and roasted red peppers baked with garlic-infused cream, this dish just can't be beat. It's perfect served with roast beef, pork or poultry.

Tips

When fresh red bell peppers are expensive, use the type in the jar; just rinse and drain before slicing. If you're using fresh, broil 1 large pepper on a baking sheet, turning often, until blackened on all sides. Let cool in a covered bowl, then remove the core and peel off the skins.

Use a mandoline slicer or a food processor with a slicing blade to make quick work of slicing the potatoes — they should be very thin for the best texture.

Although baking this dish ahead doesn't save on time in the oven, it does save on preparation time in the kitchen just before dinner. Let the baked dish cool, then cover and refrigerate for up to 1 day. Reheat, covered with foil, for about 40 minutes in a 325°F (160°C) oven; uncover and bake for 10 minutes to crisp the top.

- Preheat oven to 375°F (190°C)
- 8-cup (2 L) shallow baking dish, buttered
- Rimmed baking sheet

2 cups	table (18%) cream (or 1 cup/250 mL each milk and heavy or whipping (35%) cream)	500 mL
1 tsp	salt	5 mL
½ tsp	freshly ground black pepper	2 mL
3	cloves garlic	3
2 lbs	yellow-fleshed or oblong baking potatoes (about 4)	1 kg
½ cup	thin strips roasted red bell pepper, patted dry	125 mL
½ cup	finely shredded cheese (Oka, Gruyère, fontina or Parmesan)	125 mL

1. In a small saucepan, combine cream, salt and pepper. Using the flat side of a knife, smash garlic cloves. Add garlic to cream mixture and heat over medium heat just until steaming. Remove from heat and keep warm.

2. Peel potatoes and cut into very thin slices. Discard garlic cloves from cream mixture. Pour enough of the cream mixture into prepared dish to coat the bottom. Layer about one-third of the potato slices, overlapping as necessary, in the dish. Sprinkle with half of the red pepper strips. Pour about one-third of the cream mixture over top. Repeat layering, ending with potatoes and the remaining cream mixture. Press down potatoes with a spatula to cover them in cream. Place dish on rimmed baking sheet.

3. Bake in preheated oven for about 50 minutes or until potatoes are tender and top is golden. Sprinkle with cheese and broil until bubbled and golden. Let stand for 10 minutes before serving.

Two-Potato Dauphinois

With thin layers of golden potatoes and sweet potatoes baked with luxurious cream, this dish is fit for the most important guests. A slicing tool such as a mandoline is a real time-saver for thinly slicing potatoes, but a good sharp knife will work too.

Tip

To make this dish ahead, bake as directed, then cool, cover and refrigerate for up to 1 day. Reheat, covered with foil, for about 1 hour in a 325°F (160°C) oven; uncover and bake for 10 minutes to crisp the top.

Variation

For a smaller recipe, halve the ingredients, bake in a 6-cup (1.5 L) shallow baking dish and reduce the baking time to about 45 minutes.

- Preheat oven to 375°F (190°C)
- 13- by 9-inch (33 by 23 cm) glass baking dish, buttered
- Rimmed baking dish

1½ cups	whipping (35%) cream	375 mL
1½ cups	milk	375 mL
1½ tsp	salt	7 mL
½ tsp	freshly ground black pepper	2 mL
½ tsp	dried thyme	2 mL
¼ tsp	dried rosemary, crumbled	1 mL
2 lbs	yellow-fleshed or oblong baking potatoes (about 4)	1 kg
1 lb	sweet potatoes (about 2)	500 g

1. In a saucepan, combine cream, milk, salt, pepper, thyme and rosemary; heat over medium heat just until steaming. Remove from heat and keep warm.

2. Meanwhile, peel yellow-fleshed potatoes and sweet potatoes and cut into very thin slices. Pour enough of the cream mixture into prepared dish to coat the bottom. Layer about one-third of the yellow potato slices, overlapping as necessary, in the dish. Layer with one-third of the sweet potato slices. Pour about one-third of the cream mixture over top. Repeat layering once. Arrange remaining yellow and sweet potatoes on top, alternating and overlapping; pour the remaining cream mixture over top. Press down potatoes with a spatula to cover them in cream. Place dish on rimmed baking sheet.

3. Bake in preheated oven for about 70 minutes or until potatoes are tender and top is golden. Let stand for 10 to 15 minutes before serving.

> In October 1995, potatoes became the first vegetable grown in space.

Classic Scalloped Potatoes

Makes 6 to 8 servings

In Jennifer's family, you can't have a ham dinner without a dish of scalloped potatoes with their creamy layers of potatoes and golden brown top.

Tip

Use yellow-fleshed potatoes for an extra-golden color.

Variation

Substitute 2 small sweet potatoes for 2 of the all-purpose potatoes.

- Preheat oven to 350°F (180°C)
- 13- by 9-inch (33 by 23 cm) glass baking dish, buttered
- Rimmed baking sheet

2 tbsp	butter	30 mL
3	cloves garlic, minced	3
2	onions, thinly sliced	2
2 tsp	chopped fresh thyme (or ¾ tsp/3 mL dried thyme)	10 mL
1 tsp	salt	5 mL
¼ tsp	freshly ground black pepper	1 mL
¼ cup	all-purpose flour	60 mL
3 cups	milk (preferably 2% or whole), heated until steaming	750 mL
1 tbsp	Dijon or dry mustard	15 mL
6	all-purpose potatoes (about 3 lbs/1.5 kg), peeled and thinly sliced	6

1. In a large pot, melt butter over medium heat. Add garlic, onions, thyme, salt and pepper; sauté for about 8 minutes or until onions are softened and just starting to brown. Sprinkle with flour and sauté for 1 minute. Gradually whisk in milk and mustard; bring to a boil, whisking constantly. Reduce heat and simmer, whisking, for about 5 minutes or until thickened. Remove from heat. Add potatoes and toss gently to coat in sauce.

2. Spread half of the potatoes evenly in prepared baking dish; pour half of the white sauce over top, spreading evenly. Repeat with the remaining potatoes and sauce. Place dish on rimmed baking sheet.

3. Bake in preheated oven for about 50 minutes or until golden and bubbling and potatoes are tender. Let stand for 10 minutes before serving.

> Preserved from extinction by British potato enthusiasts, the Pink Fir Apple potato is a long, red heirloom variety that is now available commercially from specialty producers.

Chipotle Cheddar Mashed Potatoes

A dinner of meatloaf will never be the same once you've tried this zesty version of mashed potatoes.

Tip

For the best texture, cut the potatoes into even-size chunks and keep them at a gentle boil so they cook evenly and the outside doesn't get mushy before the inside is tender.

2 lbs	oblong baking or yellow-fleshed potatoes (about 4), peeled and cut into chunks	1 kg
	Cold water	
	Salt	
¾ cup	milk, heated until steaming (approx.)	175 mL
2 tbsp	chipotle barbecue sauce (or 1 minced chipotle pepper in adobo sauce)	30 mL
1 cup	shredded sharp (old) Cheddar cheese	250 mL
	Freshly ground black pepper	
	Chopped fresh chives	

1. Place potatoes in a large pot and add enough cold water to cover. Bring to a boil over high heat. Season water with salt, reduce heat and boil gently for about 20 minutes or until potatoes are fork-tender. Drain well and return to pot.

2. Using a potato masher, mash potatoes, gradually adding warm milk, until potatoes are smooth and fluffy. Mash in barbecue sauce and cheese until blended. Season to taste with salt and pepper. Serve sprinkled with chives.

> Fianna is the ultimate mashing potato. Its exceptionally floury texture makes for very light results.

Fennel Seed Mashed Potatoes

Makes 8 to 10 servings

A hint of fennel flavor adds an interesting accent to fluffy mashed potatoes. Serve them alongside a roasted rack of pork or lamb, or a veal pot roast.

Tip

Heating the milk and butter helps create fluffy mashed potatoes.

Don't be tempted to use an electric mixer to mash potatoes — it is quick but tends to make the texture gluey rather than fluffy.

4 lbs	oblong baking or yellow-fleshed potatoes (about 8), peeled and cut into chunks	2 kg
	Cold water	
	Salt	
2 tsp	fennel seeds	10 mL
2 cups	milk	500 mL
2 tbsp	butter	30 mL
	Freshly ground black pepper	

1. Place potatoes in a large pot and add enough cold water to cover. Bring to a boil over high heat. Season water with salt, reduce heat and boil gently for about 20 minutes or until potatoes are fork-tender. Drain well and return to pot.

2. Meanwhile, in a medium saucepan, over medium heat, toast fennel seeds, stirring constantly, for about 1 minute or just until fragrant. Remove from heat. Let pan cool slightly, then add milk and butter; heat over medium heat until steaming and butter is melted.

3. Using a potato masher, mash potatoes, gradually adding warm milk mixture, until potatoes are smooth and fluffy. Season to taste with salt and pepper.

> Golden Wonder is a large, relatively smooth-skinned potato that mashes well.

Golden Puffed Potato Puddings

Makes 8 servings

This recipe combines two side dish favorites — mashed potatoes and Yorkshire puddings — in one fabulous dish. The best part is there's no need to be draining and mashing potatoes in the midst of your dinner party. All of the messy work is done well ahead of time.

Tip

To make ahead, prepare the puddings through step 3, cover and refrigerate for up to 1 day. Let ramekins stand at room temperature for 30 minutes to remove the chill, then bake just before you're ready to serve them.

- Eight ¾-cup (175 mL) ramekins or other ovenproof dishes

2½ lbs	yellow-fleshed potatoes (about 6), peeled and cut into chunks	1.25 kg
	Cold water	
2 tsp	salt, divided	10 mL
4	eggs	4
½ cup	milk	125 mL
½ cup	all-purpose flour	125 mL
½ tsp	freshly ground black pepper	2 mL
2 tbsp	butter, softened (approx.)	30 mL
¼ cup	dry bread crumbs	60 mL

1. Place potatoes in a large pot and add enough cold water to cover. Bring to a boil over high heat. Add 1 tsp (5 mL) salt, reduce heat and boil gently for about 20 minutes or until potatoes are fork-tender. Drain and return to pot. Mash with a potato masher until smooth and fluffy, or press through a ricer. Let cool until steaming subsides.

2. Meanwhile, preheat oven to 425°F (220°C).

3. In a large bowl, whisk together eggs and milk. Whisk in flour, the remaining salt and pepper. Stir into potatoes until blended.

4. Generously butter ramekins and sprinkle with bread crumbs, tapping to evenly coat and shaking out excess crumbs. Spoon potato mixture into ramekins, smoothing top. Bake for about 25 minutes or until puffed, golden and hot in the center. Serve immediately in the ramekins.

Potato and Rutabaga Mash

Makes 8 servings

A touch of apple complements flavorful rutabaga in this twist on mashed potatoes. Serve it at your next holiday gathering and keep everyone guessing just how you made the potatoes taste so fabulous.

Tip

To make this dish ahead, prepare through step 3 and transfer to an 8-cup (2 L) shallow baking dish. Let cool, cover and refrigerate for up to 2 days. Reheat, covered with foil, in a 375°F (190°C) oven for about 30 minutes or until heated through.

1/4 cup	butter, divided	60 mL
1	tart apple, peeled and chopped	1
1	onion, chopped	1
1	small rutabaga, peeled and chopped (about 4 cups/1 L)	1
1/2 cup	Vegetable Stock (page 130) or ready-to-use vegetable broth	125 mL
3/4 tsp	salt, divided	3 mL
4	all-purpose or oblong baking potatoes (about 2 lbs/1 kg), peeled and cut into chunks	4
	Cold water	
1/2 cup	milk or cream (any type)	125 mL
	Freshly ground black pepper	

1. In a medium saucepan, melt half the butter over medium heat. Add apple and onion; sauté for about 5 minutes or until onion is softened. Add rutabaga, stock and 1/4 tsp (1 mL) salt; bring to a boil. Cover, reduce heat to low and simmer for about 45 minutes or until rutabaga is soft.

2. Meanwhile, place potatoes in a large pot and add enough cold water to cover. Bring to a boil over high heat. Add 1/2 tsp (2 mL) salt, reduce heat and boil gently for about 20 minutes or until potatoes are fork-tender. Drain and return to pot. Mash with a potato masher until smooth and fluffy.

3. Transfer rutabaga mixture to a food processor fitted with a metal blade and purée until smooth. Add milk and pulse to combine. Add to potatoes in pot and mash with a potato masher until blended. Season to taste with salt and pepper.

Perogies

Makes 8 to 10 servings (about 5 dozen perogies)

Pierogy, Verenyky, Pyrohy ... there are many names for these tender filled dumplings, and as many versions of the recipe as there are Eastern European cooks! Whatever the recipe, there are a few details that every Bubby or Baba will agree on: the dough must be rolled very thin and the potatoes must be dry and fluffy for the filling. Jennifer gives special thanks to her friend Michelle Deeton and Michelle's mom, Olive Deeton, for their excellent coaching to perfect this recipe.

- Rimmed baking sheet, dusted with all-purpose flour

Dough

4 cups	all-purpose flour	1 L
2 tsp	salt	10 mL
1¾ cups	buttermilk	425 mL

Filling

2 lbs	oblong baking potatoes (about 4)	1 kg
	Cold water	
	Salt	
1 tbsp	butter	15 mL
¼ cup	finely chopped onion	60 mL
1	clove garlic, minced	1
¼ tsp	freshly ground black pepper	1 mL
1½ cups	shredded sharp (old) Cheddar cheese	375 mL
	Warm water	
½ cup	butter, melted	125 mL
	Fried onions, crumbled cooked bacon and sour cream	

1. *For the dough:* In a large bowl, combine flour and salt. Using a wooden spoon, stir in buttermilk to make a ragged dough. Gather into a ball and knead on a floured surface for 2 to 3 minutes or until smooth. Cover and let rest for 20 minutes.

2. *For the filling:* Peel potatoes and cut into chunks. Place in a large pot and add enough cold water to cover. Bring to a boil over high heat. Season water with salt, reduce heat and boil gently for about 20 minutes or until soft.

3. Meanwhile, in a saucepan, melt 1 tbsp (15 mL) butter over medium heat. Add onion, garlic and pepper; sauté for about 5 minutes or until softened. Set aside.

4. Drain potatoes and return to pot over low heat. Shake pot for about 1 minute to dry potatoes. Remove from heat and, using a potato masher, mash until smooth. Sprinkle with cheese, cover and let stand for 1 minute or until cheese is melted. Add onion mixture and mash until blended. Let cool slightly.

Tips

Uncooked perogies can be frozen on baking sheet until firm, transferred to an airtight container and frozen for up to 3 months. Do not thaw before cooking, but increase the boiling time to 8 to 10 minutes.

You can add many different sautéed vegetables or herbs to the potato filling. Once you've mastered the basic filling, feel free to experiment — just make sure the filling doesn't get too sticky.

5. *To assemble:* Cut dough in half. On a floured surface, roll out half the dough to $1/8$-inch (3 mm) thickness, lightly flouring under dough as you roll and letting the dough rest while rolling if it is too elastic. Cut out 3-inch (7.5 cm) circles and gather up scraps to reroll. Roll out each circle again to make sure dough is very thin.

6. Place a heaping teaspoon (5 mL) of filling in the center of each dough circle. Dip a finger in warm water and dampen the edge on one side of the circle. Fold opposite side of dough over to make a semicircle and pinch edges to seal, squeezing out air. Place filled perogies in a single layer on floured baking sheet. Repeat with remaining dough and filling. Cook right away or cover and refrigerate for up to 4 hours.

7. Bring a large pot of water to a boil; season with salt. Add 8 to 10 perogies at a time, stirring gently, and cook for 3 to 4 minutes or until they float to the top and are tender. Remove with a slotted spoon and place in a warmed serving dish. Toss gently with some of the melted butter. Keep warm. Repeat with the remaining perogies. Serve with fried onions, bacon and sour cream.

Although potatoes have played an important role in Europe for many centuries, they originated in the Andes mountains of South America. They were first brought across the Atlantic in 1536.

Royal Sea Salt and Malt Oven Fries

Makes 4 to 6 servings

Purple Peruvian, Purple Majestic and True Blue are a just a few of the many varieties of purple potatoes, some of which have been grown for centuries (as far back as ancestors of the Incas). They usually have purple-blue skin and flesh, though some have purple skin and bright white flesh. Roasting them makes the color even more royal. When they're combined with a classic salt-and-vinegar seasoning, this side dish is certainly fit for royalty.

Variation

Substitute all-purpose or oblong baking potatoes for the purple potatoes. Cut them into lengthwise wedges slightly thicker than 1/2 inch (1 cm).

- Preheat oven to 400°F (200°C)
- Large rimmed baking sheet, lined with foil

2 lbs	purple (blue) potatoes (about 16 small)	1 kg
1/4 cup	malt vinegar, divided	60 mL
2 tbsp	vegetable or olive oil	30 mL
1/2 tsp	coarse sea salt	2 mL
1/2 tsp	freshly ground black pepper	2 mL
2 tsp	chopped fresh thyme, rosemary or dill	10 mL

1. Cut potatoes into quarters (or halves if very small). In a bowl, combine potatoes, 2 tbsp (30 mL) of the vinegar, oil, salt and pepper. Spread out in a single layer on prepared baking sheet. Roast in preheated oven for about 30 minutes, stirring twice, until potatoes are tender inside and browned on the outside.

2. Sprinkle with the remaining vinegar and season to taste with salt and pepper. Transfer to a warmed serving dish and sprinkle with thyme.

> Officially recognized in 1923, Shetland Black potatoes have yellow flesh and a dark purple ring inside.

Beet and Sweet Potato Fries with Three-Pepper Mayo

Makes 4 servings

Oven-baked root vegetables make colorful and flavorful French fries and add interest to a meal as a side dish or appetizer. Three kinds of pepper mixed into creamy mayonnaise make a zesty and luscious dip.

- Preheat oven to 400°F (200°C), with racks positioned in the bottom and top third
- Two large baking sheets, lined with parchment paper

½ cup	mayonnaise	125 mL
1 tsp	pink peppercorns, crushed	5 mL
½ tsp	drained green peppercorns, crushed	2 mL
¼ tsp	coarsely ground black pepper	1 mL
2	large beets (about 1 lb/500 g)	2
2 tbsp	olive oil, divided	30 mL
	Sea salt or fleur de sel	
	Freshly ground black pepper	
1	large sweet potato (about 1 lb/500 g)	1

1. In a small bowl, combine mayonnaise, pink peppercorns, green peppercorns and coarsely ground black pepper. Cover and refrigerate until serving, for up to 1 day.

2. Trim off leaf stalks from beets (reserving for another use, if desired) and trim off long roots. Peel beets and rinse. Cut in half crosswise, then cut lengthwise into sticks about ½-inch (1 cm) square. Toss with half the oil, ¼ tsp (1 mL) salt and ground pepper to taste. Spread out on one prepared baking sheet, leaving space between each fry. Bake on lower rack of preheated oven for 20 minutes or until starting to get tender.

3. Meanwhile, peel sweet potato and rinse. Cut in half crosswise, then cut lengthwise into sticks about ½-inch (1 cm) square. Toss with the remaining oil, ¼ tsp (1 mL) salt and ground pepper to taste. Spread out on the other baking sheet, leaving space between each fry.

4. Remove beets from oven and flip each fry over. Return to upper rack and place sweet potatoes on lower rack. Bake for about 30 minutes, flipping sweet potatoes halfway through, until beets are tender and sweet potatoes are browned and tender.

5. Season fries with salt and serve with three-pepper mayonnaise in small bowls for dipping.

Sweet Potato Rösti

Rösti have Swiss origins, though many cuisines feature similar "pancakes" made from potatoes. The use of sweet potatoes makes for an attractive and delicious addition to a holiday meal — or any meal.

Tip

The rösti can be cooked, cooled, covered and refrigerated for up to 1 day. Reheat on a baking sheet in a 375°F (190°C) oven for about 15 minutes or until heated through.

- 9-inch (23 cm) cast-iron skillet or heavy stainless-steel skillet

2	large sweet potatoes (about 1½ lbs/750 g), peeled	2
½ tsp	salt	2 mL
½ tsp	freshly ground black pepper	2 mL
3 tbsp	vegetable oil, divided	45 mL

1. Heat skillet over medium-high heat until very hot.

2. Meanwhile, using the coarse side of a box grater, shred sweet potatoes into a large bowl. Sprinkle with salt and pepper; toss to combine.

3. Add half the oil to heated skillet and swirl to coat; sprinkle shredded potatoes in an even layer in skillet, pressing lightly with a spatula. Cook for about 8 minutes or until bottom is golden and crispy. Invert a large plate over skillet and carefully invert potatoes onto plate. Add remaining oil to skillet, swirling to coat, and slide potatoes back into pan to cook the other side. Cook for about 8 minutes or until golden on the bottom and potatoes are tender. Cut into wedges to serve.

Bulgur with Cumin-Scented Sweet Potatoes

Makes 4 to 6 servings

Bulgur is toasted and cracked kernels of either hard red or soft white wheat. It comes in different textures, from fine to coarse. Coarse-grind bulgur, made from red wheat, has a toothsome texture and is nice for hot side dishes like this one. The fine and medium grinds are more tender, making them better suited to salads, such as the ever-popular tabbouleh. This hearty dish works well alongside pork chops, sausages or poultry.

Tip

If you don't have coarse bulgur, use medium bulgur; instead of cooking, simply stir into the boiling stock, remove from the heat and let stand for 15 minutes.

- Preheat oven to 450°F (230°C)
- Rimmed baking sheet, lined with foil

1 lb	sweet potato (about 1 large), peeled and cut into ½-inch (1 cm) cubes	500 g
2 tbsp	olive oil	30 mL
1 tsp	ground coriander	5 mL
1 tsp	ground cumin	5 mL
½ tsp	salt	2 mL
¼ tsp	freshly ground black pepper	1 mL
2 cups	Vegetable Stock (page 130), Chicken Stock (page 131) or ready-to-use vegetable or chicken broth	500 mL
1 cup	coarse bulgur	250 mL
2 tbsp	freshly squeezed lemon or lime juice	30 mL
	Chopped fresh cilantro	

1. On prepared baking sheet, combine sweet potato, oil, coriander, cumin, salt and pepper. Spread out in a single layer and roast in preheated oven for about 20 minutes, stirring once or twice, until sweet potatoes are golden brown on the outside and tender inside.

2. Meanwhile, in a saucepan with a tight-fitting lid, bring stock and a pinch of salt to a boil over high heat. Gradually pour in bulgur in a thin stream, stirring constantly. Reduce heat to low, cover and simmer for 15 minutes or until bulgur is tender and liquid is absorbed.

3. Using a fork, fold sweet potatoes and lemon juice into bulgur. Season to taste with salt and pepper. Serve sprinkled with cilantro.

Green Beans with Shiitakes and Onions

Makes 8 servings

Mushrooms, onions, a splash of wine and toasted hazelnuts elevate the humble green bean to something special. The beans stay vibrant and tender-crisp if blanched ahead and chilled, with a quick sauté just before serving.

Tip

To toast hazelnuts, spread on a rimmed baking sheet and bake in a 375°F (180°C) oven for about 8 minutes or until fragrant and skins start to crack. Transfer to a towel and rub off skins.

1 lb	green beans, trimmed	500 g
1 tbsp	butter	15 mL
1 tbsp	olive oil	15 mL
1	onion, halved lengthwise and thinly sliced	1
4 oz	shiitake mushrooms, stems removed, caps sliced	125 g
1/4 tsp	salt	1 mL
1/4 tsp	freshly ground black pepper	1 mL
1/4 cup	dry white wine	60 mL
1/2 cup	hazelnuts, toasted, skinned and chopped	125 mL

1. In a pot of boiling salted water, blanch green beans for about 3 minutes or until bright green. Drain and rinse under cool running water until cold. Drain well. Transfer to a bowl. Set aside until serving or cover and refrigerate for up to 1 day.

2. Just before serving, in a large skillet, heat butter and oil over medium-high heat. Add onion, mushrooms, salt and pepper; sauté for about 5 minutes or until golden brown. Add wine and boil, stirring, until almost evaporated.

3. Add green beans and 1/4 cup (60 mL) water; sauté for about 5 minutes or until beans are tender-crisp and liquid is evaporated. Stir in hazelnuts. Season with salt and pepper to taste. Transfer to a warmed serving dish.

Brussels Sprouts in Browned Butter with Pine Nuts

Makes 4 to 6 servings

The nuttiness of browned butter and pine nuts offset the flavor of Brussels sprouts, which can sometimes be strong. The key to converting those who do not usually enjoy Brussels sprouts is to be sure not to overcook them. Just-cooked sprouts are sweet, toothsome and irresistible!

Tips

Choose sprouts that are almost the same size (for even cooking) and have tight leaves. Trim off any dark stems and outer leaves before cooking.

To prevent spattering and keep the flavor from being watered down, make sure sprouts are very dry before adding them to the browned butter.

- Baking sheet or tray, lined with paper towels

1½ lbs	Brussels sprouts, trimmed	750 g
¼ cup	butter	60 mL
¼ cup	pine nuts	60 mL
1 tbsp	freshly squeezed lemon juice	15 mL
	Salt and freshly ground black pepper	

1. In a large pot of boiling salted water, cook Brussels sprouts for 5 to 8 minutes or until almost tender. Refresh under cold water and drain well. Let cool slightly.

2. Cut sprouts in half lengthwise and place cut side down on prepared baking sheet to drain. Set aside until serving or cover and refrigerate for up to 1 day.

3. If sprouts have been refrigerated, let stand at room temperature for about 30 minutes to remove the chill. In a large skillet, melt butter over medium-low heat until just starting to turn golden brown, with a nutty aroma. Stir in pine nuts and lemon juice; sauté for about 2 minutes or until butter is browned. Add Brussels sprouts, toss to coat well and heat through. Season to taste with salt and pepper. Transfer to a warmed serving dish.

Wilted Cabbage with Pan-Roasted Garlic and Almonds

Makes 6 servings

Cabbage often gets a bad rap as a boring vegetable. Dress it up with nutty browned butter and a hit of pan-roasted garlic, and no one will call it boring again.

Tip

Use a food processor fitted with a slicing blade or a mandoline slicer to shred the cabbage.

¼ cup	butter	60 mL
4	cloves garlic, minced	4
⅓ cup	chopped almonds	75 mL
6 cups	finely shredded cabbage (about ½ head)	1.5 L
2 tbsp	white wine vinegar	30 mL
	Salt and freshly ground black pepper	

1. In a large skillet, melt butter over medium-low heat. Add garlic and sauté for about 2 minutes or until fragrant and just starting to turn golden brown. Stir in almonds and sauté for about 2 minutes or until butter is browned and almonds are toasted. Working quickly, remove almonds from pan, leaving as much butter in the pan as possible; set almonds aside in a bowl.

2. Increase heat to medium-high and add cabbage to skillet. Sauté for about 3 minutes or until cabbage is just wilted. Add vinegar and toss to coat. Season to taste with salt and pepper. Transfer to a warmed serving dish and sprinkle with reserved almonds.

> Cabbage was developed from kale, beginning in first-century Germany.

Sweet and Sour Red Cabbage

Makes 8 servings

This is a classic treatment for red cabbage. The vinegar turns the cabbage a terrific fuchsia color and gives it tang that combines with the touch of sweetness for a lively flavor. Serve as a side to roast pork, ham, lamb or poultry.

Variation

For a traditional European flavor, add 1 tsp (5 mL) caraway seeds with the onion.

2 tbsp	butter	30 mL
1	small red onion, halved and thinly sliced	1
8 cups	finely shredded red (purple) cabbage (about ½ head)	2 L
¼ cup	packed brown sugar	60 mL
¼ cup	red wine vinegar	60 mL
	Salt and freshly ground black pepper	

1. In a large skillet, melt butter over medium-high heat. Add onion and sauté for about 3 minutes or until softened. Add cabbage and sauté for about 5 minutes or until wilted. Add sugar and vinegar; toss to coat. Sauté until sugar is dissolved. Season to taste with salt and pepper. Transfer to a warmed serving dish.

Red Acre is one of the best dark cabbage varieties.

Sesame-Sautéed Carrots

Makes 4 to 6 servings

Yellow, white, red and purple heirloom carrots are making a comeback and are fun to experiment with. This recipe is a terrific way to use carrots of different colors, if you've got them in your stores. A light sauté is a good way to make the most of their unusual look, since the color sometimes fades with heat. Of course, it's just as delicious with traditional orange carrots, too.

1 lb	carrots (about 5 medium)	500 g
2 tsp	canola oil	10 mL
2 tsp	toasted sesame oil	10 mL
1 tbsp	sesame seeds	15 mL
1 tbsp	freshly squeezed lemon juice	15 mL
2 tsp	liquid honey	10 mL
	Salt and freshly ground black pepper	

1. Trim off ends of carrots. Gently scrub under running water to remove any sand and grit. Cut crosswise on a diagonal into $\frac{1}{8}$-inch (3 mm) slices.

2. In a large skillet or wok, heat canola and sesame oil over high heat. Add carrots and sesame seeds; sauté for 2 to 3 minutes or until just starting to wilt. Transfer to a warmed serving dish and drizzle with lemon juice and honey; toss to coat. Season to taste with salt and pepper.

> The Dragon Carrot is an heirloom variety that is dark purple outside and orange inside.

Sage Butter Parsnip Sauté

Pungent garlic and frizzled sage add a savory depth to sweet parsnips in this easy dish. Serve it with roast beef, baked salmon or ham.

Tip

For this recipe, make sure you have extra parsnips available in case some are woody. Generally, thinner ones are more tender, but it's sometimes difficult to tell from the outside, and you might find that the core is very tough. Save those ones to use in a puréed soup and use only tender ones for this recipe.

6	parsnips (about 2 lbs/1 kg)	6
¼ cup	butter	60 mL
2	cloves garlic, minced	2
2 tbsp	slivered fresh sage leaves	30 mL
	Salt and freshly ground black pepper	

1. Peel parsnips and cut on a slight diagonal into thin slices, cutting slices from the thick ends in half. In a pot of boiling salted water, cook parsnips for about 3 minutes or until almost tender. Drain and rinse under cool running water until cold. Drain well. Transfer to a bowl. Set aside until serving or cover and refrigerate for up to 2 days.

2. If parsnips have been refrigerated, let stand at room temperature for about 30 minutes to remove the chill. In a large skillet, melt butter over medium-low heat. Add garlic and sage; sauté for about 2 minutes or until garlic is just starting to turn golden. Add parsnips and cook, gently stirring often, for about 5 minutes or until hot and tender. Season to taste with salt and pepper. Transfer to a warmed serving dish.

> Developed by Professor James Buckman in the 1850s, the Student is believed to be the oldest recognized parsnip variety in the world. Its root can grow up to 3 feet (1 m) long.

Spice-Roasted Turnip and Beet Batons

Makes 4 to 6 servings

Change up your traditional vegetable side dishes by adding a dash of spice and roasting them instead of boiling, and you'll think you're eating an entirely new food.

Tip

A sharp Y-shaped vegetable peeler is very helpful when you're peeling hard root vegetables, such as turnips and beets. If your peeler seems to be dragging the skin rather than neatly peeling it off, it's probably time to invest in a new one.

- Preheat oven to 400°F (200°C)
- Large rimmed baking sheet, lined with foil

3	large turnips (about 1 lb/500 g)	3
2	large beets (about 1 lb/500 g)	2
2 tbsp	olive oil	30 mL
1/2 tsp	curry powder	2 mL
1/2 tsp	ground cumin	2 mL
1/2 tsp	ground coriander	2 mL
1/8 tsp	cayenne pepper	0.5 mL
	Sea salt and freshly ground black pepper	

1. Peel turnips and rinse. Trim off leaf stalks from beets (reserving for another use if desired) and trim off long roots. Peel beets and rinse. Cut turnips and beets lengthwise into sticks about 1/2-inch (1 cm) square.

2. On prepared baking sheet, toss turnips and beets with oil, curry powder, cumin, coriander and cayenne. Season to taste with salt and black pepper. Spread out as much as possible. Bake in preheated oven for about 50 minutes, flipping halfway through, or until vegetables are tender and browned. Season to taste with salt and black pepper. Transfer to a warmed serving dish.

Main Courses

Turkey Breast with Apple Sausage Stuffing

Makes 6 to 8 servings

A delicious and attractive alternative to a whole roast turkey, and the perfect size for a smaller party, with enough left over for sandwiches.

Tips

Choose a mild pork sausage, such as Bavarian or Oktoberfest.

For maximum food safety, be sure the stuffing is completely cool before stuffing the turkey breast, and don't stuff the turkey until just before you plan to roast it.

1	pork sausage, casing removed	1
2	stalks celery, chopped	2
1	onion, chopped	1
2 tsp	dried sage	10 mL
1/2 tsp	celery seeds	2 mL
	Salt and freshly ground black pepper	
1/4 cup	dry sherry (optional)	60 mL
1	tart apple, diced	1
7 cups	cubed day-old bread	1.75 L
1/4 cup	Chicken Stock (page 131) or ready-to-use chicken broth	60 mL
1	boneless turkey breast (about 3 lbs/1.5 kg)	1
2 tbsp	butter, softened	30 mL

1. In a large skillet, over medium-high heat, brown sausage, breaking meat up into small pieces, for about 5 minutes or until no longer pink; drain off fat. Reduce heat to medium-low. Add celery, onion, sage, celery seeds and 1/4 tsp (1 mL) each salt and pepper; sauté for about 8 minutes or until vegetables are softened. Add sherry (if using) and boil, stirring, until most of the liquid is evaporated. Add apple and sauté for about 5 minutes or until tender. Transfer to a bowl and let cool completely.

2. Meanwhile, preheat oven 325°F (160°C).

3. Add bread and stock to sausage mixture and toss to combine. Place turkey breast on a cutting board, skin side down. Butterfly turkey by slicing it almost in half horizontally. Open up like a book, cover with thick plastic wrap and pound lightly to about 1/2 inch (1 cm) thick. Pack stuffing in an even layer on top of turkey. Starting at one narrow end, roll up turkey so skin is on top and stuffing is spiraled. Tie with kitchen string. Place seam side down in roasting pan. Spread with butter and sprinkle with salt and pepper.

4. Roast, basting occasionally, for about 1 1/2 hours or until a meat thermometer inserted in the center reads 170°F (77°C). Transfer to a cutting board, tent with foil and let rest for 15 minutes before slicing.

Quick Chili-Roasted Chicken and Vegetables

Makes 4 servings

This is a great dish when you want a roasted chicken dinner but don't have the time to roast a whole chicken. Everything cooks to perfection in the oven while you prepare a salad and set the table.

Tip

Plan ahead for a weeknight meal and cut up the carrots, zucchini and chicken up to 1 day ahead; cover and refrigerate until you're ready to cook. (Make sure to store the vegetables and chicken in separate containers.)

- Preheat oven to 425°F (220°C), with racks positioned in the bottom and top third
- Two large rimmed baking sheets

4	oblong baking potatoes, cut lengthwise into thin wedges	4
4	carrots, cut into ¾-inch (2 cm) slices	4
2	small zucchini, cut into 1-inch (2.5 cm) chunks	2
1½ cups	corn kernels (drained canned or frozen)	375 mL
1 tbsp	chili powder	15 mL
2 tsp	dried oregano or basil	10 mL
½ tsp	salt	2 mL
3 tbsp	olive oil	45 mL
¼ cup	dry bread crumbs	60 mL
1 lb	boneless skinless chicken breasts, cut into 1½-inch (4 cm) chunks	500 g

1. In a large bowl, combine potatoes, carrots, zucchini and corn. In another bowl, combine chili powder, oregano, salt and oil; pour half over vegetables and toss to coat. Divide vegetables evenly among baking sheets and spread out in an even layer.

2. Add bread crumbs to remaining spice mixture and stir to combine. Add chicken and toss to coat with crumb mixture. Arrange chicken pieces on top of vegetables, spacing out as much as possible.

3. Roast in preheated oven for about 25 minutes, switching sheets between racks halfway through, until chicken is no longer pink inside and vegetables are golden and tender.

Garlic and Herb Roasted Chicken with Sweet Onion Gravy

Makes 6 to 8 servings

The garlic infuses the meat from the inside, the herbs from the outside, and the light, sweet onion gravy is the crowning glory. Serve with mashed potatoes and a tender-crisp green vegetable.

Tip

For the best texture and more flavorful gravy, choose an air-chilled chicken.

- Preheat oven to 325°F (160°F)
- Roasting pan

1	roasting chicken (about 4 lbs/2 kg)	1
6	cloves garlic, smashed	6
2 tbsp	butter, softened	30 mL
2 tsp	dried basil	10 mL
1/2 tsp	dried rosemary, crumbled	2 mL
1/2 tsp	dried thyme	2 mL
1/2 tsp	salt	2 mL
1/4 tsp	freshly ground black pepper	1 mL

Sweet Onion Gravy

1	large sweet onion (such as Spanish or Vidalia), finely chopped	1
2 tbsp	all-purpose flour	30 mL
1/4 cup	dry white wine	60 mL
2 cups	Chicken Stock (page 131) or reduced-sodium ready-to-use chicken broth	500 mL
	Salt and freshly ground black pepper	

1. Remove giblet package from inside chicken, if necessary. Rinse chicken inside and out with cold running water and pat dry. Place garlic inside cavity. Tuck wings under back and tie legs together with string. Place breast side up in roasting pan.

2. In a small bowl, combine butter, basil, rosemary, thyme, salt and pepper. Rub all over chicken. Roast in preheated oven, basting occasionally, for about 2 1/2 hours or until juices run clear when thigh is pierced and a meat thermometer inserted in thigh reads 170°F (77°C). Transfer chicken to a cutting board and tent with foil; let rest for 15 to 20 minutes.

Tip

A probe-style digital meat thermometer with an alarm is particularly handy when you're roasting whole poultry and roasts — especially when you have other things on the go. You can keep watch as the temperature rises and put the rest of your dishes on to cook when your poultry or meat is getting close to done.

3. *For the gravy:* Meanwhile, drain off pan drippings into a measuring cup. Skim off fat, adding 2 tbsp (30 mL) back to roasting pan (or a saucepan if you can't use your roasting pan on the stovetop). Discard the remaining fat, reserving juices. Heat fat in roasting pan over medium heat on the stovetop. Add onion and sauté for about 5 minutes or until softened. Sprinkle with flour and sauté for 1 minute. Gradually whisk in wine and bring to a boil, scraping up brown bits stuck to pan. Gradually whisk in reserved juices and stock; boil gently, whisking constantly, for 5 to 10 minutes or until gravy is thickened. Season to taste with salt and pepper.

4. Carve chicken into pieces and serve with gravy.

> Sweet onion varieties must be grown in soils with a low sulfur content, to prevent the development of a pungent taste.

Chicken and Olive Ragoût with Dijon Potatoes

Makes 8 servings

The flavors in this savory ragoût actually benefit when it is made ahead, which makes it perfect for entertaining. Make it at least a day ahead and refrigerate or even freeze it. The Provençal flavors are sure to warm up the coldest winter evening, made even more festive because it is shared with friends.

Tips

Chicken thighs stay moist and tender when cooked in a ragoût. If you substitute chicken breasts, make sure to cook just until no longer pink inside to prevent them from drying out.

Keep in mind that the flavors will intensify after reheating, so season lightly to start.

• 12- to 16-cup (3 to 4 L) casserole dish, buttered

4	strips bacon, chopped	4
1 tbsp	butter, if necessary	15 mL
2 lbs	boneless skinless chicken thighs, cut into chunks	1 kg
4	carrots, chopped	4
4	cloves garlic, minced	4
½ cup	minced shallots	125 mL
1 tsp	dried thyme	5 mL
½ tsp	freshly ground pepper	2 mL
¼ tsp	salt	1 mL
⅓ cup	all-purpose flour	75 mL
2 cups	dry white wine	500 mL
1 cup	Chicken Stock (page 131) or ready-to-use chicken broth	250 mL
1	large red bell pepper, diced	1
¾ cup	mixed black and green olives	175 mL
1 tbsp	Dijon or grainy mustard	15 mL
	Chopped fresh parsley and/or thyme	

Dijon Potatoes

4 lbs	oblong baking or yellow-fleshed potatoes	2 kg
	Salt	
1¼ cups	heavy or whipping (35%) cream, heated until steaming	300 mL
1 tbsp	Dijon or grainy mustard	15 mL
	Freshly ground black pepper	

1. In a large pot, sauté bacon over medium-high heat until crisp. Using tongs, transfer bacon to a plate lined with paper towels and set aside. Drain off all but 1 tbsp (15 mL) bacon fat from pot, reserving excess fat. Add chicken to pot, in batches, and brown on all sides, heating pot and adding more reserved bacon fat between batches as necessary. Transfer chicken to a bowl and set aside.

2. Reduce heat to medium-low and add the remaining bacon fat or butter to pot. Add carrots, garlic, shallots, thyme, pepper and salt; sauté for about 10 minutes or until soft. Sprinkle with flour and sauté for 1 minute.

3. Gradually whisk in wine and stock; bring to a boil over medium heat, scraping up any brown bits stuck to pot. Boil gently, whisking often, for 5 minutes or until slightly thickened.

4. Add chicken and any accumulated juices to pot, along with red pepper, olives and mustard. Reduce heat and simmer, stirring often, for about 20 minutes or until chicken is no longer pink inside and sauce is thickened. Crumble reserved bacon and stir into sauce. Season to taste with salt and pepper. Transfer to a shallow heatproof container and let cool slightly. Refrigerate until cold.

5. *For the potatoes:* Meanwhile, peel potatoes and cut into chunks. Place in a large pot and add enough cold water to cover. Bring to a boil over high heat. Season water with salt, reduce heat and boil gently for about 20 minutes or until potatoes are fork-tender. Drain well and return to pot over low heat. Dry potatoes, shaking pot, for 1 minute. Remove from heat and, using a potato masher, mash potatoes, gradually mashing in cream and mustard, until potatoes are smooth and fluffy. Season to taste with salt and pepper. Spoon potatoes around the edge of prepared casserole dish, leaving room for chicken in the center and making sure potatoes do not extend above edge of dish. Refrigerate until cold.

6. Spoon cold chicken ragoût into center of potatoes. Cover dish with plastic wrap and refrigerate for at least 1 day or for up to 2 days.

7. Preheat oven to 350°F (180°C). Remove plastic wrap and cover dish with foil. Bake for about $1\frac{1}{2}$ hours or until potatoes and chicken are hot. Uncover and bake for about 20 minutes or until potatoes are browned and sauce is bubbling. Let stand for 10 minutes. Sprinkle with parsley and/or thyme before serving.

Sear-Roasted Steaks with Caramelized Cabbage and Onions

Makes 4 servings

Pan-sear the steaks while the cabbage and onions caramelize and finish them off in the oven for mouth-watering tenderness. Serve roasted or mashed potatoes on the side.

Tip

Don't shred the cabbage too finely for this dish. It's best to cut wedges crosswise into shreds with a sharp chef's knife, so it still has a nice texture once caramelized.

- Preheat oven to 400°F (200°C)
- 13- by 9-inch (33 by 23 cm) glass baking dish

2 tbsp	butter, divided	30 mL
1	red onion, halved and thinly sliced	1
6 cups	shredded purple (red) cabbage (about $\frac{1}{2}$ a small head)	1.5 L
2 tbsp	packed brown sugar	30 mL
	Salt and freshly ground black pepper	
$\frac{1}{4}$ cup	red wine vinegar	60 mL
4	boneless beef rib steaks or other grilling steaks, about 1 inch (2.5 cm) thick	4

1. In a large skillet, melt half the butter over medium-high heat. Add onion and sauté for about 3 minutes or until starting to soften. Add cabbage and sauté for about 5 minutes or until wilted. Stir in sugar, 1 tsp (5 mL) salt and pepper to taste. Stir in vinegar. Transfer to baking dish; set skillet aside.

2. Cover dish with foil and roast in preheated oven for about 15 minutes or until cabbage is tender. Uncover and roast, stirring once, for about 30 minutes or until starting to brown and caramelize.

3. Meanwhile, season steaks on both sides with salt and pepper. Heat skillet over high heat until hot but not smoking. Add remaining butter and swirl to coat pan. Add steaks, in batches as necessary, and brown for about 3 minutes per side, turning once. Place on top of cabbage in baking dish and drizzle with any pan drippings. Roast, uncovered, for about 10 minutes for medium-rare or until desired doneness.

Prime Rib Roast with Plenty of Onions

Makes 8 servings

With a simple mustard and herb seasoning and a bed of onions that roast almost until they're like butter, the beefy flavor of prime rib really shines. Searing the roast in a hot oven and then cooking it low and slow does take a little longer, but it seals in every drop of juice, keeping it melt-in-your-mouth tender.

Tips

A good meat thermometer is worth the investment, to make sure you get an accurate test for doneness.

The slow roasting method reduces the amount of pan drippings, so the flavor of the jus relies on good-quality broth. Use homemade broth or stock if you have it, or the highest-quality prepared broth available.

Variation

If you prefer a thickened gravy, stir 2 tbsp (25 mL) all-purpose flour into the onions and sauté for 1 minute before adding the wine.

- Preheat oven to 450°F (230°C)
- Roasting pan

4	large onions, sliced	4
2½ cups	reduced-sodium ready-to-use beef broth, divided	625 mL
1	beef prime rib premium oven roast (about 5 lbs/2.5 kg)	1
½ cup	grainy or Dijon mustard	125 mL
2 tbsp	chopped fresh rosemary (or 2 tsp/10 mL dried)	30 mL
1 tsp	salt	5 mL
1 tsp	coarsely ground black pepper	5 mL
½ cup	dry red wine	125 mL

1. Spread onions in bottom of roasting pan and drizzle ½ cup (125 mL) broth evenly over top. Place roast, rib side down, on top of onions. In a small bowl, combine mustard, rosemary, salt and pepper; rub over top and sides of roast. Roast in preheated oven for 10 minutes.

2. Reduce temperature to 275°F (140°C). Roast for 3 to 3½ hours or until a meat thermometer inserted in the thickest part of the meat reads 135°F (57°C) for medium-rare, 4 hours and 145°F (62°C) for medium, or until desired doneness. Transfer roast to a cutting board, tent with foil and let rest for 20 minutes.

3. Meanwhile, to make jus, place roasting pan over medium-high heat on stovetop (or transfer to a saucepan if you can't use your roasting pan on the stovetop) and stir in wine. Bring to a boil, scraping up any bits stuck to pan. Pour in the remaining broth and bring to a boil. Reduce heat and simmer, stirring often, for about 5 minutes or until slightly reduced. Season to taste with salt and pepper.

4. Carve roast across the grain and serve drizzled with onion jus.

Classic Beef Pot Roast

Makes 4 to 6 servings

There just doesn't seem to be a more comforting winter meal than a classic pot roast. With the meat and vegetables cooked together, all you need is some green peas on the side.

Tip

The horseradish adds a nice flavor to the pot roast. If you're not a big fan of it, use just 1 tbsp (15 mL) or replace it with Dijon mustard. If you are a fan, use 2 tbsp (30 mL) and serve more alongside.

- Preheat oven to 325°F (160°C)
- Large oven-safe pot with a lid

1	boneless beef cross rib or blade roast (3 to 4 lbs/1.5 to 2 kg), tied	1
1/3 cup	all-purpose flour	75 mL
2 tbsp	vegetable oil	30 mL
1	onion, finely chopped	1
1	carrot, finely chopped	1
1	bay leaf	1
1/2 tsp	dried thyme	2 mL
1 1/2 cups	reduced-sodium ready-to-use beef broth	375 mL
2 tbsp	cider vinegar	30 mL
1 or 2 tbsp	prepared horseradish	15 or 30 mL
4	carrots, cut into chunks	4
4	all-purpose potatoes, cut into chunks	4
	Salt and freshly ground black pepper	

1. Pat roast dry and dust with flour; set remaining flour aside. In oven-safe pot, heat oil over medium-high heat. Brown roast, turning to brown all sides. Transfer to a plate.

2. Reduce heat to medium and add onion, finely chopped carrot, bay leaf and thyme to pot; sauté for about 3 minutes or until softened. Sprinkle with the remaining flour and sauté for 1 minute. Pour in broth, vinegar and horseradish to taste; bring to a boil, scraping up brown bits stuck to pot.

3. Return roast and any accumulated juices to pot. Cover and roast in preheated oven for 1 hour. Turn roast and add remaining carrots and potatoes to pot. Cover and roast, turning roast once, for about 1 1/2 hours or until roast and vegetables are fork-tender. Transfer roast to a cutting board, tent with foil and let rest for 15 minutes.

4. Meanwhile, bring sauce to a boil over medium-high heat on the stovetop. Reduce heat and boil gently, stirring often, for 5 to 10 minutes or until desired thickness. Season to taste with salt and pepper. Discard bay leaf.

5. Carve roast across the grain into thin slices and serve with sauce and vegetables.

Maple Mustard Pork Roast with Two Potatoes

Makes 6 to 8 servings

A rib roast (equivalent to a beef prime rib) is the most flavorful and moist cut of pork (in Jennifer's opinion), but any section of the loin will work in this recipe. Serve this recipe to spark up your Sunday roast dinner. Brussels sprouts or broccoli are nice on the side.

Tip

Ask the butcher to chine the ribs for easy cutting.

- Preheat oven to 325°F (160°C)
- Large roasting pan

1	bone-in pork rib roast (3 to 4 lbs/1.5 to 2 kg), tied	1
	Salt and freshly ground black pepper	
4	yellow-fleshed or all-purpose potatoes	4
2	sweet potatoes	2
1 tbsp	vegetable oil	15 mL
2 tbsp	grainy or Dijon mustard	30 mL
2 tbsp	pure maple syrup	30 mL

1. Place roast, bone side down, in roasting pan. Sprinkle with salt and pepper. Roast in preheated oven for 30 minutes.

2. Meanwhile, cut yellow-fleshed potatoes and sweet potatoes into chunks. In a bowl, toss potatoes with oil and season with salt and pepper. In another bowl, combine mustard and maple syrup.

3. Sprinkle potatoes around roast in pan. Brush half the mustard mixture over roast. Roast for 30 minutes. Brush roast with the remaining mustard mixture and stir potatoes. Roast for 30 to 60 minutes or until a meat thermometer inserted in the thickest part of the meat (away from the bone) reads 155°F (68°C). Transfer roast to a cutting board, tent with foil and let rest for 15 minutes.

4. Stir potatoes and return to oven while roast rests, until browned and tender. Carve roast into chops between each rib and serve with potatoes.

> Hayman, an heirloom sweet potato, doesn't grow large, but it tastes great. Nancy Hall is another delicious variety.

Chorizo and Potato Torta

Makes 4 servings

Spanish tortas are often served as tapas, or "small bites." This one is perfect served with other tapas, or as a main course with tender-crisp green beans or sautéed rapini.

Tips

Chorizo sausage is available in fresh and dry-cured forms. The dry-cured works best for this recipe, but if you only have fresh, remove the casing and sauté the sausage in oil, breaking up with a spoon until no longer pink, then add the onion and spices and sauté until tender.

To serve this cold for tapas, let it cool, then cover and refrigerate for up to 1 day. Cut into small wedges while cold. Serve cold or warm slightly on a baking sheet in a 350°F (180°C) oven for 5 to 10 minutes.

- Preheat oven to 325°F (160°C)
- 9-inch (23 cm) cast-iron skillet or heavy stainless-steel skillet

2 tbsp	olive oil, divided	30 mL
6 oz	dry-cured chorizo sausage, diced (about 1)	175 g
1	small sweet onion, thinly sliced	1
¼ tsp	Spanish paprika (smoked, if desired)	1 mL
¼ tsp	freshly ground black pepper	1 mL
3	yellow-fleshed or oblong baking potatoes (about 1 lb/500 g), peeled and thinly sliced	3
8	eggs	8

1. In skillet, heat 1 tbsp (15 mL) oil over medium-high heat. Add sausage, onion, paprika and pepper; sauté for about 5 minutes or until onion is softened. Using a slotted spoon, transfer sausage and onion to a bowl, leaving fat in the pan.

2. Add potatoes to skillet, tossing gently to coat in fat. Reduce heat to low, cover and simmer for about 10 minutes or until slightly tender. Add to sausage mixture in bowl.

3. In a separate bowl, whisk eggs until frothy; pour over potato mixture and stir gently to combine. Return skillet to medium heat, add remaining oil and swirl to coat pan. Add egg mixture and cook, stirring with a heatproof spatula, for 1 minute or until eggs start to set. Spread out potatoes, smoothing top.

4. Bake in preheated oven for about 15 minutes or until potatoes are tender and top is golden brown. Let cool in pan for 5 minutes. Run a knife around the edge of the pan, invert a plate on top of the pan and flip the torta out onto the plate. Cut into wedges.

Roasted Fish Fillets with Warm Fennel Slaw

Makes 4 servings

Fish pairs naturally with the slight licorice flavor of fennel. This fresh-tasting slaw is quick to make and accents the roasted fillets beautifully.

Tip

Before purchasing fish, always learn what you can about sustainability and fishing practices. Ask your fishmonger or check online resources.

- Preheat oven to 425°F (220°C)
- Rimmed baking sheet, lined with parchment paper or foil

1	bulb fennel	1
1½ lbs	fish fillet (salmon, Artic char, striped bass)	750 g
	Salt and freshly ground black pepper	
8	lemon slices	8
2 tbsp	olive oil	30 mL
1	small onion, halved and thinly sliced	1
1	small red bell pepper, cut into thin strips	1
2 tbsp	freshly squeezed lemon juice	30 mL

1. Trim feathery fronds from fennel; chop 2 tbsp (30 mL) and set aside. Trim off long stalks and outer layer of bulb (if tough and/or bruised) and discard. Cut fennel bulb in half lengthwise and trim out root with a paring knife. Place each half cut side down and thinly slice lengthwise; set slices aside separately.

2. Place fish on prepared baking sheet and sprinkle with salt and pepper; arrange lemon slices on top and sprinkle with chopped fennel fronds. Roast in preheated oven for about 10 minutes per inch (2.5 cm) of thickness or until fish flakes easily with a fork.

3. Meanwhile, in a large skillet, heat oil over medium-high heat. Add fennel, onion, red pepper and salt and pepper to taste; sauté for about 5 minutes or until fennel is slightly tender. Add lemon juice and scrape up brown bits stuck to pan. Remove from heat.

4. Cut fish into portions and transfer to warmed serving plates. Top with fennel slaw.

Hearty Vegetable Pot Pie

Makes 8 to 10 servings

Jennifer created this recipe for a magazine article on make-ahead meals for the holidays. It's perfect when your root vegetables are getting to the end of their cellar storage life. There are a few steps, but once it's made, it's as though you have your own convenience food stashed in the freezer, ready for a potluck or a family gathering.

Tip

To make this ahead, the individual elements can be covered and refrigerated separately for up to 2 days. Proceed with step 4. To freeze, complete through step 5, wrap the dish in plastic wrap, then in foil, and freeze for up to 1 month. Let thaw in the refrigerator for 48 hours, then proceed with step 6.

• 10-cup (2.5 L) oval casserole dish or 13- by 9-inch (33 by 23 cm) glass baking dish, buttered

Pastry

2 cups	all-purpose flour	500 mL
1/2 tsp	dried tarragon	2 mL
1/2 tsp	salt	2 mL
1/8 tsp	freshly ground black pepper	0.5 mL
1/3 cup	cold butter, cut into cubes	75 mL
1/3 cup	cold shortening, cut into cubes	75 mL
1	egg	1
1 tsp	white vinegar	5 mL
	Ice water	
2 tbsp	milk or cream (any type), divided	30 mL

Filling

2 tbsp	butter	30 mL
2	onions, chopped	2
2	cloves garlic, minced	2
4 cups	sliced carrots (6 to 8)	1 L
3 cups	sliced parsnips (3 to 5)	750 mL
3 cups	sliced mushrooms	750 mL
1 tsp	dried tarragon	5 mL
1/2 tsp	salt	2 mL
1/2 tsp	freshly ground black pepper	2 mL
2 cups	frozen green peas	500 mL
2 cups	frozen corn kernels	500 mL
3 tbsp	all-purpose flour	45 mL

Sauce

3 tbsp	butter	45 mL
1/2 cup	all-purpose flour	125 mL
2 cups	milk, heated until steaming	500 mL
1 cup	Vegetable Stock (page 130) or ready-to-use vegetable broth	250 mL
2 tbsp	Dijon mustard	30 mL
1 1/2 tsp	grated lemon zest	7 mL
	Salt and freshly ground black pepper	

1. *For the pastry:* In a bowl, combine flour, tarragon, salt and pepper. Using a pastry blender or two knives, cut in butter and shortening until mixture resembles fine crumbs, with a few larger pieces. In a measuring cup,

Tip

If you want to freeze a prepared casserole without losing the use of your dish, before assembling the casserole line the dish with foil or parchment paper (moisten the parchment to make it more flexible), leaving at least a 2-inch (5 cm) overhang at the edge. Fill the dish and cover the top with another piece of foil or parchment, folding the overhang over to completely cover the top. Freeze the dish until the food is solid. Remove the liner with the frozen casserole and wrap it in plastic wrap or place in it in an airtight container. When you're ready to thaw or reheat the food, remove the liner and place the frozen food back in the dish.

using a fork, beat egg and vinegar. Add enough ice water to make $1/2$ cup (125 mL). Pour into flour mixture and stir with fork just until dough holds together. Gather into a ball and press into a disc. Wrap in plastic wrap and refrigerate for at least 30 minutes or for up to 2 days.

2. *For the filling:* In a large pot, melt butter over medium heat. Add onions, garlic, carrots, parsnips, mushrooms, tarragon, salt and pepper; cover and simmer for about 12 minutes or just until carrots start to soften. Uncover and sauté for 3 to 5 minutes or until moisture is evaporated. Transfer to a large bowl and let cool.

3. *For the sauce:* In the same pot, melt butter over medium heat. Stir in flour and sauté for 1 minute, without browning. Gradually whisk in milk and stock; bring to a boil, whisking constantly. Reduce heat to medium-low and simmer, whisking often, for about 15 minutes or until thickened to the consistency of pudding. Whisk in mustard and lemon zest, and season to taste with salt and pepper. Transfer to a bowl, place plastic wrap directly on the surface and let cool.

4. Stir peas, corn and flour into filling. Pour cooled sauce over top and fold gently to combine. Pour into prepared casserole dish, smoothing top.

5. On a lightly floured surface, roll out pastry to $1/4$-inch (0.5 cm) thickness to cover casserole. Place over filling, trimming to leave a 1-inch (2.5 cm) overhang. Reserve scraps. Pinch edges of pastry over rim of dish to seal and flute decoratively. Reroll pastry scraps and cut out shapes, as desired, to decorate top. Brush top of pastry with half of the milk and arrange shapes on top.

6. Preheat oven to 400°F (200°C).

7. Brush top of pastry with the remaining milk. Slash several steam vents and/or cut out small vents in decorative shapes evenly over pastry. Bake for 50 to 60 minutes or until pastry is golden and filling is bubbling. Let stand for 15 minutes before serving.

Farfalle with Hearty Greens

Makes 4 servings

A few simple, yet flavorful ingredients shine in this quick pasta dish. Once the water comes to a boil, you can have this on the table in less than 15 minutes.

Tips

Depending on the type of greens you're using, you may want to mix in some spinach to lighten the flavor. Collards, kale and rapini can be strong and, unless you're used to the flavor, could be overwhelming.

Save a little of the cooking water as you drain the pasta and use it to moisten the pasta as you toss in the greens, if desired.

12 oz	farfalle or other short pasta	375 g
	Salt	
1/4 cup	olive oil, divided	60 mL
1/2 cup	finely chopped shallots	125 mL
3	cloves garlic, minced	3
1/4 tsp	hot pepper flakes	1 mL
	Freshly ground black pepper	
6 cups	chopped dark leafy greens (Swiss chard, kale, collards, escarole, rapini)	1.5 L
2 tbsp	freshly squeezed lemon juice	30 mL
	Freshly grated Parmesan cheese	

1. In a large pot of boiling salted water, cook farfalle for about 8 minutes or until tender but firm, or according to package directions. Drain and return to pot.

2. Meanwhile, in a large skillet, heat 2 tbsp (30 mL) of the oil over medium heat. Add shallots and sauté for 2 minutes or until starting to soften. Add garlic, hot pepper flakes, 1/4 tsp (1 mL) salt and black pepper to taste; sauté for 2 minutes or until shallots are softened. Add greens and sauté for 3 to 8 minutes or until tender. Stir in lemon juice.

3. Add greens to pasta, along with the remaining oil, and toss gently to coat. Season to taste with salt and pepper. Serve sprinkled with Parmesan.

> Rapini is an important part of southern Italian cuisine. Rapini a Foglia D'Olivo is a rare, exceptionally flavorful variety.

Penne with Caramelized Onions and Winter Squash

Makes 4 servings

This is a nice change from a traditional tomato sauce for pasta. It sings of the flavors of fall. Serve a crispy salad with a creamy dressing on the side.

Tip

Butternut squash is the easiest squash to peel and cut into cubes; however, any hard winter squash works nicely in this dish. If you're finding your squash tricky to peel, cut it into chunks or wedges and microwave for 1 to 2 minutes, or place in a 350°F (180°C) for about 5 minutes, to soften the skin.

Variation

If you don't have fresh sage, substitute 1½ tsp (7 mL) dried and add it with the onions in step 1.

2 tbsp	butter	30 mL
3	onions, halved lengthwise and thinly sliced	3
1 tsp	granulated sugar	5 mL
½ tsp	salt	2 mL
¼ tsp	freshly ground black pepper	1 mL
1	small winter squash, cut into cubes (about 4 cups/1 L)	1
1 tbsp	chopped fresh sage	15 mL
¼ cup	dry white wine	60 mL
12 oz	penne, cavatappi or gemelli pasta	375 g
2 tbsp	olive oil	30 mL

1. In a large skillet, melt butter over medium heat. Add onions, sugar, salt and pepper; sauté for 1 minute. Reduce heat to low, cover and simmer, stirring often, for about 15 minutes or until onions start to turn golden. Stir in squash and sage. Increase heat to medium-high and boil, stirring once, for about 10 minutes or until onions are caramelized and squash is almost tender.

2. Meanwhile, in a large pot of boiling salted water, cook penne for about 9 minutes or until tender but firm, or according to package directions. Drain, reserving 1 cup (250 mL) of the cooking water. Return penne to the pot.

3. Add wine to the skillet and boil, scraping up any brown bits stuck to pan. Pour over pasta in pot. Add oil and toss gently to coat, adding just enough of the reserved cooking liquid to moisten to desired consistency. Season to taste with salt and pepper.

> Introduced in 1920, Buttercup squash is now readily available in grocery stores and is widely regarded as the best-tasting winter squash variety.

Stuffed Acorn Squash

Stuffed squash make a nice vegetarian main course for a celebratory meal or just a nice change from an ordinary main course.

Tip

To make these ahead, let the baked squash and cooked rice cool separately. Cover and refrigerate for up to 1 day. Before serving, let stand at room temperature for 30 minutes to remove the chill. Proceed as directed in step 3, but leave off the cheese, reduce the oven temperature to 350°F (180°C) and cover each squash with foil. Bake for about 30 minutes or until hot. Add cheese and bake until melted.

Variation

Use your favorite herbs in place of the basil and thyme. Add dill, rosemary, chives, tarragon or oregano to taste.

- Preheat oven to 400°F (200°C)
- Rimmed baking sheet, lined with parchment paper or buttered foil

2	acorn squash	2
2 tbsp	butter, softened, or olive oil, divided	30 mL
2	cloves garlic, minced	2
2 tbsp	minced shallots	30 mL
¾ cup	long-grain brown rice	175 mL
2 cups	Vegetable Stock (page 130) or reduced-sodium ready-to-use vegetable broth	500 mL
1	small red bell pepper, diced	1
1 tbsp	chopped fresh basil	15 mL
1 tsp	chopped fresh thyme	5 mL
1 tbsp	white wine vinegar or freshly squeezed lemon juice	15 mL
	Salt and freshly ground black pepper	
1 cup	shredded Gruyère, Swiss or Asiago cheese (optional)	250 mL

1. Cut squash in half lengthwise and scrape out seeds. Spread cut sides with 1 tbsp (15 mL) of the butter and place cut side down on prepared baking sheet. Bake in preheated oven for about 30 minutes or until tender.

2. Meanwhile, in a medium saucepan with a tight-fitting lid, melt the remaining butter over medium heat. Add garlic and shallots; sauté for about 2 minutes or until softened. Stir in rice until coated with butter. Stir in stock, increase heat to high and bring to a boil. Reduce heat to low, cover and simmer for about 45 minutes or until rice is just tender and most of the liquid is absorbed. Using a fork, stir in red pepper, basil, thyme and vinegar; cover and let stand for 5 minutes. Season to taste with salt and pepper.

3. Scrape about ½ inch (1 cm) of the flesh from inside each squash half and fold into rice mixture, using a fork and being careful not to mash rice. Place squash halves cut side up on baking sheet. Fill with rice mixture, packing lightly, and sprinkle with cheese (if using). Bake for about 5 minutes or until heated through and cheese is bubbling and melted.

Desserts and Baked Goods

Easy-as-Pie Pastry

Makes pastry for two 9-inch (23 cm) single-crust pies or one double-crust pie

This pastry has a combination of butter for flavor and shortening for flexibility. It's very tender and forgiving — just what you want in a pastry.

3 cups	all-purpose flour	750 mL
1 tbsp	granulated sugar	15 mL
1 tsp	salt	5 mL
¾ cup	cold butter, cubed	175 mL
¼ cup	cold shortening, cubed	60 mL
1	egg	1
1 tsp	white vinegar	5 mL
	Ice water	

Tips

Depending on the climate where you live, the humidity in the air and the protein content of your flour, you may need a little more flour for the right texture. Once the liquid is incorporated, if the dough feels sticky rather than ragged, gently work in more flour, a little at a time and working the dough as little as possible to prevent it from getting tough, until the dough no longer feels sticky.

The dough can be placed in a sealable plastic bag and frozen for up to 2 months. Thaw overnight in the refrigerator before rolling out.

Variation

If you plan to use this pastry for a savory pie, omit the sugar.

1. In a large bowl, stir together flour, sugar and salt. Using a pastry blender or two knives, cut in butter and shortening until mixture resembles fine crumbs, with a few larger pieces.

2. In a measuring cup, whisk together egg and vinegar. Add enough ice water to measure ⅔ cup (150 mL) liquid. Drizzle liquid over flour mixture. Using a fork, stir just until mixture holds together as a ragged dough.

3. With lightly floured hands, gather dough into a ball. Divide dough in half (or with one piece slightly larger, depending on the recipe) and press each piece into a disk. Wrap in plastic wrap and refrigerate for at least 30 minutes or until chilled.

Pear Almond Galette

Jennifer first started making galettes, or free-form pies, when she was in university, with a seriously underequipped kitchen, plenty of hungry roommates and the desire to procrastinate by baking instead of studying! This is one of her favorite creations.

Tips

Use pears that hold their shape and flavor when cooked. Bartlett, Bosc and Packham are good choices.

Toast ground almonds in a small, dry skillet over medium heat, stirring constantly, for about 3 minutes or until golden and fragrant. Immediately transfer to a heatproof bowl and let cool.

- Preheat oven to 425°F (220°C), with rack positioned in bottom third

½	recipe Easy-as-Pie Pastry (page 206)	½
⅓ cup	packed brown sugar	75 mL
⅓ cup	ground almonds, toasted (see tip, at left)	75 mL
¼ cup	all-purpose flour	60 mL
4	ripe pears	4
2 tbsp	freshly squeezed lemon juice	30 mL
1 tbsp	butter, melted	15 mL
½ tsp	vanilla extract	2 mL
½ cup	sliced almonds	125 mL
	Cream (any type) or milk	
	Coarse granulated sugar (optional)	

1. On a large piece of lightly floured parchment paper, roll out pastry to a 14-inch (35 cm) circle, dusting parchment and pastry as necessary to prevent sticking. Slide parchment and pastry onto a baking sheet.

2. In a bowl, combine brown sugar, ground almonds and flour. Sprinkle about half in a circle in the center of the pastry circle, leaving a 3-inch (7.5 cm) border.

3. Peel pears and cut in half lengthwise; trim out cores and stems. Cut lengthwise into thin slices. In a bowl, gently toss pear slices with lemon juice. Arrange on top of sugar mixture, overlapping as necessary and mounding slightly in the center.

4. Stir butter and vanilla into the remaining sugar mixture. Gently stir in sliced almonds. Sprinkle evenly over pears.

5. Gently fold edges of dough toward the center over pears, pleating as necessary, leaving about 4 inches (10 cm) in the center exposed. Brush pastry with cream, sealing well at pleats. Sprinkle pastry with coarse sugar (if using).

6. Bake in bottom third of preheated oven for 20 minutes. Reduce heat to 375°F (190°C) and bake for about 30 minutes or until crust is golden brown and juices are bubbling and thickened.

Lattice-Topped Apple Cranberry Pie

Makes 8 servings

Bursting with color and flavor, this pie is sure to impress. The lattice top is a little more work than a plain top, but the results are stunning. If you haven't made one before, use a few of the pastry strips to practice weaving on the parchment paper before you try it on the pie.

Tip

Rolling out the pastry on parchment paper makes it easy to transfer to the pie plate and helps you avoid adding too much flour, which would make the pastry tough.

Variation

To make a solid top instead of the lattice, roll out the top pastry into a circle; cut out three 1-inch (2.5 cm) shapes from the circle to let steam escape. Place on pie and fold top pastry over edge of bottom pastry to seal, then flute edge. Cut several more steam vents in top crust with the tip of a knife, then brush with egg wash and sprinkle with sugar. You can also sprinkle the top with cinnamon.

- Preheat oven to 425°F (220°C), with rack positioned in bottom third
- 9-inch (23 cm) deep-dish glass pie plate

1	recipe Easy-as-Pie Pastry (page 206)	1
⅔ cup	granulated sugar, divided	150 mL
7 cups	thinly sliced peeled tart cooking apples (about 5 large)	1.75 L
1 tbsp	freshly squeezed lemon juice	15 mL
3 tbsp	all-purpose flour	45 mL
½ tsp	ground cinnamon	2 mL
1 cup	fresh or frozen cranberries	250 mL
1	egg	1

1. On a floured piece of parchment paper, roll out slightly more than half the pastry and fit into pie plate; trim pastry to edge of plate.

2. Set 2 tsp (10 mL) of the sugar aside for topping. In a large bowl, toss apples with lemon juice. Sprinkle with the remaining sugar, flour and cinnamon; toss to coat evenly. Gently stir in cranberries. Spread into pie shell.

3. In a small bowl, whisk egg with 1 tsp (5 mL) water. Brush edge of pastry with some of the egg wash.

4. On floured parchment, roll out the remaining pastry to a circle about 2 inches (5 cm) larger than the diameter of the pie. Cut into ½-inch (1 cm) thick strips. Lay one strip of pastry across the center of the pie, letting each end hang over the edge a little. Lay another strip crosswise. Continue layering, weaving strips over and under to form a lattice. Tuck ends of lattice strips under bottom pastry edge. Flute edge around pie. Brush pastry strips with the remaining egg wash and sprinkle with the reserved sugar.

5. Bake in bottom third of preheated oven for 15 minutes. Reduce heat to 350°F (180°C) and bake for about 40 minutes or until apples are tender, filling is bubbling and pastry is golden.

Maple Pecan Crumble Apple Pie

Makes 8 servings

This pie is a twist
on the traditional,
with the addition of
maple and pecans.

Tips

Choosing the right apples
is the key to a successful
pie. Make sure you use a
variety that holds its flavor
and texture when baked,
such as Northern Spy,
Crispin (Mutsu), Ida Red
or Granny Smith.

You can find maple sugar
granules at farmers'
markets and specialty
food stores.

- Preheat oven to 425°F (220°C), with rack positioned in bottom third
- 9-inch (23 cm) deep-dish glass pie plate

Maple Pecan Crumble

1/2 cup	all-purpose flour	125 mL
1/4 cup	maple sugar granules or packed brown sugar	60 mL
Pinch	ground cinnamon	Pinch
3 tbsp	cold butter, cut into cubes	45 mL
1/3 cup	pure maple syrup	75 mL
1 cup	chopped pecans	250 mL
1/2	recipe Easy-as-Pie Pastry (page 206)	1/2
8 cups	sliced peeled tart cooking apples (about 6 large)	2 L
1/3 cup	pure maple syrup	75 mL
1/4 cup	all-purpose flour	60 mL
1/2 tsp	ground cinnamon	2 mL

1. *For the crumble:* In a bowl, combine flour, maple sugar and cinnamon. Using a pastry blender or two knives, cut in butter until crumbly. Drizzle with maple syrup and toss to combine. Stir in pecans. Set aside.

2. On a floured piece of parchment paper, roll out pastry and fit into pie plate; trim and flute edge.

3. In a bowl, combine apples and maple syrup; toss to coat. Sprinkle with flour and cinnamon; toss to coat evenly. Spread into pie shell and sprinkle with crumble.

4. Bake in bottom third of preheated oven for 15 minutes. Reduce heat to 350°F (180°C) and bake for about 40 minutes or until apples are tender and topping is crisp and golden.

> A hand-crank apple peeler is a fast way to remove peel and core from apples before cooking. It's also fun enough that kids will fight over who gets to use it.

Pear, Cherry and Ginger Crumble

Makes 4 servings

Take a bit of a shortcut by using ginger snaps in the topping for this decadent, warming dessert.

Tip

Use pears that hold their flavor when cooked. Bartlett, Bosc and Packham are good choices.

Variations

Use lemon snaps in place of the ginger snaps

Double the recipe and bake in an 8-inch (20 cm) square glass baking dish.

- Preheat oven to 350°F (180°C)
- 4-cup (1 L) shallow glass baking dish or four 1-cup (250 mL) ramekins or ovenproof bowls, buttered
- Rimmed baking sheet

3 cups	sliced peeled pears	750 mL
¼ cup	dried cherries, chopped	60 mL
2 tbsp	granulated sugar	30 mL
2 tbsp	cornstarch	30 mL
¼ tsp	ground ginger	1 mL
Pinch	ground cinnamon	Pinch

Cookie Crumble

¾ cup	finely crushed thin ginger snaps	175 mL
2 tbsp	all-purpose flour	30 mL
2 tbsp	butter, melted	30 mL

1. In a bowl, combine pears, cherries, sugar, cornstarch, ginger and cinnamon. Spread into prepared baking dish and place on rimmed baking sheet to catch any drips.

2. *For the crumble:* In a bowl, toss together crushed ginger snaps and flour. Drizzle with butter and toss until flour is moistened. Sprinkle evenly over fruit in baking dish.

3. Bake in preheated oven for about 45 minutes or until fruit is bubbling around the edges and center is hot.

> Bartlett pears cook to a soft consistency; Boscs remain more firm.

Classic Apple Crisp

This is one of those standby desserts every baker should have in his or her repertoire. It can be a weeknight treat for the family or a dessert for a potluck, or it can be dressed up for company with a custard sauce or maple-sweetened whipped cream.

Variations

Add ½ cup (125 mL) chopped pecans, walnuts or almonds to the topping after cutting in the butter.

Add ½ cup (125 mL) raisins or dried cherries or 1 cup (250 mL) wild blueberries with the apples.

- Preheat oven to 375°F (190°C)
- 8-cup (2 L) shallow glass baking dish

6 cups	sliced peeled tart cooking apples (see tip, page 209)	1.5 L
¼ cup	packed brown sugar	60 mL
2 tbsp	all-purpose flour	30 mL
½ tsp	ground cinnamon	2 mL
2 tbsp	unsweetened apple juice or cider or freshly squeezed lemon juice	30 mL

Crisp Topping

1 cup	quick-cooking rolled oats	250 mL
¾ cup	packed brown sugar	175 mL
½ cup	all-purpose flour	125 mL
½ tsp	ground cinnamon	2 mL
½ cup	cold butter, cut into pieces	125 mL

1. In a bowl, combine apples, brown sugar, flour, cinnamon and apple juice. Spread into prepared baking dish.

2. *For the topping:* In a bowl, combine oats, brown sugar, flour and cinnamon. Using a pastry blender or two knives, cut in butter until crumbly.

3. Sprinkle crumb mixture over fruit. Bake in preheated oven for about 45 minutes or until fruit is bubbling, liquid is thickened and topping is golden and crisp. Let stand for at least 5 minutes before serving or let cool to room temperature.

> Rome Beauty apples are terrific for baking.

Apple Pear Cobbler

Cobbler combines tender fruit with a fluffy biscuit topping and is a warming, comforting dessert for cold winter evenings. Serve with a scoop of ice cream or a dollop of sweetened whipped cream to dress it up.

Tip

Use any apples or pears that hold their flavor when cooked. They can be firm or soft varieties, but avoid those that are best suited to eating fresh, such as Royal Gala or Pink Lady apples or Anjou pears, as they'll be bland once baked.

- Preheat oven to 375°F (190°C)
- 8-inch (2 L) square glass baking dish, buttered

3 cups	sliced peeled cooking apples	750 mL
2 cups	sliced peeled pears	500 mL
¼ cup	granulated sugar	60 mL
1 tbsp	all-purpose flour	15 mL
2 tbsp	freshly squeezed lemon juice or unsweetened apple juice	30 mL

Topping

¼ cup	granulated sugar	60 mL
½ cup	milk	125 mL
¼ cup	plain yogurt (not fat-free)	60 mL
¼ cup	butter, melted	60 mL
1 cup	all-purpose flour	250 mL
1 tsp	ground cinnamon or ginger	5 mL
½ tsp	baking powder	2 mL
¼ tsp	baking soda	1 mL
¼ tsp	salt	1 mL
	Granulated sugar	

1. In prepared baking dish, combine apples, pears, sugar, flour and lemon juice. Cover and bake in preheated oven for about 10 minutes or until fruit starts to soften and juice is bubbling.

2. *For the topping:* Meanwhile, in a large bowl, whisk together sugar, milk, yogurt and butter. Without stirring, add flour, cinnamon, baking powder, baking soda and salt. Using a fork, stir just until moistened.

3. Uncover baking dish and pour batter over fruit, spreading gently to cover evenly. Sprinkle with sugar. Bake, uncovered, for about 30 minutes or until a tester inserted in the center of the topping comes out clean. Let stand for at least 5 minutes before serving or let cool to room temperature.

Walnut and Orange Baked Apples

Makes 6 servings

Sweetened baked apples are always lovely, but they're even better with the addition of walnuts and a hint of orange.

Tip

Use cooking apples that hold their shape. If you like tart apples, try Northern Spy, Crispin (Mutsu), Ida Red or Granny Smith. Try Golden Delicious if you prefer a sweeter apple.

Variation

Substitute lemon zest for the orange zest and almonds for the walnuts.

- Preheat oven to 350°F (180°C)
- Large shallow baking dish, buttered

6	large cooking apples (see tip, at left)	6
1/3 cup	packed brown sugar	75 mL
1 tbsp	butter, softened	15 mL
1/4 tsp	ground cinnamon or ginger	1 mL
1/2 tsp	grated orange zest	2 mL
2/3 cup	freshly squeezed orange juice, divided	150 mL
1/3 cup	chopped toasted walnuts	75 mL

1. Using an apple corer, remove core from apples, almost but not all the way through to the bottom. Using a vegetable peeler or a paring knife, remove a 3/4-inch (2 cm) wide strip of skin from around the top of each apple. Place apples in prepared baking dish.

2. In a bowl, mash together brown sugar, butter, cinnamon and orange zest. Stir in about 1 tbsp (15 mL) of the orange juice, just enough to moisten the sugar. Stir in walnuts. Pack evenly into the cavity of each apple; sprinkle any excess over top. Pour remaining orange juice evenly over top.

3. Cover with foil and bake in preheated oven for about 20 minutes or until apples are almost tender. Uncover and bake, basting with juices a few times, for about 20 minutes or until apples are tender. Serve hot or let cool slightly.

Caramelized Apples with Cinnamon Sugar Twists

This comforting dessert has all the flavors of the French classic tarte Tatin, but is prepared with much less fuss. Make the elements ahead of time and reheat just before serving to save on last-minute preparations. For extra decadence, serve with a dollop of freshly whipped cream or a scoop of vanilla ice cream.

Tip
Use tart cooking apples that hold their shape, such as Northern Spy, Crispin (Mutsu), Ida Red or Granny Smith.

• Baking sheet, lined with parchment paper or greased

Caramelized Apples

4	tart cooking apples, peeled and cut into thick wedges	4
2 tbsp	freshly squeezed lemon juice	30 mL
¼ cup	butter	60 mL
½ cup	granulated sugar	125 mL

Cinnamon Sugar Twists

	All-purpose flour	
8 oz	frozen puff pastry, thawed (see tip, at left)	250 g
2 tbsp	granulated sugar	30 mL
2 tbsp	butter, melted	30 mL
1 tsp	ground cinnamon	5 mL

1. *For the apples:* In a bowl, toss apples with lemon juice; set aside. In a large, heavy skillet, melt butter over medium-high heat. Add sugar and cook, stirring often, for about 8 minutes or until caramel in color. Drain apples and add to skillet, drizzling syrup over apples. Reduce heat and simmer, basting often, for about 15 minutes or until apples are tender and caramelized. (The caramel will harden when the apples are first added, but will soften again when the juices are released.) Transfer to a serving or baking dish.

2. *For the twists:* On a lightly floured surface, roll out pastry to a 14- by 10-inch (35 by 25 cm) rectangle. In a bowl, combine sugar, butter and cinnamon. Looking at the rectangle like a book, brush one side with a thin coating of the sugar mixture. Fold other half over to enclose coating. Roll out again to a 12- by 10-inch (30 by 25 cm) rectangle. Brush the entire surface with the remaining sugar mixture. Trim edges as necessary to straighten. Cut crosswise into twelve 10-inch (25 cm) long strips. Working with one strip at a time, hold opposite ends and twist several times with the coated side facing out (like a candy cane). Place twists at least ½ inch (1 cm) apart on prepared baking sheet. Refrigerate for 30 minutes, until chilled, or for up to 8 hours.

Puff pastry packages vary in weight depending on the brand you buy. Use half a package, which may be anywhere from 7 to 9 oz (210 to 270 g). For the best flavor, buy pastry that is made with real butter, if possible.

The caramelized apples can be cooled, covered and refrigerated for up to 2 days.

3. Preheat oven to 425°F (220°C). Bake twists for about 15 minutes or until golden brown. Serve warm or let cool completely and store in a cookie tin or wrapped in foil for up to 1 day.

4. If necessary, preheat oven to 350°F (180°C). Reheat apples in a covered baking dish for about 20 minutes or until warmed through. If made ahead, heat the twists on a baking sheet for 2 to 3 minutes alongside the apples. Spoon apples and syrup into serving bowls and serve twists on the side.

The Granny Smith apple was discovered in the 1860s in Australia by Maria Ann Smith. It is thought to have developed as a chance seedling from French crabapples. It is now appreciated worldwide for its crisp, juicy texture and tart flavor.

Poached Pear, Brie and Pecan Napoleons

The classic elegance of a cheese course is incorporated into a stunning and delicious dessert in this twist on the layered napoleon. This dessert is made in stages that you can start three days before you plan to serve it. It takes a bit of patience, but the results are well worth it and your guests will be wowed! Garnish with strips of candied lemon peel or candied pecan halves and a sprinkle of cinnamon.

Tips

Use pears that hold their shape and flavor when cooked. Bartlett, Bosc and Packham are good choices.

At the end of step 2, the pears in their liquid can be covered and stored in the refrigerator for up to 3 days.

The cooled baked phyllo squares can be stored in a cookie tin at room temperature for up to 2 days.

Poached Pears

½ cup	granulated sugar	125 mL
¾ cup	ruby port	175 mL
1	strip of lemon zest	1
2 tbsp	freshly squeezed lemon juice	30 mL
1	piece (3 inches/7.5 cm) cinnamon stick	1
3	ripe pears (Bartlett or Bosc)	3
3	sheets phyllo pastry	3
¼ cup	butter, melted	60 mL
½ cup	finely chopped pecans	125 mL
7 oz	Brie cheese, cut into 24 thin squares	210 g
	Confectioner's (icing) sugar	
	Pecan pieces, toasted (optional)	

1. *For the pears:* In a shallow pot, combine sugar, port, lemon zest, lemon juice, cinnamon stick and 1½ cups (375 mL) water. Bring to a boil over medium heat, stirring until sugar is dissolved.

2. Meanwhile, peel pears and cut in half lengthwise; trim out cores and stems. Add pears to pot and cover surface of liquid with parchment or waxed paper. Reduce heat and simmer gently, turning once, for about 15 minutes or until pears are tender. Let cool in liquid.

3. Drain liquid from pears and reserve; discard lemon zest and cinnamon stick. Place pears flat side down on a cutting board and slice horizontally in half; set aside and let warm to room temperature.

4. In a saucepan, bring reserved liquid to a boil over high heat; reduce heat and boil gently until syrup is thickened and glossy. Transfer to a heatproof dish and let cool slightly.

5. Preheat oven to 400°F (200°C), with rack positioned in the bottom third.

Tip

The napoleons can be assembled through step 7 and held at room temperature for up to 2 hours before heating to serve.

Variation

For a shortcut dessert with the same great flavors, make the poached pears and the reduced syrup; slice the pears and arrange them in individual gratin dishes. Drizzle with syrup, top with slices of Brie and chopped pecans and broil just before serving.

6. Place 1 sheet of phyllo on a work surface, keeping remaining phyllo covered with a damp tea towel. Brush phyllo lightly with butter and sprinkle with two-thirds of the pecans. Place another sheet of phyllo on top; brush with butter. Using a sharp knife, cut crosswise into 4 strips; cut each strip into 3 squares. Place on large baking sheets, leaving at least $1/2$ inch (1 cm) between squares. Place remaining sheet of phyllo on work surface; brush one side with butter and sprinkle with the remaining pecans. Fold the other side over the pecans like closing a book; brush top with butter. Using a sharp knife, cut into 6 squares; place on baking sheet. Bake, in batches as necessary, in bottom third of preheated oven for about 5 minutes or until golden brown. Let cool on baking sheets on a wire rack.

7. *To assemble:* For each napoleon, place 1 phyllo square on a baking sheet lined with parchment paper or an oven-safe serving plate. Place 1 piece of Brie on top, then 1 slice of pear and another piece of Brie. Place another phyllo square on top and repeat the layering with Brie and pear; top with 1 more phyllo square. Repeat to make 6 napoleons.

8. Preheat oven to 350°F (180°C). Bake napoleons for about 3 minutes or just until Brie is starting to melt. If on a baking sheet, use a thin spatula to transfer to serving plate. Drizzle with thickened port syrup and sprinkle with confectioner's sugar. Garnish with toasted pecan pieces, if desired.

Chocolate Citrus Trifle

Makes 8 servings

Airy chocolate cake, a softly set, rich chocolate custard and liqueur-spiked citrus segments offer a different twist on traditional trifle. Each element can be done ahead, as can the assembly of the trifles, so they're ready and waiting in the fridge when it's time for dessert. In fact, they benefit from standing, so there's no fuss when you're ready to serve except to add the final garnish. For traditionalists, a dollop of sweetened whipped cream before the chocolate shavings is always a nice touch.

Tip

Use whatever sweet citrus fruit you have in your stores: oranges, tangerines, clementines, mandarins, blood oranges or a combination. A little grapefruit mixed in with other citrus is nice, too.

- Preheat oven to 375°F (190°C)
- 8-inch (20 cm) square metal cake pan, lined with parchment paper
- Eight 8- to 12-oz (250 to 375 mL) old-fashioned, highball, parfait or wine glasses

Cake

3	eggs	3
	Warm water	
1/3 cup	all-purpose flour	75 mL
1/4 cup	unsweetened cocoa powder, sifted	60 mL
Pinch	salt	Pinch
1/2 cup	granulated sugar	125 mL
1 tsp	vanilla extract	5 mL
2 tbsp	butter, melted	30 mL

Chocolate Custard

6 oz	bittersweet (dark) chocolate, finely chopped	175 g
3 cups	milk	750 mL
1/3 cup	granulated sugar, divided	75 mL
4 tsp	cornstarch	20 mL
3	egg yolks	3
1 1/2 tsp	vanilla extract	7 mL

Macerated Citrus

3 cups	citrus segments with juices (see tip, at right)	750 mL
1/3 cup	Grand Marnier or other orange-flavored liqueur, or brandy	75 mL
	Bittersweet (dark) chocolate shavings	

1. *For the cake:* Place eggs (in shells) in a bowl and cover with warm water; let eggs warm to slightly above room temperature, refreshing with more warm water if it cools. In another bowl, whisk together flour, cocoa and salt.

2. Drain water from eggs and crack into a straight-sided bowl. Add sugar. Using an electric mixer, beat until very pale, quadrupled in volume and ribbons fall slowly from beater when lifted. Beat in vanilla. Sprinkle with half the flour mixture and fold just until combined. Gently fold in the remaining flour mixture. Fold in butter. Pour into prepared pan, smoothing top.

Tip

To make restaurant-worthy citrus segments, use a small serrated knife to cut a slice off the top and bottom of the fruit. Place one flat side down on a cutting board and cut off the peel in strips, including the white pith. Carefully trim off any remaining white pith. Holding the fruit over a bowl to catch the juices, carefully cut between the fruit and the membrane of one segment, through to the center of the fruit. Cut along the membrane on the other side of the segment to release the segment into the bowl. Repeat with the remaining segments. Squeeze juices from membranes into bowl, then discard the membranes.

3. Bake in preheated oven for about 25 minutes or until top springs back when lightly pressed. Let cool in pan on a wire rack for 15 minutes. Run a knife around edge of cake and invert onto rack. Peel off paper and let cool completely.

4. *For the custard:* Place chocolate in a heatproof bowl. In a medium saucepan, heat milk and half the sugar over medium heat just until steaming. In a bowl, whisk the remaining sugar, cornstarch and egg yolks until blended. Gradually pour in hot milk, whisking constantly. Return to saucepan. Cook over medium-low heat, whisking constantly, for about 12 minutes or until slightly thickened and bubbles just rise to the surface. Remove from heat and strain through a sieve into the bowl with chocolate. Add vanilla and stir until chocolate is melted. Place plastic directly on the surface and refrigerate for at least 4 hours, until completely chilled, or for up to 1 day.

5. *For the citrus:* In a bowl, combine citrus segments and liqueur. Let stand for 2 to 4 hours or until fruit is well flavored with liqueur.

6. *To assemble:* Cut cake in half horizontally. Cut each half into 36 squares. Place 3 squares in each glass. Using about one-third of the citrus mixture, divide evenly and spoon on top of cake. Spoon in a heaping tbsp (15 mL) of custard. Repeat layers once with cake, citrus and custard. Top with remaining cake, then custard and citrus. Cover and refrigerate for at least 2 hours, until chilled, or for up to 8 hours.

7. Serve sprinkled with chocolate shavings.

Pear Upside-Down Cake

This updated version of an old classic uses much less butter and sugar for the fruit layer, allowing the lovely pear flavor to shine. The parchment paper provides insurance that the fruit will come out on top of the cake and won't stick to the pan.

Tips

When baking, avoid fat-free yogurt and any yogurt that contains gelatin, as it doesn't react well to heat and can cause rubbery baked goods.

This cake is best served the day it is made. For best results, time it so the cake comes out of the oven just before you sit down for your main course, so you can enjoy it warm.

- Preheat oven to 350°F (180°C)
- 9-inch (23 cm) round metal cake pan, bottom lined with parchment paper

Topping

3	ripe pears	3
¼ cup	packed brown sugar	60 mL
2 tbsp	unsweetened pear nectar or apple juice	30 mL
1 tbsp	butter, softened	15 mL

Cake

1½ cups	all-purpose flour	375 mL
1½ tsp	ground cinnamon	7 mL
1 tsp	baking powder	5 mL
½ tsp	baking soda	2 mL
¼ tsp	salt	1 mL
¼ tsp	ground ginger	1 mL
⅔ cup	packed brown sugar	150 mL
½ cup	butter, softened	125 mL
1	egg	1
1 tsp	vanilla extract	5 mL
⅔ cup	plain yogurt (not fat-free)	150 mL

1. *For the topping:* Peel pears and cut in half lengthwise; trim out cores and stems. Cut lengthwise into thin slices. In a bowl, mash together brown sugar, pear nectar and butter; sprinkle evenly in bottom of prepared pan. Arrange pear slices decoratively in pan, overlapping as necessary and leaving a ½-inch (1 cm) border without fruit. Set aside.

2. *For the cake:* In a bowl, combine flour, cinnamon, baking powder, baking soda, salt and ginger.

3. In a separate bowl, using an electric mixer, beat brown sugar and butter until fluffy. Beat in egg and vanilla until blended. Using a wooden spoon or rubber spatula, stir in flour mixture alternately with yogurt, making three additions of flour and two of yogurt. Gently drop batter by spoonfuls over pears and carefully smooth top.

4. Bake in preheated oven for 50 to 60 minutes or until a tester inserted in the center comes out clean. Let cool in pan on a wire rack for 10 minutes. Invert a large plate on top of pan and flip over to unmold cake onto plate. If necessary, rearrange pear slices.

Classic Carrot Cake

Makes 10 to 12 servings

This cake is lightened up from the oil-laden versions of old, but the taste captures the essence of the timeless favorite.

Tip

If you have a dark metal pan, keep an eye on the cake as it bakes to make sure the edges aren't getting too dark. If they do, you may need to reduce the oven temperature to 325°F (160°C) about halfway through baking.

Variations

Add 1 cup (250 mL) chopped toasted pecans or walnuts and/or $\frac{1}{2}$ cup (125 mL) raisins or dried cranberries with the carrots.

Add 1 tbsp (15 mL) grated orange zest with the vanilla.

- Preheat oven to 350°F (180°C)
- 10-inch (25 cm) metal Bundt pan, buttered

2 cups	all-purpose flour	500 mL
2 tsp	baking powder	10 mL
2 tsp	ground cinnamon	10 mL
1 tsp	baking soda	5 mL
1 tsp	salt	5 mL
1 tsp	ground ginger	5 mL
$\frac{1}{2}$ tsp	ground nutmeg, preferably freshly grated	2 mL
$\frac{1}{4}$ tsp	ground allspice	1 mL
4	eggs	4
$1\frac{1}{3}$ cups	packed brown sugar	325 mL
$\frac{1}{2}$ cup	vegetable oil or melted butter	125 mL
1 tsp	vanilla extract	5 mL
1 cup	unsweetened applesauce	250 mL
2 cups	shredded carrots (about 4)	500 mL
$\frac{1}{2}$ cup	drained canned crushed pineapple (about one 8 oz/227 mL can)	125 mL
	Confectioner's (icing) sugar	

1. In a bowl, combine flour, baking powder, cinnamon, baking soda, salt, ginger, nutmeg and allspice.

2. In a separate bowl, whisk together eggs, brown sugar, oil and vanilla until blended. Stir in flour mixture alternately with applesauce, making three additions of flour and two of applesauce. Stir in carrots and pineapple. Spread into prepared pan, smoothing top.

3. Bake in preheated oven for 60 to 70 minutes or until a tester inserted in the center comes out clean. Let cool in pan on a wire rack for 15 minutes. Transfer cake to rack to cool completely. Serve dusted with confectioner's sugar.

Double Apple Coffee Cake

Makes 10 to 12 servings

Though the flavor of this cake is reminiscent of a crisp fall day, it's absolutely delicious at any time of year. For a fancier presentation, serve with a custard sauce or whipped cream with a touch of sugar and cinnamon.

Tips

Use any apples that hold their flavor when cooked. They can be firm or soft varieties, but avoid those that are best suited to eating fresh, such as Royal Gala or Pink Lady apples, as they'll be bland once baked.

Cardamom is a pungent spice used in Scandinavian baking and East Asian cooking. It adds depth to the spice flavor in this cake and complements apples nicely.

- Preheat oven to 350°F (180°C)
- 9-inch (23 cm) springform pan, bottom lined with parchment paper

1½ cups	all-purpose flour	375 mL
1 tsp	baking powder	5 mL
1 tsp	ground cinnamon	5 mL
½ tsp	baking soda	2 mL
¼ tsp	salt	1 mL
¼ tsp	ground cardamom (optional)	1 mL
⅔ cup	packed brown sugar	150 mL
½ cup	butter, softened	125 mL
1	egg	1
2 tsp	vanilla extract	10 mL
¾ cup	unsweetened applesauce	175 mL
1½ cups	diced peeled cooking apples	375 mL
2	cooking apples, thinly sliced (peeled if desired)	2
	Ground cinnamon	

1. In a bowl, combine flour, baking powder, cinnamon, baking soda, salt and cardamom (if using).

2. In a large bowl, using an electric mixer, beat brown sugar and butter until fluffy. Beat in egg and vanilla until blended. Using a wooden spoon or rubber spatula, stir in flour mixture alternately with applesauce, making three additions of flour and two of applesauce. Stir in diced apples.

3. Spread batter in prepared pan, smoothing top. Arrange apple slices on top in a spiral pattern, overlapping slightly as necessary.

4. Bake in preheated oven for 50 to 60 minutes or until a tester inserted in the center comes out clean. Let cool in pan on a wire rack for 20 minutes. Run a knife around the edge of the cake and remove ring. Serve warm or let cool completely.

Rhubarb Streusel Coffee Cake

Makes 8 to 10 servings

If you've grown rhubarb in your root cellar (see page 101), dazzle guests with this moist cake topped with a crispy streusel, long before their garden rhubarb is ready.

Tip

Be sure to chop the rhubarb into fairly small pieces so they cook evenly in the batter.

- Preheat oven to 350°F (180°C)
- 9-inch (23 cm) springform pan, bottom lined with parchment paper

Streusel

⅓ cup	all-purpose flour	75 mL
⅓ cup	packed brown sugar	75 mL
⅓ cup	quick-cooking rolled oats	75 mL
½ tsp	ground cinnamon or ginger	2 mL
¼ cup	butter, melted	60 mL

Cake

1½ cups	all-purpose flour	375 mL
1 tsp	baking powder	5 mL
1 tsp	ground cinnamon or ginger	5 mL
½ tsp	baking soda	2 mL
¼ tsp	salt	1 mL
⅔ cup	packed brown sugar	150 mL
½ cup	butter, softened	125 mL
1	egg	1
2 tsp	vanilla extract	10 mL
¾ cup	plain yogurt (not fat-free)	175 mL
2 cups	chopped fresh rhubarb, divided	500 mL

1. *For the streusel:* In a bowl, mash together flour, brown sugar, oats, cinnamon and butter until crumbly. Set aside.

2. *For the cake:* In a bowl, combine flour, baking powder, cinnamon, baking soda and salt.

3. In a separate bowl, using an electric mixer, beat brown sugar and butter until fluffy. Beat in egg and vanilla until blended. Using a wooden spoon or rubber spatula, stir in flour mixture alternately with yogurt, making three additions of flour and two of yogurt. Gently stir in half the rhubarb. Spread into prepared pan, smoothing top.

4. Sprinkle the remaining rhubarb over batter in pan, then sprinkle with streusel. Bake in preheated oven for 50 to 60 minutes or until a tester inserted in the center comes out clean. Let cool in pan on a wire rack for 20 minutes. Run a knife around the edge of the cake and remove ring. Serve warm or let cool completely.

Ginger Streusel Coffee Cake

Makes 10 to 12 servings

When you have gingerroot in your stores, you can create this lovely coffee cake any time you need something to serve to guests or to bring to a potluck.

Tips

Peel the gingerroot using a vegetable peeler or paring knife, then use the fine side of a box cheese grater or a Microplane-style grater to grate the gingerroot very finely (so it's almost a purée).

When baking, avoid fat-free yogurt and any yogurt that contains gelatin, as it doesn't react well to heat and can cause rubbery baked goods.

- Preheat oven to 350°F (180°C)
- 9-inch (23 cm) springform pan, bottom lined with parchment paper, sides buttered

Streusel

⅓ cup	packed brown sugar	75 mL
¼ cup	all-purpose flour	60 mL
3 tbsp	butter, softened	45 mL

Cake

2 cups	all-purpose flour	500 mL
1 tsp	baking powder	5 mL
½ tsp	baking soda	2 mL
½ tsp	salt	2 mL
¾ cup	packed brown sugar	175 mL
½ cup	butter, softened	125 mL
2	eggs	2
3 tbsp	finely grated gingerroot	45 mL
2 tsp	vanilla extract	10 mL
¾ cup	plain yogurt (not fat-free)	175 mL

1. *For the streusel:* In a bowl, mash together brown sugar, flour and butter until crumbly. Set aside.

2. *For the cake:* In a large bowl, combine flour, baking powder, baking soda and salt.

3. In a separate bowl, using an electric mixer, beat brown sugar and butter until fluffy. Beat in eggs, one at a time, until blended. Beat in ginger and vanilla. Using a wooden spoon or rubber spatula, stir in flour mixture alternately with yogurt, making three additions of flour and two of yogurt.

4. Spread batter in prepared pan, smoothing top. Sprinkle with streusel. Bake in preheated oven for 50 to 60 minutes or until a tester inserted in the center comes out clean. Let cool in pan on a wire rack for 20 minutes. Run a knife around the edge of the cake and remove ring. Serve warm or let cool completely.

Double Ginger Pound Cake

Makes 1 loaf, about 12 slices

For ginger lovers, the more spicy ginger flavor, the better. This sweet cake has a double punch from ground and fresh ginger. It's perfect with a steaming cup of tea.

Tip

If you add the minced ginger directly to the liquid ingredients, it can curdle the milk, so it's best to add it just as you combine the batter. The batter may still look a little curdled, but it will bake up just fine.

This cake is best eaten within a day or two of baking. If you have leftovers, toast slices and spread them with a little butter or pear or peach jam for a real treat.

- Preheat oven to 350°F (180°C)
- 8- by 4-inch (20 by 10 cm) metal loaf pan, buttered

2$\frac{1}{3}$ cups	all-purpose flour	575 mL
1 tbsp	ground ginger	15 mL
1$\frac{1}{2}$ tsp	baking powder	7 mL
$\frac{1}{2}$ tsp	salt	2 mL
3	eggs	3
1 cup	granulated sugar	250 mL
$\frac{3}{4}$ cup	butter, melted	175 mL
$\frac{3}{4}$ cup	milk	175 mL
1 tsp	vanilla extract	5 mL
2 tbsp	minced gingerroot	30 mL

1. In a large bowl, combine flour, ground ginger, baking powder and salt.

2. In another bowl, whisk together eggs, sugar, butter, milk and vanilla. Pour over dry ingredients and add minced ginger. Stir just until moistened.

3. Spread batter in prepared pan, smoothing top. Bake in preheated oven for about 1 hour or until a tester inserted in the center comes out clean. Let cool in pan on a wire rack for 15 minutes. Transfer cake to rack to cool completely.

> *Zingiber* ginger is the most common edible variety. Young roots are mild, while the juice from older ones is extremely potent.

Sweet Lemon Parsnip Loaf

Makes 1 loaf, about 12 slices

Parsnips sound like an odd ingredient for a sweet loaf, but once you try it you'll be amazed at how well it works with the delicate spices and burst of fresh lemon.

Tip

If you don't have buttermilk on hand, sour fresh milk by placing 1 tbsp (15 mL) freshly squeezed lemon juice in a glass measuring cup, then filling to ¾ cup (175 mL) with milk. Let stand for 5 minutes, then stir.

Variations

Add 1 cup (250 mL) chopped toasted pecans with the parsnips.

Make mini loaves in four or five 5- by 3-inch (12.5 by 7.5 cm) buttered pans, decreasing the baking time to about 40 minutes.

- Preheat oven to 350°F (180°C)
- 9- by 5-inch (23 by 12.5 cm) metal loaf pan, buttered

2½ cups	all-purpose flour	625 mL
2 tsp	ground ginger	10 mL
1 tsp	baking powder	5 mL
½ tsp	baking soda	2 mL
½ tsp	salt	2 mL
½ tsp	ground allspice	2 mL
½ tsp	ground nutmeg	2 mL
¾ cup	packed brown sugar	175 mL
2	eggs	2
¾ cup	buttermilk or sour milk (see tip, at left)	175 mL
½ cup	butter, melted	125 mL
1 tbsp	grated lemon zest	15 mL
1¼ cups	shredded parsnips	300 mL

1. In a large bowl, combine flour, ginger, baking powder, baking soda, salt, allspice and nutmeg.

2. In another bowl, whisk together brown sugar, eggs, buttermilk, butter and lemon zest. Pour over dry ingredients and sprinkle with parsnips. Stir just until moistened.

3. Spread batter in prepared pan, smoothing top. Bake in preheated oven for 60 to 70 minutes or until a tester inserted in the center comes out clean. Let cool in pan on a wire rack for 15 minutes. Transfer cake to rack to cool completely.

> Kral Russian parsnips have a short wedge shape that makes them easy to pull out of the ground.

Spiced Pumpkin Loaf

Makes 1 loaf, about 12 slices

Pumpkin and warm spices are a natural match. This moist and nutritious loaf is great for breakfast, as a snack or, with a dollop of sweetened whipped cream, as a not-too-sweet dessert.

Tip

To make pumpkin purée, cut a pie pumpkin in half lengthwise. Scoop out seeds and loose pulp. Place cut side down in a glass baking dish and pierce the skin several times. Pour in enough water to fill the dish about $1/4$ inch (0.5 cm). Bake in a 375°F (190°C) oven for 50 to 70 minutes or until fork-tender (add more water if the dish gets dry and the pumpkin starts to brown too much). Let cool, then scoop pumpkin from skin, discarding skin. Purée pumpkin in a food processor or with an immersion blender until smooth. One $2^1/_2$-lb (1.25 kg) pumpkin yields about $2^1/_2$ cups (625 mL) purée.

- Preheat oven to 350°F (180°C)
- 9- by 5-inch (23 by 12.5 cm) metal loaf pan, buttered

$3/4$ cup	buttermilk or sour milk (see tip, page 226)	175 mL
1 cup	raisins	250 mL
$2^1/_2$ cups	all-purpose flour	625 mL
1 tbsp	ground cinnamon	15 mL
2 tsp	baking powder	10 mL
2 tsp	ground ginger	10 mL
1 tsp	salt	5 mL
$3/4$ tsp	ground allspice	3 mL
$3/4$ tsp	ground nutmeg	3 mL
$1/2$ tsp	baking soda	2 mL
$3/4$ cup	packed brown sugar	175 mL
$1/2$ cup	butter, softened	125 mL
2	eggs	2
$1^1/_3$ cups	cooked pumpkin purée (see tip, at left)	325 mL
1 tsp	vanilla extract	5 mL

1. In a measuring cup, combine buttermilk and raisins; set aside.

2. In a bowl, combine flour, cinnamon, baking powder, ginger, salt, allspice, nutmeg and baking soda.

3. In a large bowl, using an electric mixer, beat brown sugar and butter until fluffy. Beat in eggs, one at a time, until blended. Beat in pumpkin purée and vanilla until blended. Using a wooden spoon or rubber spatula, stir in flour mixture alternately with buttermilk mixture, making three additions of flour and two of buttermilk; stir just until blended.

4. Spread batter in prepared pan, smoothing top. Bake in preheated oven for about 75 minutes or until a tester inserted in the center comes out clean. Let cool in pan on a wire rack for 15 minutes. Transfer cake to rack to cool completely.

Apple Oat Muffins

Makes 12 muffins

These are among the most popular muffins at the café Jennifer co-owns with her husband, Jay Nutt. Customers love the simple flavor of apples and oats.

Tips

When baking, avoid fat-free yogurt and any yogurt that contains gelatin, as it doesn't react well to heat and can cause rubbery baked goods.

Muffins are best within a day of baking them. Wrap extra cooled muffins individually in plastic wrap, then place in an airtight container or freezer bag and freeze for up to 2 months.

Variation

Add ½ cup (125 mL) chopped toasted walnuts or pecans with the apples.

- Preheat oven to 375°F (190°C)
- 12-cup muffin pan, greased or lined with silicone or paper liners

1½ cups	all-purpose flour	375 mL
1 cup	quick-cooking rolled oats	250 mL
½ cup	whole wheat flour	125 mL
2 tsp	baking powder	10 mL
1 tsp	ground cinnamon	5 mL
¼ tsp	baking soda	1 mL
¼ tsp	salt	1 mL
⅔ cup	packed brown sugar	150 mL
1	egg	1
1 cup	plain yogurt (not fat-free)	250 mL
¾ cup	milk	175 mL
¼ cup	butter, melted, or vegetable oil	60 mL
1½ cups	diced peeled apples (about 2)	375 mL
	Quick-cooking rolled oats	

1. In a large bowl, combine all-purpose flour, oats, whole wheat flour, baking powder, cinnamon, baking soda and salt.

2. In a bowl, whisk together brown sugar, egg, yogurt, milk and butter. Pour over dry ingredients and sprinkle with apples. Stir just until moistened.

3. Spoon batter evenly into prepared muffin cups. Sprinkle oats on top, pressing lightly so they stick. Bake in preheated oven for 20 to 25 minutes or until tops are firm to the touch. Let cool in pan on a wire rack for 10 minutes. Transfer muffins to rack to cool completely.

Pear Ginger Muffins

Makes 12 muffins

These are a little like soft gingerbread cake, but not quite as sweet. They're lovely for breakfast or as an afternoon snack.

Tips

Peel the gingerroot using a vegetable peeler or paring knife, then use the fine side of a box cheese grater or a Microplane-style grater to grate the gingerroot very finely (so it's almost a purée).

Muffins are best within a day of baking them. Wrap extra cooled muffins individually in plastic wrap, then place in an airtight container or freezer bag and freeze for up to 2 months.

- Preheat oven to 375°F (190°C)
- 12-cup muffin pan, greased or lined with silicone or paper liners

1½ cups	all-purpose flour	375 mL
1 cup	whole wheat flour	250 mL
2 tsp	baking powder	10 mL
½ tsp	baking soda	2 mL
½ tsp	salt	2 mL
½ tsp	ground cinnamon	2 mL
½ tsp	ground ginger	2 mL
½ cup	packed brown sugar	125 mL
1	egg	1
1 cup	milk	250 mL
½ cup	light (fancy) molasses	125 mL
¼ cup	butter, melted, or vegetable oil	60 mL
1 tbsp	grated gingerroot	15 mL
1 cup	diced pears (peeled, if desired)	250 mL

1. In a large bowl, whisk together all-purpose flour, whole wheat flour, baking powder, baking soda, salt, cinnamon and ground ginger.

2. In another bowl, whisk together brown sugar, egg, milk, molasses, butter and grated ginger. Pour over dry ingredients and sprinkle with pears. Stir just until moistened.

3. Spoon batter evenly into prepared muffin cups. Bake in preheated oven for 20 to 25 minutes or until tops are firm to the touch. Let cool in pan on a wire rack for 10 minutes. Transfer muffins to rack to cool completely.

Carrot Bran Muffins

Makes 12 muffins

Carrots add great flavor to bran muffins, and the touch of honey not only adds a nice taste but keeps them moist, too.

Tips

When baking, avoid fat-free yogurt and any yogurt that contains gelatin, as it doesn't react well to heat and can cause rubbery baked goods.

These muffins are best within 2 days of baking them. Wrap extra cooled muffins individually in plastic wrap, then place in an airtight container or freezer bag and freeze for up to 2 months.

- Preheat oven to 375°F (190°C)
- 12-cup muffin pan, greased or lined with silicone or paper liners

1½ cups	bran cereal, such as All-Bran or 100% Bran	375 mL
1½ cups	shredded carrots (about 3)	375 mL
¾ cup	plain yogurt (not fat-free)	175 mL
½ cup	milk or unsweetened applesauce	125 mL
1 cup	all-purpose flour	250 mL
½ cup	whole wheat flour	125 mL
2 tsp	baking powder	10 mL
1 tsp	ground cinnamon	5 mL
½ tsp	baking soda	2 mL
¼ tsp	salt	1 mL
1	egg	1
½ cup	liquid honey	125 mL
¼ cup	butter, melted or vegetable oil	60 mL

1. In a bowl, combine bran cereal, carrots, yogurt and milk; let stand for 5 minutes.

2. In a large bowl, whisk together all-purpose flour, whole wheat flour, baking powder, cinnamon, baking soda and salt.

3. Whisk egg, honey and butter into cereal mixture. Pour over dry ingredients and stir just until moistened.

4. Spoon batter evenly into prepared muffin cups. Bake in preheated oven for about 25 minutes or until tops are firm to the touch. Let cool in pan on a wire rack for 10 minutes. Transfer muffins to rack to cool completely.

Condiments

Pickled Ginger

Makes three 4-ounce (125 mL) jars

Why buy commercially prepared pickled ginger when it's simple to make yourself and the taste is outstanding?

Tips

Be sure to use gingerroot with taut, shiny skin, juicy flesh and no signs of mold.

Use a Y-shaped vegetable peeler to peel the skin from gingerroot, then use a mandoline, Microplane-style slicer or sharp knife to cut crosswise into paper-thin slices. You'll need about 8 oz (250 g) gingerroot to get 1½ cups (375 mL).

The ginger may turn pink once it's pickled. There is nothing wrong with the pickles; it's just a reaction between the acid and the pigment in the ginger. Commercially prepared pickled ginger often has food coloring added to make sure it turns pink.

This is a small batch of pickled ginger, so you can just store it in the refrigerator and the jars don't need to be processed in a boiling water canner. Follow proper, modern canning procedures if you want to make a larger batch and store the jars at room temperature.

- Three 4-ounce (125 mL) canning jars with two-piece metal lids or plastic storage lids

Day 1

1½ cups	very thinly sliced peeled gingerroot	375 mL
½ tsp	pickling or canning salt	2 mL

Day 2

¼ cup	granulated sugar	60 mL
¾ cup	natural rice vinegar	175 mL
¼ cup	water	60 mL

Day 1

1. In a non-reactive bowl, combine ginger and salt; toss to combine. Cover and refrigerate for at least 8 hours or for up to 24 hours.

Day 2

1. Place jars on a rack in a pot. Fill pot and jars with water. Bring to a simmer over medium heat. Simmer gently for at least 10 minutes to sterilize jars; keep hot. Wash lids.

2. In a colander, drain ginger, gently squeezing out excess liquid; set aside.

3. In a medium saucepan, combine sugar, vinegar and water. Bring to a boil over medium-high heat, stirring often to dissolve sugar. Boil for 1 minute. Add ginger and simmer until heated through.

4. Empty water from jars and drain well. Using a slotted spoon, pack ginger into hot jars, leaving room for liquid and leaving 1 inch (2.5 cm) headspace. Pour in hot pickling liquid, leaving ½ inch (1 cm) headspace. Remove air bubbles and adjust headspace as necessary by adding hot pickling liquid. Wipe rims. Place lid discs on jars and screw bands down until fingertip-tight (or use plastic storage lids). Let jars cool completely. Refrigerate for at least 5 days before serving or for up to 3 months.

Quick Carrot Pickles

Makes two pint (500 mL) jars

These are among the easiest pickles to make, and you'll be delighted with what the dilly taste and tangy crunch do to a humble carrot stick.

Tips

When cutting the carrots, it is easiest to cut them crosswise into 4-inch (10 cm) lengths and then into sticks. You may just need to cut the narrow end of the carrot in half lengthwise; it's okay not to have squared-off sticks.

Avoid very large carrots, which often have a woody core and make unpleasant pickles.

This is a small batch of pickles, so you can just store them in the refrigerator and the jars don't need to be processed in a boiling water canner. Follow proper, modern canning procedures if you want to make a larger batch and store the jars at room temperature.

Two 1-pint (500 mL) canning jars with two-piece metal lids or plastic storage lids

5	carrots (about 1 lb/500 g)	5
1 tbsp	granulated sugar	15 mL
2 tsp	pickling or kosher salt	10 mL
2 cups	white vinegar	500 mL
¾ cup	water	175 mL
2	dill heads	2
2	dill sprigs	2
½ tsp	dill seeds	2 mL

1. Place jars on a rack in a pot. Fill pot and jars with water. Bring to a simmer over medium heat. Simmer gently for at least 10 minutes to sterilize jars; keep hot. Wash lids.

2. Cut carrots into 4- by ½- by ½-inch (10 by 1 by 1 cm) sticks, or the length that will fit in jars allowing for 1 inch (2.5 cm) headspace. Set aside.

3. In a pot, combine sugar, salt, vinegar and water. Bring to a boil over medium-high heat, stirring often until sugar and salt are dissolved. Boil for 1 minute. Reduce heat to low and keep liquid hot.

4. Empty water from jars and drain well. Place 1 dill head in each hot jar. Pack carrot sticks into jar, leaving room for liquid. Add 1 dill sprig and ¼ tsp (1 mL) dill seeds. Pour in hot pickling liquid, leaving ½ inch (1 cm) headspace. Wipe rim. Place lid disc on jar and screw band down until fingertip-tight (or use plastic storage lid). Let jars cool completely. Refrigerate for at least 5 days before serving or for up to 1 month.

> Fine-grained and flavorful, the very rare Early Horn carrot was developed in the Netherlands in the early 1600s.

Barrel-Fermented Dill Pickles

Makes five quart (1 L) jars

These are the richly flavored dills of deli fame. You may know them as crock-cured dill pickles or deli dills. Regardless of what you call them, they're made to accompany a deli meat sandwich.

Tips

To weigh down the plate, you can use sterilized glass jars with tight-fitting lids full of water or a large, heavy-duty sealable plastic bag filled with cooled extra brine (don't use water, just in case it leaks, because water would dilute the brine and ruin the fermentation).

You may need extra brine to cover the cucumbers or to add later in the fermenting process if too much evaporates or is skimmed off. Use ¼ cup (50 mL) pickling or canning salt dissolved in 4 cups (1 L) water and ½ cup (125 mL) white vinegar (or multiply in the same proportions for more). Extra brine can be stored in an airtight container in the refrigerator for up to 2 months. Let warm to room temperature before adding to crock.

- Cheesecloth
- Five 1-quart (1 L) canning jars with two-piece metal lids or plastic storage lids

Day 1

1 cup	pickling or canning salt	250 mL
¼ cup	pickling spice	60 mL
16 cups	water	4 L
2 cups	white vinegar	500 mL
6 lbs	3- to 4-inch (7.5 to 10 cm) pickling cucumbers (66 to 72)	3 kg
2 cups	packed dill sprigs	500 mL

Final Day

5 tsp	dill seeds	25 mL

Day 1

1. In a pot, combine salt, pickling spice, water and vinegar. Bring to a boil over high heat, stirring often until salt is dissolved. Let cool to room temperature.

2. Meanwhile, scrub cucumbers gently under running water. Trim off ⅛ inch (3 mm) from each end.

3. In a large crock, glass bowl or other non-reactive container, layer cucumbers and dill sprigs, using about one-third of each per layer. Pour brine over cucumbers and place a plate on top to weigh down cucumbers. Fill a couple of glass jars with water (see tip, at left) and place on plate to keep it weighted. Cover with several layers of cheesecloth. Let stand in a warm and dry area (50°F to 60°F/10°C to 15.5°C) of the root cellar for about 6 weeks.

During Fermentation

1. Skim off scum daily and check to make sure pickles are fermenting. You should see some slight bubbling, and the aroma will change. Add more brine (see tip, at left) if necessary to make sure pickles are covered. If there are any signs of mold or a foul aroma, discard pickles and liquid. Let ferment until bubbles stop and pickles are well flavored.

Here are the keys to success with these pickles: make sure there is brine covering the cucumbers, be diligent about skimming the brine while they ferment, and make sure they're at the right temperature.

To extend the shelf life of the pickles and store the jars at room temperature rather than in the refrigerator, process the hot filled jars in a boiling water canner for 15 minutes. Be sure to follow proper, modern canning procedures.

Final Day

1. Place jars on a rack in a pot. Fill pot and jars with water. Bring to a simmer over medium heat. Simmer gently for at least 10 minutes to sterilize jars; keep hot. Wash lids.

2. Place a colander over a large bowl and line colander with several layers of cheesecloth. Drain pickles, in batches as necessary, straining the liquid through the cheesecloth. Set pickles aside. Discard cheesecloth, including spices and dill.

3. Line colander with several layers of clean cheesecloth and set over a pot. Strain pickling liquid once again to filter out any solids. Bring liquid to a boil over high heat. Reduce heat and boil gently for 5 minutes. Reduce heat to low and keep liquid hot.

4. Working with one jar at a time, empty water from jar and drain well. Place 1 tsp (5 mL) dill seeds in hot jar. Pack cucumbers into jar, leaving about 1 inch (2.5 cm) headspace. Pour in hot pickling liquid, leaving $1/2$ inch (1 cm) headspace. Remove air bubbles and adjust headspace as necessary by adding hot pickling liquid. Wipe rim. Place lid disc on jar and screw band down until fingertip-tight (or use plastic storage lid). Let jars cool completely. Use immediately or refrigerate for up to 2 months.

> Pickling cucumbers have softer skin than slicing cukes. Bush Pickle and Carolina are two varieties that are good for pickling.

Classic Sauerkraut

Makes five to six pint (500 mL) jars

Making your own sauerkraut does take time but, amazingly, with just two ingredients, some water and natural fermentation in your root cellar, you can create a unique flavor that can't be beat.

Tips

You may need extra brine to cover the cabbage in step 4 of Day 1, to add later in the fermenting process if too much evaporates or is skimmed off, or when canning. Use 1½ tbsp (22 mL) pickling or canning salt and 4 cups (1 L) water, prepared according to step 1 of Day 1 (or multiply in the same proportions for more). Extra brine can be stored in an airtight container in the refrigerator for up to 2 months. Let warm to room temperature before adding to crock.

If you want to make a larger batch of sauerkraut, feel free to multiply the recipe in batches of 5 lbs (2.5 kg), up to 5 times. Just make sure you have a container large enough to allow for plenty of liquid and bubbling action above the cabbage during fermentation. The raw-pack method is best for larger batches; fill jars in batches that will fit into the canner.

- Cheesecloth
- Five to six 1-pint (500 mL) canning jars with two-piece metal lids or plastic storage lids

6 tbsp	pickling or canning salt, divided	90 mL
8 cups	water	2 L
5 lbs	green cabbage (about 1 large)	2.5 kg

Day 1

1. In a pot, combine 3 tbsp (45 mL) of the salt and the water. Bring to a boil over medium-high heat, stirring often until salt is dissolved. Boil for 1 minute. Let cool to room temperature.

2. Meanwhile, cut cabbage lengthwise into 6 or 8 wedges. Cut out core. Cut each wedge crosswise into very thin slices. You should have about 28 cups (7 L).

3. In a large crock, glass bowl or other non-reactive container, combine cabbage and the remaining salt; let stand for about 15 minutes or until wilted.

4. Pour brine over wilted cabbage, pressing to immerse cabbage. The liquid should cover the cabbage by at least 1 inch (2.5 cm). Add extra brine (see tip, at left), if necessary. Place a plate on top to weigh down cabbage. Fill a couple of glass jars with water (see tip, page 234) and place on plate to keep it weighted. Cover with several layers of cheesecloth. Let stand in a warm and dry area (50°F to 60°F/10°C to 15.5°C) of the root cellar for about 6 weeks.

During Fermentation

1. Check every few days to make sure cabbage is fermenting. You should see bubbles form, and the aroma will change. Skim off any scum that forms and add extra brine (see tip, at left) if necessary to make sure cabbage is covered. If there are any signs of mold or a foul aroma, discard cabbage and liquid. Let ferment until bubbles stop and sauerkraut is well flavored.

Tips

Use a cotton apron instead of a towel to cover the crock — use the ties on the apron to wrap around the crock and secure the apron.

Successful fermentation requires the correct air temperature. If the air is too cool, fermentation will be very slow or may not occur at all, which can allow mold to form. If the air is too warm, the sauerkraut can become overfermented and have a soft, unpleasant texture and flavor. Place a thermometer next to the crock and check it often, relocating the sauerkraut if necessary.

To extend the shelf life of the sauerkraut and store the jars at room temperature rather than in the refrigerator, process the hot filled jars in a boiling water canner for 20 minutes for raw pack jars or 10 minutes for hot pack jars. Be sure to follow proper, modern canning procedures.

Final Day

1. Place jars on a rack in a pot. Fill pot and jars with water. Bring to a simmer over medium heat. Simmer gently for at least 10 minutes to sterilize jars; keep hot. Wash lids.

Raw Pack

1. Working with one jar at a time, empty water from jar and drain well. Pack sauerkraut and brine into hot jars, packing sauerkraut lightly but ensuring that there is enough brine to keep it moist, leaving $1/2$ inch (1 cm) headspace. Add extra brine (see tip, page 236) if necessary to fill jars. Remove air bubbles and adjust headspace as necessary by adding brine. Wipe rim. Place lid disc on jar and screw band down until fingertip-tight (or use plastic storage lid). Let jars cool completely. Use immediately or refrigerate for up to 2 months.

Hot Pack

1. In a large pot, heat sauerkraut and brine over medium-high heat, stirring often, just until brine starts to simmer. Do not boil. Remove from heat.

2. Working with one jar at a time, empty water from jar and drain well. Pack hot sauerkraut and brine into hot jars, packing sauerkraut lightly but ensuring that there is enough brine to keep it moist, leaving $1/2$ inch (1 cm) headspace. Add heated extra brine (see tip, page 236) if necessary to fill jars. Remove air bubbles and adjust headspace as necessary by adding hot brine. Wipe rim. Place lid disc on jar and screw band down until fingertip-tight (or use plastic storage lid). Let jars cool completely. Use immediately or refrigerate for up to 2 months.

Preserved Lemons

Makes one quart (1 L) jar

Chef Neil Baxter of Rundles Cooking Classes in Stratford, Ontario, first introduced Jennifer to the delightful flavor of preserved lemons. They complement Moroccan foods in a way that just can't be matched by any other ingredient.

Tip

It is easiest to use a wide-mouth jar. Instead of a canning jar, you can use the type with the glass lid and rubber sealer, as long as it has a tight seal when closed.

• 1-quart (1 L) canning jar with plastic storage lid or two-piece metal lid

Day 1

5	lemons	5
1/3 cup	pickling or canning salt	75 mL
3	whole cloves	3
1	piece (3 inches/7.5 cm) cinnamon stick	1

After 1 Week

1 cup	freshly squeezed lemon juice (approx.)	250 mL

Day 1

1. Place jar on a rack in a pot. Fill pot and jar with water. Bring to a simmer over medium heat. Simmer gently for at least 10 minutes to sterilize jar; keep hot. Wash lid.

2. Scrub lemons gently under running water. Trim off stem end. Working with one lemon at a time, place stem end down on cutting board and, using a serrated knife, cut lemon lengthwise into sixths, almost but not all the way through. Repeat with the remaining lemons.

3. Empty water from jar and drain well. Holding a lemon over the jar, pack a scant 1 tbsp (15 mL) of the salt inside the cuts of the lemon and place in the jar, cut side up. Repeat with the remaining lemons, packing tightly to fit as necessary. Add cloves and cinnamon stick. Sprinkle the remaining salt over top. Wipe rim and place lid on jar (or place lid disc on jar and screw band down until fingertip-tight). Shake jar gently.

4. Place jar in a warm and dry area (50°F to 60°F/10°C to 15.5°C) of the root cellar for 1 week, gently rotating jar daily to swirl accumulating juices and salt around the lemons.

Tips

Add thin slices of preserved lemon rind to Moroccan tagines.

Simmer a slice of preserved lemon when cooking rice. Discard before serving.

Use a twist of preserved lemon to add punch as a cocktail garnish.

After 1 Week

1. Remove lemons from jar and place them back in the jar in reverse order (so the ones from the bottom are now on top). Add enough of the lemon juice to cover the lemons by about $1/2$ inch (1 cm). Store in a warm and dry area of the root cellar for 3 weeks. The lemon rind should be translucent and most of the salt should be dissolved. After 3 weeks, transfer the jar to the refrigerator and store lemons for up to 1 year.

To Use

1. Cut the desired size piece of lemon, returning the remaining lemon to the jar. Scrape flesh and membranes, and some of the white pith if it is thicker than $1/8$ inch (3 mm), from the lemon rind. Cut rind into thin slices or mince to use in recipes.

> Unlike table salt, pickling salt contains no iodine or anti-caking agents, which can cause cloudy brine and darken pickles and preserves.

Preserved Oranges

Makes one quart (1 L) jar

The floral flavor of orange rind gets even more intense when it's preserved in salt. This ages-old practice can add new life to your cooking.

Tip

It is easiest to use a wide-mouth jar. Instead of a canning jar, you can use the type with the glass lid and rubber sealer, as long as it has a tight seal when closed.

- 1-quart (1 L) canning jar with plastic storage lid or two-piece metal lid

Day 1

5	small oranges	5
⅓ cup	pickling or canning salt	75 mL
2	bay leaves	2
½ tsp	black peppercorns	2 mL

After 1 Week

1 cup	freshly squeezed orange juice (approx.)	250 mL

Day 1

1. Place jar on a rack in a pot. Fill pot and jar with water. Bring to a simmer over medium heat. Simmer gently for at least 10 minutes to sterilize jar; keep hot. Wash lid.

2. Scrub oranges gently under running water. Trim off stem end. Working with one orange at a time, place stem end down on cutting board and, using a serrated knife, cut orange lengthwise into sixths, almost but not all the way through. Repeat with the remaining oranges.

3. Empty water from jar and drain well. Holding an orange over the jar, pack a scant 1 tbsp (15 mL) of the salt inside the cuts of the orange and place in the jar, cut side up. Repeat with the remaining oranges, packing tightly to fit as necessary. Add bay leaves and peppercorns. Sprinkle the remaining salt over top. Wipe rim and place lid on jar (or place lid disc on jar and screw band down until fingertip-tight). Shake jar gently.

4. Place jar in a warm and dry area (50°F to 60°F/10°C to 15.5°C) of the root cellar for 1 week, gently rotating jar daily to swirl accumulating juices and salt around the oranges.

Tips

Simmer a slice of preserved orange with a beef or pork stew.

Finely minced preserved orange rind adds depth to spicy curries.

After 1 Week

1. Remove oranges from jar and place them back in the jar in reverse order (so the ones from the bottom are now on top). Add enough of the orange juice to cover the oranges by about $1/2$ inch (1 cm). Store in a warm and dry area of the root cellar for 3 weeks. The orange rind should be translucent and most of the salt should be dissolved. After 3 weeks, transfer the jar to the refrigerator and store oranges for up to 1 year.

To Use

1. Cut the desired size piece of orange, returning the remaining orange to the jar. Scrape flesh and membranes from the orange rind. Cut rind into thin slices or mince to use in recipes.

> Peppercorns are the world's most widely traded spice. Vietnam produces one-third of world output.

Preserved Limes

The color of preserved limes is a little dark and dull, but the taste is anything but! The depth of flavor that comes from even the smallest piece will amaze you.

Tip

It is easiest to use a wide-mouth jar. Instead of a canning jar, you can use the type with the glass lid and rubber sealer, as long as it has a tight seal when closed.

• 1-quart (1 L) canning jar with plastic storage lid or two-piece metal lid

Day 1

10	limes	10
⅓ cup	pickling or canning salt	75 mL
3	whole green cardamom pods	3
1	bay leaf	1

After 1 Week

1 cup	freshly squeezed lime juice (approx.)	250 mL

Day 1

1. Place jar on a rack in a pot. Fill pot and jar with water. Bring to a simmer over medium heat. Simmer gently for at least 10 minutes to sterilize jar; keep hot. Wash lid.

2. Scrub limes gently under running water. Trim off stem end. Working with one lime at a time, place stem end down on cutting board and, using a serrated knife, cut lime lengthwise into quarters, almost but not all the way through. Repeat with the remaining limes.

3. Empty water from jar and drain well. Holding a lime over the jar, pack a heaping teaspoon (5 mL) of the salt inside the cuts of the lime and place in the jar, cut side up. Repeat with the remaining limes, packing tightly to fit as necessary. Add cardamom pods and bay leaf. Sprinkle the remaining salt over top. Wipe rim and place lid on jar (or place lid disc on jar and screw band down until fingertip-tight). Shake jar gently.

4. Place jar in a warm and dry area (50°F to 60°F/10°C to 15.5°C) of the root cellar for 1 week, gently rotating jar daily to swirl accumulating juices and salt around the limes.

Tips

Use a small piece of preserved lime rind instead of lime leaves in recipes. Discard rind before serving.

Instead of salting the glass rim for a margarita, serve a sliver of preserved lime for garnish, rubbing it around the rim before adding it on top of the drink or perching it on the edge of the glass.

After 1 Week

1. Remove limes from jar and place them back in the jar in reverse order (so the ones from the bottom are now on top). Add enough of the lime juice to cover the limes by about $1/2$ inch (1 cm). Store in a warm and dry area of the root cellar for 3 weeks. The lime rind should be almost translucent and most of the salt should be dissolved. After 3 weeks, transfer the jar to the refrigerator and store limes for up to 1 year.

To Use

1. Cut the desired size piece of lime, returning the remaining lime to the jar. Scrape flesh and membranes from the lime rind. Cut rind into thin slices or mince to use in recipes.

> Cardamom pods are produced by members of the ginger family. Malabar and Mysore are two varieties.

Three-Onion Relish

Makes three 8-ounce (250 mL) jars

Top a juicy steak with this relish and you'll never go back to a bottled sauce. It's also wonderful as a sandwich spread.

Tips

This relish looks nice if you cut the onions in half lengthwise, then crosswise into thin slices.

Be sure to wash the leeks well to remove all of the sand and grit. Trim off the root end and dark green parts, then cut the white and light green portion in half lengthwise. Rinse well between the layers and drain, then cut crosswise into thin slices.

You can store this relish in airtight containers instead of jars, but sterilized jars do keep it a better quality for a longer time.

- Cheesecloth
- Three 8-ounce (250 mL) canning jars with two-piece metal lids or plastic storage lids

3 cups	thinly sliced onions	750 mL
1 cup	sliced leeks (white and light green parts only)	250 mL
2 tbsp	pickling or canning salt	30 mL
¾ cup	granulated sugar	175 mL
1 tsp	coriander seeds, crushed	5 mL
½ tsp	dried thyme	2 mL
1 cup	cider vinegar	250 mL
¼ cup	thinly sliced green onions	60 mL

1. In a large non-reactive bowl, combine onions, leeks and salt. Cover and let stand at a cool room temperature for 2 hours.

2. Meanwhile, place jars on a rack in a pot. Fill pot and jars with water. Bring to a simmer over medium heat. Simmer gently for at least 10 minutes to sterilize jars; keep hot. Wash lids.

3. In a colander lined with cheesecloth, working in batches, drain onion mixture and rinse well. Drain again and squeeze out excess liquid. Set aside in colander to continue draining.

4. In a pot, combine sugar, coriander seeds, thyme and vinegar. Bring to a boil over medium heat, stirring often until sugar is dissolved. Increase heat to medium-high, add drained onions and return to a boil, stirring often. Reduce heat and boil gently, stirring often, for about 15 minutes or until onions are translucent and mixture is slightly thickened. Stir in green onions and return to a boil, stirring often.

5. Empty water from jars and drain well. Ladle hot relish into hot jars, leaving ½ inch (1 cm) headspace. Remove air bubbles and adjust headspace as necessary by adding hot relish. Wipe rims. Place lid discs on jars and screw bands down until fingertip-tight (or use plastic storage lids). Let jars cool completely. Use immediately or refrigerate for up to 1 month.

Red Onion Marmalade

Makes two 8-ounce (250 mL) jars

Once you try this savory marmalade, you'll be thinking up more and more ways to serve it. The sweet flavor with a touch of tang complements meats, poultry, fish, cheeses and vegetable dishes wonderfully.

Tips

It's best if you chop the onions by hand for this marmalade. Using a power tool or manual chopper will make the onions mushy and the marmalade won't have nearly as nice a texture.

You can store this marmalade in airtight containers instead of jars, but sterilized jars do keep it a better quality for a longer time.

* Two 8-ounce (250 mL) canning jars with two-piece metal lids or plastic storage lids

6 cups	chopped red onions	1.5 L
1 cup	granulated sugar	250 mL
1 tsp	pickling or canning salt	5 mL
¼ cup	water	60 mL
¾ cup	cider vinegar	175 mL

1. Place jars on a rack in a pot. Fill pot and jars with water. Bring to a simmer over medium heat. Simmer gently for at least 10 minutes to sterilize jars; keep hot. Wash lids.

2. In a large pot, combine onions, sugar, salt and water. Bring to a boil over medium heat, stirring often until sugar is dissolved. Reduce heat to low, cover and simmer, stirring occasionally, for about 20 minutes or until onions are softened. Uncover, increase heat to medium-low and boil gently, stirring often, for about 30 minutes or until onions are deeply caramelized. Increase heat to medium-high, add vinegar and return to a boil, stirring often. Reduce heat and boil gently, stirring constantly, for about 5 minutes or until mixture is slightly thickened.

3. Empty water from jars and drain well. Ladle hot marmalade into hot jars, leaving ½ inch (1 cm) headspace. Remove air bubbles and adjust headspace as necessary by adding hot marmalade. Wipe rims. Place lid discs on jars and screw bands down until fingertip-tight (or use plastic storage lids). Let jars cool. Use immediately or refrigerate for up to 1 month.

Pear, Sweet Onion and Almond Chutney

Makes one pint (500 mL) jar

A subtle sherry undertone, mild pears and sweet onions make for a pleasant combination in this easy chutney. The toasted almonds add flavor and a nice contrast in texture to the tender pears.

Tips

Choose fragrant but firm pears and use a variety that keep their flavor when cooked, such as Bartlett, Bosc or Packham.

You can store this chutney in airtight containers instead of a jar, but a sterilized jar does keep it a better quality for a longer time.

Serve this chutney with sharp or creamy cheeses, spice-rubbed chicken or pork, or grilled fish. Top baguette slices with pâté and a spoonful of warmed chutney for a simple appetizer.

- 1-pint (500 mL) canning jar with two-piece metal lid or plastic storage lid

2 cups	chopped peeled pears	500 mL
½ cup	finely chopped sweet onion	125 mL
¼ cup	packed brown sugar	60 mL
½ tsp	kosher or sea salt	2 mL
Pinch	freshly ground black pepper	Pinch
½ cup	dry sherry	125 mL
2 tbsp	white wine vinegar	30 mL
⅓ cup	chopped toasted almonds	75 mL

1. Warm jar by filling it with hot water. Set aside. Wash lid.

2. In a saucepan, combine pears, onion, brown sugar, salt, pepper, sherry and vinegar. Bring to a boil over medium-high heat. Reduce heat and simmer, stirring occasionally, for about 15 minutes or until pears are tender and liquid is syrupy. Stir in almonds.

3. Empty water from jar and pour in hot chutney, gently inserting a narrow spatula to remove air bubbles. Wipe rim. Place lid disc on jar and screw band down until fingertip-tight (or use plastic storage lid). Let jars cool completely. Refrigerate for at least 2 days before serving or for up to 1 month.

Pumpkin Orange Chutney

Makes one pint (500 mL) jar

The burst of fresh orange and liqueur is a wonderful way to accent sweet pumpkin. You can decide whether you prefer a chunkier or smoother texture by adjusting the cooking time.

Tips

If you don't have a sweet pie pumpkin, hubbard squash makes a good substitute.

You can store this chutney in airtight containers instead of a jar, but a sterilized jar does keep it a better quality for a longer time.

Use this colorful, gently spiced chutney to spruce up roasted turkey or chicken, braised or roasted lamb or pork roast. It also works as a dressing for a grain salad or as an appetizer in toast cups, warmed and topped with a touch of creamy blue cheese.

* 1-pint (500 mL) canning jar with two-piece metal lid or plastic storage lid

2 cups	diced peeled pie pumpkin	500 mL
1/2 cup	finely chopped red onion	125 mL
2	whole cloves	2
1	piece (2 inches/5 cm) cinnamon stick	1
1/4 tsp	kosher or sea salt	1 mL
1/2 cup	water	125 mL
1/3 cup	packed brown sugar	75 mL
1/3 cup	cider vinegar	75 mL
1/2 cup	chopped seedless orange with juices	125 mL
2 tbsp	Grand Marnier or other orange-flavored liqueur (optional)	30 mL

1. Warm jar by filling it with hot water. Set aside. Wash lid.

2. In a saucepan, combine pumpkin, onion, cloves, cinnamon stick, salt and water. Bring to a boil over medium-high heat; reduce heat, cover and simmer for about 3 minutes or until pumpkin is starting to soften.

3. Stir in brown sugar and vinegar. Increase heat to medium-low and simmer, uncovered, stirring occasionally, for about 5 minutes, until pumpkin is just fork-tender and liquid is syrupy (for a chunky texture), or for about 10 minutes, until pumpkin is starting to break down (for a smoother texture). Stir in orange with juices and liqueur (if using); simmer for 3 minutes or until orange starts to release juices. Discard cloves.

4. Empty water from jar and pour in hot chutney, gently inserting a narrow spatula to remove air bubbles. Wipe rim. Place lid disc on jar and screw band down until fingertip-tight (or use plastic storage lid). Let jars cool completely. Refrigerate for at least 1 day before serving or for up to 1 month.

Roasted Garlic

Makes about ½ cup (125 mL)

Roasting garlic mellows the sharper flavors and enhances the sweet and savory ones. Use it in salad dressings or pastas, add it to soups or gravies, or spread it on toasted baguette slices.

Variation

If you only need a few cloves of roasted garlic and don't want to turn the oven on, peel as many cloves as you need and trim off the root end. In a cast-iron or other heavy skillet, heat a thin layer of olive oil over medium-low heat. Add garlic and stir to coat in oil; reduce heat to low, cover and cook, stirring occasionally, for about 20 minutes or until garlic is soft. Using a slotted spoon, transfer garlic to a bowl; mash with a fork.

● Preheat oven to 375°F (190°C)

4	large heads garlic	4
1 tbsp	olive oil	15 mL
	Salt and freshly ground black pepper	

1. Rub off loose papery skins from outside of garlic heads, but do not peel. Trim about ¼ inch (0.5 cm) off the top of each head, or enough to expose the tops of the cloves. Place in the center of a large piece of foil. Drizzle oil over the exposed cloves and season to taste with salt and pepper. Wrap foil loosely around garlic, sealing edges well. Place on a baking sheet.

2. Bake in preheated oven for about 45 minutes or until garlic is very soft. Let stand, wrapped, until cool enough to handle. Squeeze garlic from skins into a bowl; discard skins. Mash garlic with a fork. Use immediately or transfer to a jar with a tight-fitting lid and refrigerate for up to 3 days.

3. To freeze roasted garlic, drop dollops (about 1 tbsp/ 15 mL) of mashed roasted garlic on a baking sheet lined with parchment paper and freeze until solid. Transfer to an airtight container, or wrap in plastic and place in a freezer bag, and store in the freezer for up to 3 months.

> Garlic varieties that produce large cloves include Amish Rocambole, German Extra Hardy, Kettle River Giant, Korean Mountain, Martin's Heirloom, Metechi, Red Estonian, Xian and Zemo.

Rhubarb Ginger Compote

Makes about 2 cups (500 mL)

Cellar-grown, or "forced," rhubarb (see page 101) is more tender than garden-grown, so it just needs a quick simmer and you've got a lovely, vibrant compote. Serve it over angel food cake or ice cream, or on its own with crisp cookies on the side.

Tip

Peel the gingerroot using a vegetable peeler or paring knife, then use the fine side of a box cheese grater or a Microplane-style grater to grate the gingerroot very finely (so it's almost a purée).

½ cup	granulated sugar, or to taste	125 mL
1 tsp	finely grated gingerroot	5 mL
4 cups	chopped rhubarb	1 L

1. In a saucepan, combine sugar, ginger and ¼ cup (60 mL) water. Bring to a boil over medium heat, stirring to dissolve sugar. Add rhubarb and return to a boil. Reduce heat and simmer, stirring occasionally, for about 10 minutes or until rhubarb is soft and compote is thickened. Add more sugar to taste, if desired. Serve warm or let cool, transfer to a clean jar or airtight container and refrigerate for up to 1 week.

> Canada Red rhubarb produces shorter stalks that are very tender and sweet (at least, as rhubarb goes).

Spiced Pear Butter

Makes about 2 cups (500 mL)

The almost creamy texture of pear butter makes a nice change from jam. The touch of spice adds depth to the floral sweetness of the pears. Pear butter can be used for sweet or savory dishes.

Tips

Use any pears that hold their flavor when cooked. They can be firm or soft varieties, but avoid those that are best suited to eating fresh, such as Anjou pears, as they'll be bland once cooked.

Make canapés by spreading pear butter on fresh baguette slices and topping with crumbled blue cheese or a slice of Camembert; broil to warm the cheese, if desired.

Variation

For a more savory version, omit the cinnamon, stir 1/4 cup (60 mL) white balsamic vinegar into the purée with the sugar and increase the pepper to 1/4 tsp (1 mL).

3 lbs	ripe pears (about 9)	1.5 kg
1 cup	unsweetened pear nectar or apple juice	250 mL
2 tbsp	freshly squeezed lemon juice	30 mL
3/4 cup	granulated sugar	175 mL
3/4 cup	packed brown sugar	175 mL
1/2 tsp	ground cinnamon	2 mL
1/4 tsp	ground ginger	1 mL
1/4 tsp	ground nutmeg, preferably freshly grated	1 mL
Pinch	salt	Pinch
Pinch	freshly ground black pepper (optional)	Pinch

1. Cut pears into quarters and trim out cores, stems and blossom ends. In a large pot, combine pears, pear nectar and lemon juice. Bring to a boil over high heat. Reduce heat to low, cover and simmer, stirring occasionally, for about 45 minutes or until pears are very soft. Let cool slightly.

2. Using a rubber spatula, press pears and liquid through a mesh sieve into a clean pot, discarding skins (or pass through a food mill fitted with a fine plate).

3. Stir granulated sugar, brown sugar, cinnamon, ginger, nutmeg, salt and pepper (if using) into purée. Bring to a boil over medium heat, stirring often to dissolve sugar. Reduce heat and boil gently, stirring often and reducing heat further as mixture thickens, for about 45 minutes or until thick enough to mound on a spoon (it will thicken more upon cooling). Let cool. Use immediately or transfer to a jar or airtight container and refrigerate for up to 3 weeks.

Honeyed Apple Butter

Makes about 2½ cups (625 mL)

If you have soft apples that are at the end of their storage life for eating out of hand but are still good quality, this is the perfect recipe to capture their flavor.

Tips

Use any apples that hold their flavor when cooked. Soft varieties such as McIntosh, Empire, Cortland, Gravenstein and Pippin work well and have great flavor. Avoid those that are best suited to eating fresh, such as Red Delicious, Royal Gala or Pink Lady, as they'll be bland once cooked.

Spread apple butter on crackers or bread and top with aged Cheddar cheese — the combination is fabulous.

Variation

For a slightly spiced version, add ½ tsp (2 mL) ground cinnamon and ¼ tsp (1 mL) ground ginger with the honey.

2 lbs	soft cooking apples (about 6 large)	1 kg
2½ cups	unsweetened apple cider or juice	625 mL
½ cup	liquid honey	125 mL
Pinch	salt	Pinch

1. Cut apples into quarters and trim off stems and blossom ends (there's no need to core them). In a large pot, combine apples and cider. Bring to a boil over high heat. Reduce heat to low, cover and simmer, stirring occasionally, for about 45 minutes or until apples are very soft. Let cool slightly.

2. Using a rubber spatula, press apples and liquid through a mesh sieve into a clean pot, discarding skins and cores (or pass through a food mill fitted with a fine plate).

3. Stir honey and salt into purée. Bring to a boil over medium heat, stirring often. Reduce heat and boil gently, stirring often and reducing heat further as mixture thickens, for about 30 minutes or until thick enough to mound on a spoon (it will thicken more upon cooling). Let cool. Use immediately or transfer to a jar or airtight container and refrigerate for up to 3 weeks.

> In 1977, Kimmswick, Missouri (population about 100), started its annual Apple Butter Festival. The two-day event now attracts almost 100,000 visitors.

All-Purpose Homemade Applesauce

Makes about 2 cups (500 mL)

Applesauce is one of those staple ingredients that is invaluable to have on hand. You can use it as an ingredient in baked goods, add it to yogurt for breakfast, or serve it as a topping for pancakes or a simple dessert. Use apples from your stores to cook up this version any time you need it.

Tip

Jennifer likes to cook the apples with the peel on (when using red apples) to give the sauce a rosy hue, but you can peel them before chopping if you prefer a pale yellow sauce.

Variations

If desired, sweeten applesauce to taste with granulated sugar, brown sugar, maple sugar granules, pure maple syrup or liquid honey.

Add $1/8$ tsp (0.5 mL) ground cinnamon (or to taste) with the water. Or simmer a 2-inch (5 cm) piece of cinnamon stick with the apples and discard before storing the sauce.

| 5 | soft cooking apples, chopped (about $1\frac{1}{2}$ lbs/750 kg) | 5 |
| 1 tbsp | freshly squeezed lemon juice | 15 mL |

1. In a saucepan, combine apples, lemon juice and $\frac{1}{4}$ cup (60 mL) water. Bring to a boil over medium heat. Reduce heat to low, cover and simmer, stirring occasionally, for about 20 minutes or until apples are very soft.

2. Using a rubber spatula, press sauce through a mesh sieve into a bowl, discarding skins. Use immediately or let cool, transfer to a clean jar or airtight container and refrigerate for up to 1 week or freeze for up to 3 months.

> There are more than 7,500 known varieties of apples in the world. For this recipe, use any apples that hold their flavor when cooked. Soft varieties such as McIntosh, Empire, Cortland, Gravenstein and Pippin work well and have great flavor. Avoid those that are best suited to eating fresh, such as Red Delicious, Royal Gala or Pink Lady, as they'll be bland once cooked.

Rumtopf

Jennifer has vivid memories of the shock of her first taste of rumtopf at a very young age. Many years later, she learned to appreciate the bold flavor of rum-soaked fruit — especially delicious served over ice cream. It's traditionally served at Christmastime, which is coincidentally just about the perfect length of time after the fruit harvest for the fullest flavor to develop. Jennifer sends thanks to her friend Christa Graf for helping her research this traditional method.

Suggested Fruits

Strawberries, raspberries, sweet cherries, blackberries, blueberries, gooseberries, halved sweet seedless grapes, halved sliced apricots, sliced plums, sliced peaches

1. Clean and sterilize an 8-cup (2 L) glass jar with a tight-fitting lid or a stoneware pot.

2. As soft fruits come into season, combine each 8 oz (250 g) fruit with $1/2$ cup (125 mL) granulated sugar and let stand for about 30 minutes or until fruit starts to soften and release juices. Pour into the jar and add enough rum to cover the fruit by about $1/2$ inch (1 cm).

3. Cover jar with plastic wrap, then a lid, and store in the root cellar. It's best to wait 1 to 2 weeks before the next addition of fruit. Do not mix the fruit as you add each new layer. You'll be able to fit about six additions of fruit in an 8-cup (2 L) jar.

4. Once the last fruit layer is added, fill the jar with rum to within $1/2$ inch (1 cm) of the rim, cover with plastic and lid and store in the root cellar for at least 2 months or for up to 6 months.

5. You can use a little of the rumtopf at a time; just be sure to use a sterilized metal ladle with a long handle so you can reach the bottom of the jar and get a sampling of each type of fruit. Top up with more rum, as necessary, to make sure the fruit is well covered in liquid.

Tips

To sterilize jar, place jar on a rack in a pot. Fill pot and jar with water. Bring to a simmer over medium heat. Simmer gently for at least 10 minutes.

You can vary the fruits to your taste or according to what you can easily purchase or harvest. Just add each fruit as it comes into season.

A kitchen scale is handy to measure the weight of the fruit. Since each fruit has a different density, the volume will vary. You don't have to add exactly 8 oz (250 g) fruit each time; the important part is the ratio of 2 parts fruit to 1 part sugar for each addition.

This is a relatively small batch, but it can certainly be doubled or tripled and made in a bigger jar or a traditional stoneware rum pot.

Resources

Products

Blast Gate Hardware

Lee Valley Tools
www.leevalleytools.com
(800) 267-8767

Google "dust collection hardware" for more contacts

Concrete Waterproofing

Everdure Caltite
www.caltite.com
(206) 764-3000 (U.S.)
(905) 761-7062 (Canada)
(44) 1293-447-878 (U.K.)

Electric Cooling Technology

Store It Cold
CoolBot window air conditioner control
www.storeitcold.com
(888) 871-5723

Euro Panel Manufacturing
Walk-in coolers
www.europanel.org

U.S. Cooler
Walk-in coolers
www.uscooler.com

Walk In Cooler Central Market
Walk-in coolers
www.walkincooler.com

Google "walk-in cooler" for more contacts

Shelf Hardware

Lee Valley Tools
Hanging and wall-mounted shelf hardware
www.leevalleytools.com
(800) 267-8767

Spray Foam Products

BetterFoam.com
www.betterfoam.com
(888) 849-3626

Energy Efficient Solutions
www.diysprayfoam.net
(877) 464-5828

Tiger Foam Insulation
www.tigerfoam.com
(800) 664-0063

Google "DIY spray foam" for more contacts

Tile Installation Accessories

Schluter Systems
Uncoupling membrane; KERDI
   waterproofing mat; KERDI-BOARD
   tile backer board
www.schluter.com
www.kerdi-board.com
(800) 667-8746

Books

Building with Structural Insulated Panels (SIPs): Strength and Energy Efficiency Through Structural Panel Construction
Michael Morley (Newtown, CT: Taunton Press, September 2000)

Remodel Plumbing
Rex Cauldwell (Newtown, CT: Taunton Press, May 2005)

Setting Tile
Michael Byrne (Newtown, CT: Taunton Press, May 1995)

Wiring a House
Rex Cauldwell (Newtown, CT: Taunton Press, January 2010)

Working with Concrete
Rick Arnold (Newtown, CT: Taunton Press, May 2003)

Acknowledgments

The phrase "too many cooks spoil the broth" certainly doesn't apply to the creation of a book — especially one that encompasses two very different disciplines: construction and cooking. Many people combined their talents to create this one, and we truly appreciate all of their efforts.

Thank you to our publisher, Bob Dees, for your vision and support; to Marian Jarkovich for your marketing expertise; and to Nina McCreath of Robert Rose Inc. Thank you to Kevin Cockburn for the useful and attractive design, as well as to Andrew Smith, Joseph Gisini and Daniella Zanchetta at PageWave Graphics. Thanks to photographer Colin Erricson, food stylist Kathryn Robertson and props stylist Charlene Erricson for the beautiful cover. Thanks also to proofreader Sheila Wawanash for your keen eye and Gillian Watts for carefully providing the index.

From Steve:

First of all, thanks to my wife, Mary, for saying yes so many years ago to leaving family and friends to work with me to build our own life in a quiet, rural community where old-fashioned root cellars are still part of the scene. Thanks also to my five children, Robert, Katherine, Joseph, Jacob and Ellie, for your constant interest in how Dad's book is coming along. May you all learn to love the satisfaction of well-stocked cellars of your own. Thanks especially to Mom and Dad for your lifelong encouragement and faith that my crazy ideas are worth a try.

Thanks to Bob for convincing me that the world really does need a new root cellar book, and to Sue for your diligence, skill and patient logic as an editor. Thank you, Jennifer, for your appetizing recipes and kind partnership in filling the pages of our book. Thanks also to Jim, Robert, Chuc and Linda for your sober second look at my construction and cellar details. Thanks to Len for your amazing skill as an illustrator. I never would have attempted a book like this without you.

Thanks also to root cellaring people I've never met. My hat goes off to the Bailey and Taylor families, the original settlers who built the ancient limestone cellars near my home. And to the Native peoples whose food storage pits near a lake I love stand as visible proof of an ancient partnership with the land. Above all, thanks to God for making good things grow, and for the power of a root cellar to preserve them.

From Jennifer:

To Sue Sumeraj, our editor, logician, motivator and logistics chief: once again, you have excelled at taking many random files and working them into a practical volume that readers will certainly appreciate. I can't thank you enough!

To my co-author, Steve, thanks for working on this project with me and for your never-ending enthusiasm.

Thank you to the food editors, especially Jody Dunn, Barb Holland, Dana McCauley, Rob McCormick and Lucy Waverman, who challenge me to create new recipes and allow me to share them with readers far beyond my kitchen. In particular, thank you to Elizabeth Baird: you gave a fresh-out-of-school home economist the best possible training in writing recipes and anticipating what cooks at home need to know for success, and your diligence is my constant reminder.

To Teresa Makarewicz, my friend and colleague, our virtual water cooler chats bring me much enjoyment and sanity.

Thank you to all of my family and friends who cheer me on, spread the word about my books and keep eating my experiments with enthusiasm. Mom, words will never be enough to express my thanks to you — for everything, always. Dad, I miss you every minute of every day and take comfort in knowing that your strength will always be with me. Alicia, John, Ryder, Brent, Melanie, Dale, Rick, Zoey and Jack, thanks for making me feel lucky to be your sister and auntie.

To Jay, my husband, protector, co-worker, co-teacher, grocery shopper, sounding board, ideas guy and best friend, thank you for being all of that for me no matter what. I'm sure glad Fate stepped in twelve years ago and made sure we were in the same place at the same time.

Library and Archives Canada Cataloguing in Publication

Maxwell, Steve, 1963–
    The complete root cellar book : building plans, uses and 100 recipes /
    Steve Maxwell and Jennifer MacKenzie.

Includes index.
ISBN 978-0-7788-0243-3

1. Vegetables—Storage. 2. Root cellars. 3. Root cellars—Design and construction.
4. Cookery (Vegetables). I. MacKenzie, Jennifer II. Title.

TX612.V4M39 2010   641.4'52   C2009-906695-5

Index